Passport to Peckham

BY THE SAME AUTHOR:

Under Siege: Literary Life in London, 1939–45 (1977)
In Anger: Culture in the Cold War, 1945–60 (1981)
Too Much: Art and Society in the Sixties, 1960–75 (1986)
The Heritage Industry: Britain in a Climate of Decline (1987)
Future Tense: A New Art for the Nineties (1990)
Culture and Consensus: England, Art and Politics since 1940 (1995)
Cultural Capital: The Rise and Fall of Creative Britain (2015)

Passport to Peckham

Culture and Creativity in a London Village

Robert Hewison

Copyright © 2022 Goldsmiths Press
First published in 2022 by Goldsmiths Press
Goldsmiths, University of London, New Cross
London SE14 6NW

Printed and bound by Versa Press, USA
Distribution by the MIT Press
Cambridge, Massachusetts, and London, England

Copyright © 2022 Robert Hewison

The right of Robert Hewison to be identified as the Author of this work has been asserted by him in accordance with sections 77 and 78 in the Copyright, Designs and Patents Act 1988.

Every effort has been made to trace copyright holders and to obtain their permission for the use of copyright material. The publisher apologises for any errors or omissions and would be grateful if notified of any corrections that should be incorporated in future reprints or editions of this book.

All Rights Reserved. No part of this publication may be reproduced, distributed or transmitted in any form or by any means whatsoever without prior written permission of the publisher, except in the case of brief quotations in critical articles and review and certain non-commercial uses permitted by copyright law.

A CIP record for this book is available from the British Library

ISBN 978-1-913380-06-9 (hbk)
ISBN 978-1-913380-05-2 (ebk)

www.gold.ac.uk/goldsmiths-press

Contents

Preface ... vii
A Note on the Sources ... ix

1. Now, 2022 ... 1
2. Is There Life In Peckham? 1087–1960 ... 11
3. Only Fools and Housing, 1900–1990 ... 37
4. Only Artists: Peckham Painters (and Others), 1891–2000 ... 69
5. "We Are Trying To Build A Bit of Ordinary London": Politics and Planning, 1965–2000 ... 99
6. An Elective Montmartre: Renewal, 1990–2010 ... 123
7. "Incidental Person": John Latham and Flat Time House, 1985–2021 ... 141
8. Bold Tendencies: Culture and Creativity, 2000–2021 ... 163
9. On Road: Culture and Resistance, 1948–2021 ... 193
10. Next: The Space of Possibilities, 2022– ... 213

Index ... 233

Preface

I neither live nor work in Peckham, but I know people who do. Through them I have become fascinated by this ordinary and unusual part of London. I started to explore it in 2016, curious to know more about the artists who live there. It was a change from the books I usually write and, as I explain later in my introductory chapter, it turned into an experiment in a different way of doing cultural history. As I investigated, it became clear that a lot more people than artists live in Peckham, and that their lives have not been easy. Peckham began to reveal itself to me. Its history and the politics of its space became more and more interesting. But I allowed myself the freedom not to trace every possible connection, follow every lead, or tell every story that I heard. For practical reasons, most studies of this kind end up doing that, but I want to be honest.

The licence I gave myself turned out to be just as well because, as I was getting into my stride, the 2020 lockdowns came to hamper my research. Archives and libraries closed, and I could not meet as many people as I would have liked, for I strongly believe in meeting people face to face. Those that I have been able to see have been generous with their time and their comments, and I have shared as much as possible of the writing process with them. Interviewees specifically quoted in the text are thanked in the "sources" section that ends each chapter, but I would like to begin by thanking my former editor at Verso, Leo Hollis, for the very best critical advice. Tom Phillips got me started. Eileen Conn submitted to interrogation, and then closely read the final manuscript, picking up many mistakes. Benedict O'Looney was generous with time and photographs; Jonathan Wilson welcomed me to Copeland Park and, in a sense, Hannah Barry gave me the idea in the first place. Russell Newell, who has contributed two fine photographs, became an important interpreter of community feelings that I would otherwise have found difficult to access.

Many people have helped in different ways, and I would like to thank: David Atua, Hakim Baghari, Humphrey Barclay, Gareth Bell-Jones, John Boughton, Dhanveer Singh Brar, Charmaine Brown, Clive Burton, Lewis Chaplin, Tim Crook, Anne and Trevor Dannatt, Bill Feaver, Martin

Gayford, Camilla Goddard, Sophie Green, Margot Heller, Julian Henriques, Lucy Inglis, John D. Johnson, John Kieffer, John Kinrade, Noa Latham, John-Paul Latham, Harriet Latham, Gavin McKinnon-Little, John McTernan, Fred Manson, Lala Meredith-Vula, Siwan Moriarty, Jane Muir, Simon Mundy, Amanda Pryce, George Rowlett, Ben Sassoon, Richard Sennett, Raqib Shaw, Mickey Smith, Martin Stellman, the late Barbara Stevini, John-Paul Stonard, Liz Tang, David Thorp, Lily Tonge, Corinne Turner, Richard Wentworth, Natalie Wongs, Trix Worrell, Roger Young.

I would also like to thank especially Josephine Berry for spotting the opportunity, Susan Kelly of Goldsmiths Press for bringing it to fruition, and it goes without saying – which is why I say it – that EJB has been totally supportive throughout.

College House Cottage, 2021

A Note on the Sources

I have chosen not to snag the reader with footnotes. Instead, they can find my key sources in the section at the end of each chapter. I hope that this feels more like a dialogue, but I acknowledge all the printed sources, as well as oral contributions. The photographic contributions are noted separately.

Quotations from Caleb Femi's poems "On Magic/Violence" and "On the Other Side of the Street", in *Poor* (Penguin Books, 2020) are by kind permission of Caleb Femi and Penguin Books.

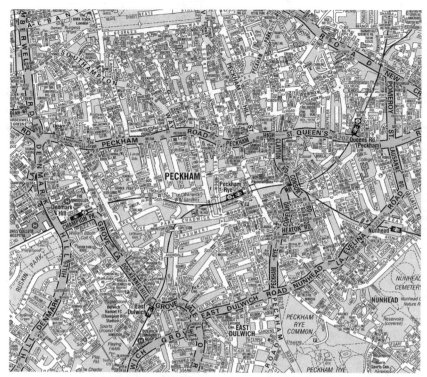

Figure 1.1 Peckham 2022 (image credit: AZ Copyright (c) Collins Bartholomew Ltd 2021 (c) Crown Copyright and database rights 2021 Ordnance Survey 10018598).

1

Now, 2022

"The city is an oeuvre, closer to that of a work of art than to a simple material product."
Henri Lefebvre, "The Specificity of Cities", in *Writing on Cities*, 1966

In 1948 Ealing Studios released its latest comedy, *Passport to Pimlico*. It is not about the whole of Pimlico, but takes us to a fictional Miramont Place: "a village within a village", a small community undergoing the irksome deprivations and bureaucratic irritations of post-World War II austerity. In a situation that will become familiar here, the locals are battling with the borough council over proposals to redevelop an urban space. They want a lido; the council wants a factory. A chance discovery from Pimlico's past on the bombsite in question allows them to create a temporary utopia, released from regulation and rationing. But the free-for-all of crooks and dealers that follows – an invasion by practitioners of what we now call the neoliberal economy – divides the community until they reach an accommodation with the council, and, by extension, with authority. The planners and developers are frustrated; nonetheless, traditional hierarchical order is restored.

There is more than another pleasing alliteration in the title of this book, *Passport to Peckham*. Peckham is far larger than Miramont Place, and it has a considerably more varied population than the White, lower-middle class and working class in Ealing Studios' comedy. But it is still a village – not "village" in the sales-speak of developers and estate agents – but a locally focused community, with all the tensions of village life, including struggles over living space and quarrels between allies. It began as a village, so small that it lacked a church. Its medieval street pattern created traffic problems that plague it still. It is also a village because it is informal, organic, without exact boundaries, and, more importantly, it is thought of as a place, rather than an administrative unit. Nobody planned Peckham.

As I explain further in the next chapter, the boundaries of my portrait of Peckham are fluid. At its centre are the electoral wards clustered round the heart of the original settlement, the junction of Peckham High Street and Rye Lane (Figures 1.1 and 2.3). Beyond the western and eastern edges of this map lie two important institutions that have given the place a distinctive flavour, a specifically cultural economy: Camberwell Art School and Goldsmiths College. Technically, Goldsmiths is in neighbouring New Cross, in the Borough of Lewisham, but for a time Goldsmiths had a key outpost over on Peckham's western border, not far from Camberwell Art School and another important institution, the South London Gallery. They are the subject of Chapter 4. The northern limit of my imprecise geography is the south side of Burgess Park, through which an older boundary, the Surrey Canal, used to flow. My southern limit runs from Goose Green to Peckham Rye Common, places that were there before the houses came.

Since I have explained why I use "village" in my subtitle, I should also explain those other terms, "culture" and "creativity". Not easy to do in short order, and this book explores their meanings through what people do. My working definition of culture is Raymond Williams's phrase: "a whole way of life". By this I mean culture as the signs, symbols, customs, costumes, and cuisines that give each of us an individual sense of identity, and through which collectively we make sense of the world. It is sometimes thought of as what we do when we are not working, but the way we work shapes what we do and who we are. At times, culture can be an unwholesome way of life.

Culture embraces my third term, "creativity", which is both the spontaneous invention that generates those expressive signs and symbols, and the crafted innovations of art. Peckham may not have been planned, but it certainly was created, and continues to be so. Art, as it has been taught and understood in the cultural institutions that I mentioned earlier, is, among other things, a response to place, and a means of shaping our understanding of it. Peckham was not designed, but it has generated contingencies over which individuals have done their best to exercise an imaginative control, in order to have a better place to live. That is why Chapter 7 is devoted to a single artist, John Latham, who lived and died in Peckham, and whose struggles with authority – between what will be later described as the vertical and the horizontal worlds – serve as a case study. He has left a lasting memorial to the distinctive way in which he understood those worlds. What first attracted me to Peckham was the number of artists who have chosen to live there; there are many more at work here, as well as poets, photographers, writers, actors, craftspeople, than I have been able to meet or mention.

As that suggests, art means a great deal more than painting and sculpture. I draw on novels, plays, poetry, music, and films as ways of understanding how people respond to the place that is Peckham. Chapter 3 begins and ends with television sitcoms set in Peckham. The first shows how – as in *Passport to Pimlico* – White working-class experience involves a resistance to authority. Resistance, and nonconformity, including crime, are important themes in this book. Another is the need for people to have their own sense of agency. The second sitcom invites consideration of comedy as a means of processing immigrant experience. In between is a discussion of the racism that newcomers have suffered under the disastrous housing policies of the post-war period. Another sitcom features in Chapter 9, this time one reflecting the later migration that has made Peckham the overseas capital of West Africa. These migrations have brought changes in culture that perfectly match Raymond Williams's meaning of the word, and have found expression in music, plays, films, and poetry.

As these changes – and the conflicts that they bring – continue, the 21st century has introduced an economic concept that Raymond Williams would have thought an oxymoron: "the creative industries". Artists, as described above, have been subsumed into a larger policy concept that emerged at the start of the 21st century. Architecture, design, fashion, digital innovation are all in their distinct ways creative, and they have been bundled in with the traditional arts, with film and television, to manufacture an "industry" where the signs and symbols of cultural production have become commodities for cultural consumption, with clubs, bars, and restaurants as important sites. "The creative industries" is no more than a label for many different activities, but language has its own policy power.

The difference between these creative industries and actual industry is that most of their creation is done by small units, start-ups, and single traders whose businesses are, to say the least, precarious. But they have a sense of independence, an idea of self-realisation which may be illusory, but which compensates for the hard work they put in, and the risky rewards they get out. These young, educated, and overwhelmingly White "creatives" have given Peckham a new sense of identity. One of the stories of this book is how, more than once, one way of life has replaced another, and in my conclusion I try to find ways in which there can be change without destructive loss.

The "passport" of my title is offered as an invitation to the past, present, and future of a few square miles of what one distinguished architectural historian described as "a forgotten part of London – from the air, just a part of the interminable London carpet and a part with no decipherable pattern". Yet there is a pattern to be deciphered, which is why we begin with a contemporary artist who has made his own Peckham pattern, one that exists through place and across time. Similarly, I have chosen to present my material in an overlapping chronology – hence the eccentric dates at the start of each chapter – because, in addition to physical geography and geology, the accumulation of history has created patterns that survive from the 19th century into the 21st. The challenges of 2020 and 2021 demand that we rethink the future.

This is an experiment in writing cultural history from the ground up. It is rooted in a piece of ground – roughly four square miles – and it looks to see what themes and questions grow out of it. There are aspects of this "London carpet" that are unique; the individuality of everyone who lives there must be respected, and Peckham has a distinctive presence. But there are also universal issues: above all, how do we live in a 21st-century city? Will the Covid pandemic change the use of social space? Can there be justice in the struggle over land use and property? How can the "horizontal" world of ordinary people – an idea further developed in the concluding chapter – resist the "vertical" power of commerce and the state? These questions are applicable not just to London, but to any large cluster of population, anywhere in the world.

Peckham is only one tile in the London carpet, and London is a world city. As an inner suburb it has its own relation to the metropolitan centre, although my main concern is the relationship between Peckham and its enclosing local authority, the London Borough of Southwark. In socio-geographic terms, Peckham is a pivot between the borough's formerly industrial dockland – now its corporate north – and the affluent domesticity of its furthest south. It is more a middle than a centre, and there will be comparisons made with the shape of a dumb-bell, or an old sock (Figure 5.2). However well intentioned, Southwark's central ambitions have produced fierce local resistance in Peckham.

It will be shown how "planning" produced the dystopia of the North Peckham estates, and then has sought to dissolve it, but without being able to resolve the deeper structural challenges of land values, social and economic opportunity, education, and employment. These problems have been made worse by racism. Nearly half the population of Peckham are from Black or Minority Ethnic backgrounds, though it is as similarly working- and middle-class as the longer-resident population. Historically, all were incomers, since the land was built over in the 19th century. The latest arrivals, now third- and fourth-generation, are citizens with as equal rights as anybody, but in spite of the enterprise they show, they are still treated as separate, and second-class. This produces a corresponding self-alienation, as Chapter 9 suggests.

Artists have likewise seen the opportunities that de-industrialisation and depopulation have created, and have in turn contributed to the process of change in Peckham. Thanks in part to the presence of two art schools, some, like their fellow incomers, have been there for a long time, but they have social advantages that can cause resentment from those experiencing disadvantage in terms of education, employment, and housing. This generates a dynamic tension, and it is important to recognise that the disadvantaged own a culture as expressive as the one that is institutionally acknowledged, however much it challenges the official culture acceptable to the privileged.

This friction is felt in the process known as gentrification, a term coined in the 1960s. It has not had a good press. The architectural critic Owen Hatherley has summed it up as: "working-class people give way to artists who give way to bankers". It has been most theorised in the United States, especially in New York City, where parts of the urban landscape appear to have been transformed in this way. The American sociologist Richard Sennett has written:

What we call "gentrification" is much more than artist-trendies colonizing colourful neighbourhoods, media-trendies following in their wake, attracting digital billionaires still struggling with pimples who price out both the natives and the first pioneers. Gentrification is more fundamentally a process by which the bottom 70–75 per cent becomes vulnerable to expulsion by the top quarter of people in a city, either through raised rents or by poor homeowners being seduced into selling out.

I show that the process is more nuanced than that, and Peckham is not Manhattan. But as in the United States there is a debate to be had. Its resolution will settle Peckham's future.

In the United States, since the publication of her study *Loft Living* in 1982, the sociologist Sharon Zukin has become increasingly critical of an earlier defender of New York's urban space, Jane Jacobs. Jacobs's campaigning book against urban renewal as it was imposed in the 1950s, *The Death and Life of Great American Cities*, led to conflict with America's most powerful town planner, Robert Moses. Her argument that places such as Greenwich Village could be revived by the influx of middle-class homeowners who would respect the texture of the streetscape and preserve the original community helped to defeat Moses's plans to drive an expressway through Lower Manhattan. The Village was saved, but the consequences were that it became subject to gentrification, and the original community was displaced. For Zukin, gentrification is "the overlay of renewal on top of abandonment". For all that Jacobs defeated Moses:

> Despite her good intentions, Jacobs's ideal vision of urban life has shaped two important vehicles that enable developers to pursue their goals: elected officials' rhetoric of growth and media representation of cultural consumption.

This is a quotation from Zukin's *Naked City: The Death and Life of Authentic Urban Places*, whose title is an ambivalent nod to Jacobs, and her book argues that gentrified communities have lost their authenticity. The rhetoric of growth and the celebration of cultural consumption can be heard in Peckham. So is the argument over whether recent changes have left Peckham an "authentic place" or not. In her case-study discussion of the process of change in Williamsburg, Brooklyn, by which a formerly rundown quarter, largely occupied by people of colour, has become a hip White bohemia, Zukin suggests that there is a "Williamsburg paradigm" that describes this process. What I offer is a "Peckham paradigm". By this I mean that, notwithstanding its particularities, the experiences through which Peckham and its people have gone – and are still going – exemplify distinct processes of urban change, and the cultural shifts that go with them.

In theory, within the general context of economic and demographic change, there are two principal ways through which established urban spaces change their character: regeneration and gentrification. Regeneration may have begun as a biological term for regrowth, but in policy terms it has come to mean something external, official, planned, and imposed. In contrast, gentrification is seen as internal, unofficial, untidy, and spontaneous. Yet since they both produce urban change, they should not be treated as opposing binaries, but as opposite ends of a spectrum that runs from massive top-down projects to bottom-up home improvements. Regeneration is a matter of public policy – "planning" – with the stated intention of producing economic and social improvement. Regeneration and gentrification often occur simultaneously and, as I show in Chapter 5, regeneration can have a covertly gentrifying agenda. Gentrification may be more informal, but it too is economically driven, and can be regulated by planning laws; it is also the result of hundreds of individual decisions and it has its own internal momentum. It is the difference between Robert Moses and Jane Jacobs.

The interaction of regeneration and gentrification can be seen in the Peckham paradigm. It starts with a settled milieu, such as Peckham became between the arrival of the railways in the 1860s and World War I (Figure 2.4). A not very exciting place, with pockets of deprivation: a racially homogeneous population, if stratified by class; a mixture of light industries, and a secure social pattern of local shopping, schools, churches, pubs, entertainment, and public space. World War I brings full employment, which continues thanks to London's privileged position during the depression of the early 1930s.

Then comes disruption. In this case, World War II brings not only significant physical destruction through bombing (Figure 2.9), but a movement away by both people and business, beginning a process of depopulation and de-industrialisation, leading to neglect of the urban space. Churches have been destroyed, others become redundant, pubs and cinemas close, department stores follow. Transport is difficult.

After a period of apparent social stasis – reflected in Muriel Spark's novel *The Ballad of Peckham Rye* – the place becomes a neglected milieu. There is unemployment, urban decay, planning blight. Education is poor. The area gains a reputation for crime. Race becomes a source of tension. A wave of migrants see the opportunities in the neglected building stock. So do artists, who are also in search of inexpensive working space. And then, there is an upswing. There is slum clearance and new social housing. This is not without problems. The first wave of state- and council-driven regeneration is a failure, exacerbated by economic recessions and political prejudice. The cultural clash of White residents – represented most obviously by the police, but also in the elected members of Southwark Council – and new Black immigrants leads to tensions that flare into riots, as in 1981 and 1985, and again in 2011.

In spite of this, the upswing continues as a second wave of regeneration tries to rectify the errors of the first, and there is a moment of public investment in private housing renewal. Thanks to the long boom of the 1990s, house prices rise, but not yet to the point where artists are unable to invest, or take up the opportunities for workspace created by the shift from an economy of production to one of consumption. This is literally so, as new bars and restaurants open. Self-starting cultural facilities appear. So do estate agents. Gentrification has begun.

This creates a new milieu, but it is not yet entirely settled. Some migrants move out because they have moved up the economic ladder; others are forced out by the rising cost of living there. The same is true of artists, but there is a re-industrialisation by the creative industries. If Owen Hatherley's definition is correct, the next stage is the arrival of bankers and others attracted by the "buzz" – that edginess associated with marginal areas whose real threats most would run a mile from – which will begin to fade as the area becomes homogenised by new-builds and refurbishments favoured by a largely White middle class. Shopping returns. House prices continue to rise.

Once this new milieu has settled, the cycle is over, and the paradigm of change is complete. Holland Park and Notting Hill Gate have been through this cycle; Hackney and Hoxton appear to be on their way. Dialectically, the next stage can only be a new disruption. In the case of Peckham, however, disruption has arrived before the cycle is complete. First came the post-2008 recession, and then the violent upset caused by the Covid-19 crisis of 2020. As I argue in my concluding chapter, this has drawn a line across what appeared to be the inexorable progress of gentrification, with its losses and gains – for there are gains for the winners. Covid has caused severe short-term damage to the arts, and long-term damage to the economy. It has already changed the way we think about living and working in cities. Yet the uncertainty generated may yet prove an opportunity to review how we got here, and decide how best to move forward. In a narrow focus, Peckham's local authority is the villain of the piece, and rightly so, but no local authority on its own can resolve the deep structural problems that a right-wing government appears to ignore.

It may well be that the Peckham paradigm is too neat and abstract for a study whose specificity comes from concentrating on these few square miles. This book is not academically neat in subject matter or approach, because Peckham is not neat. It is real. This is an empirical study that has had to become in part a participant observation. The ability to participate depends on circumstance, and the willingness and availability of people to talk with. The narrative does not have the smoothness of generality. Individual stories run up against each other. The only over-arching frame is time, and history. Here, history is made up of opposing stories that interlock because they are all about the same place: the extraordinary ordinary place that is Peckham.

Sources

The epigraph comes from Henri Lefebvre's essay "The Specificity of Cities" in his *Writing on Cities*, ed. E. Kofman and E. Lebas (Blackwell, 1966). Charles Barr uses the phrase "village within a village" in his study of *Passport to Pimlico* in *Ealing Studios* (Cameron & Tayleur in association with David & Charles, 1977). The bombsite image held symbolic power for Londoners. The plot turns on the discovery of a buried charter revealing the area to be part of Burgundy, linking "heritage" with recovery. Raymond Williams's phrase comes from his introduction to *Culture and Society 1780–1950* (Chatto & Windus, 1958; Penguin,1961). Williams spent a lifetime trying to define what he said in *Keywords* (Fontana, 1976) was: "one of the two or three most complicated words in the English language". For the rest of the "London carpet" quotation and its source, see the end of Chapter 2.

    Owen Hatherley was writing in *The London Review of Books*, 17 November 2016. Richard Sennett is quoted from his *Building and Dwelling: Ethics for the City* (Allen Lane, 2018). Sharon Zukin's *Naked City: The Death and Life of Authentic Urban Places* was published by Oxford University Press in 2010. She attributes the term "Williamsburg paradigm" to a catalogue essay by Jonathan Fineberg. I got the idea of a Peckham paradigm from her.

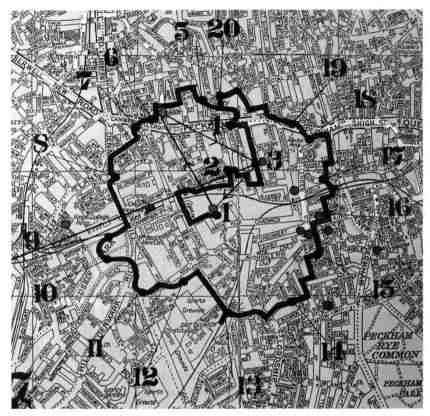

Figure 2.1 Tom Phillips, *South London Dreaming* (2006), detail.

2

Is There Life In Peckham? 1087–1960

"Is there life on Mars? Is there life on Mars? Is there life in Peckham?"

Alexei Sayle, "Ullo John! Gotta New Motor?", 1982

It is 6 June; rain is streaming down the street and the wind is tearing the leaves from the trees. The artist Tom Phillips and his assistant Alice Wood are getting ready to complete another section in the forty-fourth iteration of Phillips's long-running project, *20 SITES n YEARS*. Every year since 1973, at this time, Phillips makes a photographic record of 20 chosen places on the circumference of an imaginary circle centred on 102 Grove Park, SE5, his South London home when the work began (Figures 2.1 and 2.2).

The rules of this project require that each new photograph is framed identically to its predecessor, made at the same time of year, at the same time of day. There are secret marks at each location to show him where to stand, and he carries a notebook recording angles and lines of sight. In the early years, the images were always made with the same camera and with the same film stock, but cameras have accidents, and the film stock is not manufactured any more. The medium has become its own message about memory and the passage of time.

The photographs are ordinary, even banal. They have what Phillips calls: "a calculated style-lessness". Across the accumulation of years, trees grow and die, shopfronts change, graffiti are sprayed, over-painted, and rewritten; whole buildings disappear and new ones take their place. Cities do not stay still. The longer the project continues – for the *n* in the title is the algebraic symbol that signals that the series has no finite number – the more artful it becomes.

In view of the wind and weather this morning, it is lucky that Phillips does not have very far to go. The subject is the house where he now lives,

57 Talfourd Road, SE15. He chose it as one of his 20 sites because his mother bought it in 1953 for £500 to use as a rooming house, "and save the family from bankruptcy". In 1960, after reading English at Oxford, he started studying at Camberwell School of Art, just 200 yards down the road, so it was logical that he should have a bedsit there. Later, after he married and moved westward to Grove Park, he rented the front bedroom of 96 Sheney Road as a studio, and then began to use one of the rooms at Talfourd Road, gradually taking over the whole house. He moved in permanently in 1984. His mother's ashes are buried beneath a gingko tree in the front garden, in a pot made by her son. Each year the photograph shows that the tree has grown taller.

Various rules and traditions have also grown up. Because in 1973 the first image of 57 Talfourd Road captured a random passer-by, Phillips has taken to inviting people to repeat that anonymous person's first action. Today, I walk by. Several times. Until the artist is satisfied. The image will join its predecessors in the care of the Tate Gallery.

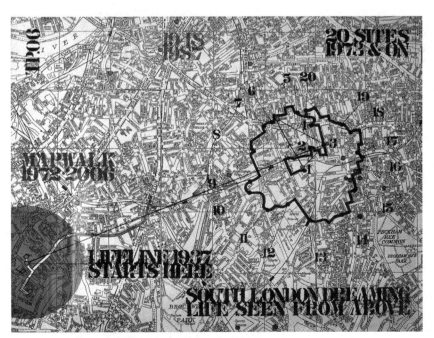

Figure 2.2 Tom Phillips, *South London Dreaming* (2006).

In the late 1950s the Situationists, a quarrelsome international bunch of avant-garde artists and revolutionary Marxists, set out to liberate everyday life through the practice of what they called psychogeography. One way of doing this was to go for a walk. They called it a *dérive* – a seemingly aimless drift through the streets of a city. They claimed it put them in touch with the city's psychic undercurrents, its fixed points and forbidden zones, its creative vortices and black holes.

Phillips's *20 Sites* is the opposite of a *dérive*. As the rigour of its process shows, his art is governed by self-imposed rules, but, paradoxically, these restrictions release spontaneity and lead to revelation. Walking generates its own visual and mental material, to the point of subjecting the artist to semiotic overload. For Phillips:

Structuralism, the ecological movement and many developments in art itself, have made the drabbest moments in sensual existence so indigestibly rich that, in order to survive the mere act of going to get the newspaper in the morning, one has in a large degree to screw down the experiential valves.

Open those valves, and objects found on a walk to the newsagent's – discarded bits of electrics, stones, bus tickets – become portraits of the people of Peckham.

One seed for his project was the mysterious land drawings visible from the air in Peru. Phillips became like a suburban Richard Long, the sculptor who has walked all over the world, taking photographs, making trails, leaving marks – though, as Phillips points out, in his own case he has travelled hardly four miles in his lifetime, having been born in neighbouring Clapham.

Philips sought out the land lines of South London for his first endeavour, *Mapwalk*, made in 1972 (Figure 2.2), but this only showed him that "Peckham is not Peru, and it was harder than I thought to extrapolate symbols of any great eloquence from these mean streets." Having sketched out a hieroglyph on a map, and then set out to explore it on foot, "at ground level I apprehended no magical feeling whatsoever". The banality of South London defeated him. Then, he began to practise making the perfect circle that Giotto was said to be able to draw freehand. The idea for *20 Sites* arrived. He took a line for a walk, attempting to describe a perfect circle with a half-mile radius around his Grove Park house. By doing so, he produced a physical, mental, and visual space, summarised in his screen-print *South London Dreaming* (Figure 2.2).

And still he makes his rounds.

We are exploring the production of a space, Peckham. As the previous chapter explained, this is about changes in urban living from the pavement up, and traces Peckham's history from village beginnings to becoming a settled milieu before 1914, then through the development and disruption caused by two wars, followed by post-war neglect, social decay, and then the slow upswing towards becoming a new, multicultural place, with the issues that brings. Towards the end of the 20th century Peckham was dismissed as no more than a drab inner-city suburb, with a bad reputation for deprivation and crime. No taxi would go there. Now, it is known as the last bohemia in Zone 2 – the name also of a group of Drill musicians linked by the police to a local gang. It may well be that the delicate balance that gives Peckham its character is about to be destroyed by planning, by what has become known as gentrification, or by the impact of Covid-19 and recession. Alternatively, it will simply change into something else. The way it came to be whatever it is, however, is important for how future city-dwellers across the world decide to live.

But then, where is Peckham? It is as much an idea as a place. Though it appears on maps, it has never had an administrative identity of its own. Even the origins of the name are uncertain. Before the creation of the London County Council in 1888, when the area was transferred from Surrey to become part of the county of London, it was administered by the chosen members of the vestry of the parish of St Giles, Camberwell. Between 1885 and 1997 it returned its own Member of Parliament, but the constituency is now merged with that of neighbouring Camberwell. Between 2002 and 2018 its central electoral wards were Peckham and Livesey to the north, The Lane and Nunhead below them, and Peckham Rye to the south of The Lane. As we will discover, ward names and boundaries keep changing, but this area is our main focus. In 2018 Livesey spread east and became Old Kent Road; The Lane became Rye Lane; Nunhead became Nunhead and Queen's Road.

Peckham is between places, absorbed into larger identities. It is not pretty, but has a personality of its own. Like most such marks on the map, it began as a village: a "T"-shaped cluster of houses around a junction of routes. The Manor of "Pecheham" was recorded in 1087 in the Domesday Book (the m is abbreviated

Figure 2.3 Peckham in Greenwood's map of 1830. Principal development is along the High Street, the crooked crossbar to the T-shape formed with the down stroke of the southward route to Peckham Rye. The Peckham branch of the Surrey Canal reaches down from the north.

in the manuscript). This translates from the Anglo-Saxon *peac-ham* as "village beside a hill". Later, a stream that flows northeast through Peckham Rye towards the Thames became known as the Peck, so we can read "Peckham" as place of the Peck – "rye" being the Old English for brook. By 1832 most of the Peck was a buried sewer. In 2003 a sculpture by local artist Randy Klein was installed on a traffic island at the top of Rye Lane to mark the Peck river.

The nearest hill is One Tree Hill to the southeast, but further north and east the land rises to the vast Victorian Nunhead Cemetery, with Telegraph Hill behind it. To the west stand Herne Hill and Denmark Hill, now topped by King's College and Maudsley hospitals; to the southwest lies the altogether smarter Dulwich Village, the Chelsea of South London, and to the south rises Sydenham Hill, where the Crystal Palace once glittered, following its re-erection after the Great Exhibition in Hyde Park of 1851. It burnt down in 1936, and its foundations now support the spire of the BBC's most celebrated transmitter mast.

This saucer of land, at the southern edge of the Thames flood plain, two miles across and three miles deep, is slashed from west to east by a railway that runs from a cutting and tunnel through Denmark Hill, out along an embankment, and over useful railway arches to Peckham Rye Station, where the tracks split – east towards Queen's Road station or Nunhead, while another line runs south and west from Peckham Rye to East and then North Dulwich (Figure 1.1).

Like the people of Peckham, this study conforms to no administrative or political definitions; its boundaries are fluid. It defines itself by what it is.

As a boy, the future poet and painter William Blake would make long *dérives* from his home in Soho. At the age of nine or ten (he was born in 1757), while wandering through the hayfields and across ancient common land at Peckham Rye, he had a vision; he looked up and saw a tree filled with angels, with "bright angelic wings bespangling every bough like stars". Another time, he saw angelic figures walking among the haymakers. In 1830 an Inclosure Act settled the land ownership in the area, with Peckham Rye established as common land. In 1868, in the face of attempted privatisation of the Rye by local landowners, Peckham Rye Common was formally acquired as public land; in 1894 the newly founded London County Council created the regulated space of Peckham Rye Park by adding land along its southern border from a former farm and market garden, once the site of Peckham Manor. By then, comfortable houses lined the green. In 1923 the Rye acquired a lido at its northern tip, closed in 1987 and finally demolished in 1995, with only a bruise in the ground and the remains of a fountain to mark its passing. At the north end of the Rye the rural curve of what was originally called South Street, now Rye Lane, led up to the crooked crossbar of the High Street and the centre of the old village, with Camberwell to the west, New Cross to the east (Figure 2.3).

When Blake wandered this way, the land between the drovers' highways to London, principally the Old Kent Road to the east, which carried the main traffic to central London, was divided among detached villas, estates, farms, and market gardens. Along with the village of Camberwell, and parts of Dulwich to the southwest, Peckham was in the parish of St Giles. The medieval church of St Giles, built on a Saxon site, stood at the northern foot of Denmark Hill, on the Peckham Road between Camberwell and New Cross. To accommodate the growing population, the church was enlarged twice, in 1786 and 1825. Destroyed by fire in 1841, and rebuilt in Gothic Revival style by the rising young architect George Gilbert Scott, it became one of the largest parish churches in the country, reflecting both population increase and middle-class prosperity.

The east window of the new church was partly designed by the equally rising young art critic John Ruskin, whose upwardly mobile parents had moved from Bloomsbury in the 1830s to one of the substantial semi-detached houses built for the burgeoning bourgeoisie who were escaping central London to live in the better air at the top of Herne Hill. Camberwell Grove, with its fine Georgian houses, climbing south from St Giles, was the earliest part of the parish to take on a *sub*urban character: connected to the urban space of London, no longer rural, but not yet absorbed by the city. On higher, healthier ground, and with the wealthiest inhabitants, this part of the parish was not only physically but socially superior to Peckham. In his memoirs Ruskin writes of the area in the 1880s as still one of "leafy seclusion ... certain Gothic splendours, lately indulged in by our wealthier neighbours, being the only serious innovations". Ruskin's name would later be celebrated in the area.

The "plains of Peckham", as Ruskin called them, were thought sufficiently salubrious, however, for the Licenced Victuallers Institution to build its neo-classical "Asylum" for retired publicans near the Old Kent Road in 1827. Progressively extended in the 19th century, the barrack-like housing is still there, owned by Southwark Council, but the elegant porticoed chapel, war-damaged, has become semi-derelict, though used for arts events. As the old agrarian aspects of the area, represented, for instance, by two taverns called The Kentish Drovers, faded away, so did connections with more ancient, earthy traditions. The riotous summer carnival of Peckham Fair was suppressed in 1827, the Camberwell Fair in 1855.

With the opening of the Camberwell New Road from Vauxhall Bridge in 1818, piecemeal and small-scale development began to spread between Camberwell and the fields of Peckham Village, absorbing the old estates and villas. Highshore Road, Elm Grove, Holly Grove, and Choumert Road covered former fields with mainly small-scale two-storey houses, either flat-fronted semi-detached Georgian townhouses or more suburban stuccoed villas. Much of this land immediately to the west of Rye Lane was developed by the French emigré George Choumert (1746–1831), hence the recurrence of his surname in street names. In 1876 the redevelopment of the gardens behind houses in Rye Lane led to the creation of Choumert Square, which is not a square at all, but a delightful secret alley of miniature houses and gardens.

In 1857 the British Land Company began to lay out houses in Talfourd Road and Denman Road. Talfourd and Denman were both lawyers. Sir Thomas Talfourd (1797–1854) was also a playwright (as was his son Francis), and latterly a judge. As a radical MP he is celebrated as a pioneer of copyright law, and is the dedicatee of Charles Dickens's *Pickwick Papers*. (Dickens rented a house for his lover Nelly Ternan in Linden Grove, off Nunhead Lane, handy for Peckham Rye Station.) The first house to be built in Talfourd Road, number 92, retains some of the cottage that had previously stood on the site. In 1872 the developers moved on to Bellenden Road, part of a second wave of more intensive building once the railways had come, during a general boom in suburban construction to provide for the lower-middle class and respectable working class who were moving out of inner London. Building in the area reached its peak. Led by the opening of Holdron's double-arcaded store in Rye Lane in 1882, followed in 1894 by Jones and Higgins's department store at the junction with Peckham High Street, with its distinctive pinnacled tower modelled on the clock tower in Piazza San Marco, Venice (Figure 2.4), Rye Lane became one of South London's smartest shopping streets, as chain stores such as Freeman, Hardy and Willis, Woolworths, and Marks and Spencer (all there by 1914) took advantage of the rising concentration of customers. In 1935 Holdron's, imitating new shops in the area, built a new block in art deco style (Figure 8.3). Rye Lane's reputation as a "Golden Mile" survived into the 1960s.

Figure 2.4 Peckham High Street in 1905, looking east towards the tower of Jones and Higgins. The head of the "Golden Mile".

One driver of Peckham's development was the need to accommodate London's growing population of the dead. There are five cemeteries within a mile of the Rye. The biggest, 52-acre All Saints' Cemetery, opened in 1840 above Nunhead, to the east of Rye Lane, and was declared full in 1969, though following a restoration programme burials continue. By the 1880s the land below it was built over by the developer Edward Yates with typically bow-fronted two-storey terraces. The Victorian sociologist Charles Booth thought some of them "badly built". Previously, the east side of Rye Lane had been mainly fronted by nurseries and market gardens. The last nursery closed in the 1870s, when the De Crespingy Estate, a Huguenot family present since 1741 and significant landowners on the eastern side of Rye Lane, decided to create Moncrieff Street. The influence of the De Crespingys and Choumerts meant that the area was sometimes known as the French Quarter.

In 1841 the living population of Peckham was 12,563; by 1900 it was 90,033, and the original more expansive and leafy suburban character of the area had almost disappeared, with little land left to build on. In 1900 Peckham, Camberwell, and Nunhead were merged as the Metropolitan Borough of Camberwell, which in turn was absorbed by the Borough of Southwark in 1965, when the Greater London Council was created to replace the LCC.

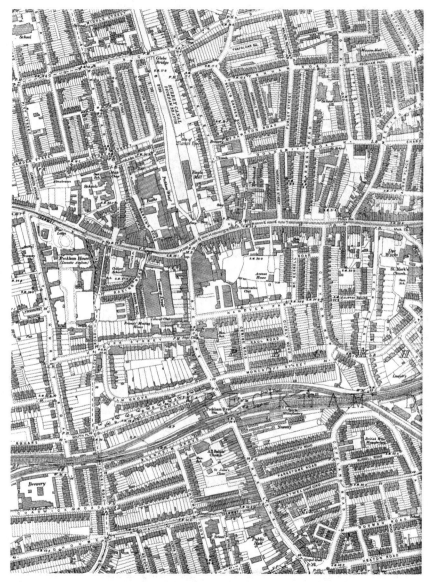

Figure 2.5 Central Peckham in 1897. Image courtesy Benedict O'Looney.

Peckham developed no specialist industry to speak of, once the fields had gone, although the cutting of the Surrey Canal from the Thames at Rotherhithe between 1801 and 1811, with a spur running south almost as far as Peckham High Street (Figure 2.3), together with the construction in 1833 of the nearby South Metropolitan Gas Works, created a semi-industrial area. The gas works' builder, George Livesey, paid for a public library to be built in the Old Kent Road. Closed in 1966, it re-opened in 1974 as the Livesey Museum, a children's museum, and was once more closed by Southwark Council in 2008. Southwark found that covenants agreed at its foundation meant it could not dispose of the building and, after it was squatted, approved its re-opening as an education centre. The western side of the canal, the gas works, and the associated commercial operations and warehouses gave the area to the east, known as Peckham New Town, a rougher character. The New Town had originally been developed by the Hill family, who gave their name to Peckham Hill Street, running north along the canal from Peckham High Street, and which is not a hill at all. By the 1880s the streets to the north of Peckham Road and the High Street were becoming slums.

The railways changed everything; the main lines out of Victoria Station, Charing Cross, and London Bridge were first developed without providing for short-distance commuting, which was done by horse-drawn omnibus – Thomas Tilling started his Peckham service to Oxford Street in 1848 – and then tramways (Figure 2.4). In 1854 the London, Brighton and South Coast Railway Company opened a spur line down to the newly relocated Crystal Palace, abandoned in 1964. In 1865, the year after the Cheap Trains Act introduced "workers' trains", offering cheap travel before 7 a.m. and after 6 p.m., the Chatham and Dover Rail Company opened Peckham Rye Station, which became an important four-track junction, linked to both London Bridge and Victoria Stations (Figure 2.6). The tracks formed a bow shape that framed the station and created workspaces in the railway arches west of the station and on the other side of Rye Lane. The station is an imposing building, with fine-wrought iron, and a large waiting room on the top floor (Figures 2.6, 8.6 and 8.7). In 1890 this became a billiard hall. After it closed in 1960 its windows were blocked up, and the elegant room disappeared from sight and memory, until a campaign to restore it began in 2006, followed by the station's heritage listing in 2008. Down the track further east, Queens Road Station opened in 1866, while the tramline network continued to develop.

Figure 2.6 Peckham Rye Station in 1892, with one of its two elevated rail lines on the left (image credit: local professional photographer Gustave Beneditti).

In 1867 the businessman George Bussey built "A Museum of Fire Arms" immediately behind buildings on the east side of Rye Lane, and almost opposite the square in front of Peckham Rye Station, with its own rifle-range running in parallel to the southern arm of the railway track. This was built over by 1887 and became "The Sports Manufactory" (Figure 2.7). The building between it and Rye Lane was rebuilt and in 1908 opened on the ground floor as a 400-seat "cinematograph", The Electric Theatre, with a billiards hall above; by 1924 it had become part of Holdron's department store. Its current use as restaurant, bar, and offices reflects the new Peckham.

Because the ground had good water, soda water and R. White's lemonade was produced in the area. In 1885 Louis Gandolfi established a business making superior glass-plate wooden cameras, run by himself and his successors until 1982. Other Peckham products were pickles, paper, birdcages, and sausages (Figure 10.1). The Bussey factory became celebrated for the manufacture of cricket bats; the great late-Victorian cricketer W.G. Grace popularised the Bussey brand, and the open space of Peckham Rye was known for its cricket pitches. More than 100 years later the new

Figure 2.7 Peckham Rye Station in 1910, looking east. The Bussey factory is on the right, fronted by what was then part of Holdron's store (image credit: Southwark Local History Library).

occupants of the Bussey Building and its neighbouring galleries and studios took to playing cricket in the next-door alley, from which emerged the Bussey Cricket Club, which plays regular fixtures.

The railways ended what little remained of the exclusivity of the area, opening it up to lower-middle-class occupation. The workers' trains and the tramway network made it possible to commute to central London and the docks and industries in Bermondsey on the south of the Thames. The west–east route through Peckham Rye Station created its own social demarcation, with a more middle-class atmosphere south of the line and west of Rye Lane, which remains. Peckham no longer supplied London with vegetables, milk and hay, but people. The philanthropist William Rossiter, founder of the South London Art Gallery in the Peckham Road (Figure 4.1), described the area in 1894 as: "the vast dormitory of the great majority of the men who work in central London". Mary Watts, wife of the painter G.F. Watts and a collaborator in Rossiter's project, described Camberwell as:

[a] thoroughly artisan and neglected neighbourhood, remarkable for the number of its public houses and the vigour of its language; for the long hours of labour and the utter absence of any means of education beyond the day schools; for the enormous number of its children, and for their uncivilized behaviour.

In 1900 there were more of the capital's 120,000 clerks living in Peckham than in any other part of London, but the London docks, warehouses, transport systems, and factories – mainly consisting of quite small businesses – also drew on South London for its labour. Dockers and printers, both independent-minded professions – the one because of its casualisation, the other for its unionisation – settled near their work.

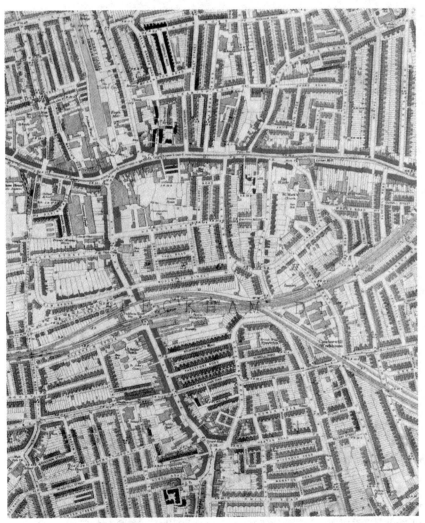

Figure 2.8 Charles Booth, "Poverty Map" of central Peckham. The bow-shaped curve of the railway runs left to right; darker areas show greater affluence.

When Charles Booth produced his magnificent 17-volume sociological study *Life and Labour of the People of London* between 1889 and 1903, which focused on the extent of poverty and social deprivation in the capital, he was not sure what to make of South London: "South of the Thames lies a huge metropolitan suburb of which I have found it difficult to form any but the most vague conception, so immense is it in size, so invertebrate in character." He thought South London dull: "There is something wanting. There seems to be a lack of spontaneous social life, among the people, perhaps due to the want of local industries. There is altogether less going on." Nonetheless, in the area that he described as a stockinged-foot shape between the Peckham and Walworth Roads on the south and west and the Old Kent Road on the northeast, he found: "a new population. There is no doubt some jerry building, and there are some dismal spots where poverty gathers head; but looked at generally, the houses appear to be quiet and decent dwellings of quiet and decent people."

Booth's colour-coded street maps of prosperity and social deprivation show a "well-to-do middle class" occupation of the main routes: Peckham Road, Peckham High Street and Queen's Road, Rye Lane and Peckham Rye, and, running north, Asylum Road, where the retired publicans lived among late-Georgian houses. But the majority of the area was "mixed, some comfortable, some poor", or "fairly comfortable. Good ordinary earnings." Booth supplied commentaries on the 134 sectors into which he divided the whole of London. These confirm his comment: "South London poverty lightens everywhere as we recede from the river."

To the north of the High Street, at Peckham New Town, whose inhabitants found "precarious work" at the gas works and around the Peckham canal, Booth calculated the poverty rate at 45.5%. By contrast, in sector 120, which ran from Camberwell Grove to Rye Lane, the rate was 5.9%: "There are a few poor streets near the tramway stables at Peckham. Shopkeepers in Rye Lane. Central part of the block is middle class; many keep a servant or two. Closely built estate on the west [developed by the British Land Company], occupied by clerks, mechanics and other workers." Camberwell Grove was suitably recorded as "well-to-do, large houses and mansions; people keep several servants". Towards the east of the sector there was "an increasing admixture of clerks and working people; fewer keep servants, near eastern boundary entirely working class. Very few poor. Large shopkeepers at Rye Lane."

Across Peckham High Street, to the north and east, in Booth's sector 119, its southern limit the High Street and Queen's Road, its northern the Commercial Road, the inhabitants were almost entirely working-class, with a 23.6% poverty rate. Conditions were worse in sector 121, comprising Nunhead and Peckham Rye East, at 40.6%, although "Near Peckham Rye people are comfortable; many keep servants. Some shopkeepers at Rye Lane and Nunhead. Remainder of district working class. Near Nunhead cemetery some very poor and improvident people; labourers and gravediggers. Many houses badly built, occupied by poor folk."

Though the celebrity of the shopping in Rye Lane grew in the 1930s, when new stores were built and the area in front of Peckham Rye Station was enclosed with vaguely art deco buildings, Peckham gradually became just another part of the "invertebrate" sprawl of South London, with its more than 30 churches, missions, and chapels, 20 schools, 300 pubs, two public meeting halls, and at least two lunatic asylums – there is a Harris Academy on the former site of one of them. Opened in 1898, the impressive Crown Theatre in Peckham High Street became a cinema in 1911, and was replaced in 1932 with the first Gaumont Palace Cinema to open in London – now in turn replaced by flats. There is a local tradition that King Charles II visited his actress mistress Nell Gwyn when she was playing in Peckham, but the first solid evidence for a theatre behind 100 Peckham High Street dates from 1780. (Another tradition is that while out hunting in the area Charles II encountered a species of butterfly known as the Camberwell Beauty, though it was not formally identified until 1748.) The High Street theatre closed in 1822 and became a Quaker School. This too closed shortly after 1880, but the shell of the theatre was incorporated into newer buildings and was rediscovered by local historian William Marshall in 1983. Reversing the process, in 1904 what is thought to have been a former Quaker Hall at 22 Elm Grove became the Peckham Liberal Club, a working men's club that has proved its usefulness right into the 21st century.

Before World War I there were five cinemas in Rye Lane, the most impressive being the Tower Cinema, with room for 2,000, which opened in 1914. The cinema survived until 1956, but was compulsorily purchased for a planned road scheme. All but the shortened tower was demolished, and when the road scheme was abandoned, the space became a car park. A makeover in 1999 filled the window above the entrance with a design depicting Blake's Peckham Rye vision.

With the outbreak of war in 1914 the insecurity and casualisation of labour that had produced many of the problems noted by Charles Booth virtually ceased, though hardship was never far away. London's labour market remained buoyant during the depression of the 1930s, with the arrival of new industries such as motor cars and electrical goods. Between 1903 and 1935 Edison Bell manufactured records in Glengall Road, near the canal, though breaking off to produce munitions during World War I. Edward Turner, designer of the Triumph motorcycle, ran a motorbike shop in Peckham High Street. While London remained Britain's key distribution centre, its manufacturing was for the most part a matter of small firms and skilled labour, unlike the mass, factory culture of the north of England. With work more settled, communities became more settled, though there was still pressure on health and housing, as a remarkable social enterprise in Peckham shows.

London's poor had long been the subject of charitable good works such as Octavia Hill's housing schemes, her Kyrle Society "for the diffusion of beauty" among the working classes, the Red Cross Cottages she built in north Southwark, and her work with the Charity Organisation Society. Public schools established "missions" bringing Christianity and good works. Peckham was no exception; the United Girls' Schools Mission, a consortium of girls' private schools led by Wycombe High School, established itself at 19 Peckham Road in 1906, moving in 1930 into a former Wesleyan chapel on the corner of Staffordshire Street and Goldsmith Road. There it provided social welfare for all ages, and launched London's first nursery school – evacuated, not very happily, to Glyndebourne, home of the opera company – at the start of World War II. A financial crisis in 2012 forced the organisation into administration and its buildings were sold off, although it continues to make small grants to local causes. In 2014, after being squatted for more than a year, the former Wesleyan chapel was converted into studio and gallery space under the name Assembly Point.

Shorter-lived than the Peckham Settlement, but far more radical in conception, was the Peckham Experiment. In 1926 two doctors, Innes Pearse and George Williamson (they married in 1950), opened what they called the Pioneer Health Centre in a house at 142 Queen's Road, the area having been chosen for the nationally average condition of its population. They took the sensible view that most medical practices, whether fee-paying or charitable, addressed sickness rather than health; the answer was to run a service based on the idea of a club for families, who would pay a subscription and receive social as well as health benefits as a result. Though medical doctors, they referred to themselves as "biologists", and gave advice rather than treatments. Initially, 112 families took part, but in 1929 the Centre closed as a first step towards a much bigger project.

In 1935 the Peckham Experiment relaunched in a modern, purpose-built building in St Mary's Road, north of Maxwell Fry's elegant flats at Sassoon House, opened in 1932. Dr Pearse's account of the scheme explained that the area had also been chosen because of the varied types of family living within a mile of the centre: "mainly artisans, occupied in every sort of skilled work, but also independent tradesmen, employers of labour, various grades of civil servants and municipal officers, clerical workers, some professional men as well as a few unskilled labourers". Wages varied from one pound five shillings a week to £1,000 a year. The spirit of Charles Booth's "quiet and decent people" seems to have lived on in this group of "sturdy people who have succeeded in keeping themselves in as fit a state as is possible in the face of present social conditions".

This was not easily done, as Dr Pearse's description of Peckham's housing in the 1930s shows.

The houses in the district, each with a garden behind, are mainly of two or three stories, built originally to house one family, but most of them now occupied by as many separate families as there are floors to the house. Little alteration has been made in these houses to adapt them to their latter day use, so that the accommodation is far from modern, and the sanitary arrangements inappropriate for the families they serve.

The new Pioneer Health Centre offered a vision of the future. Designed by the engineer-architect E. Owen Williams at a cost of £38,000, it is a white concrete-and-glass building with a sympathetic, rhythmically bowed frontage, on three platform floors over cantilever pillars, with a glazed-over swimming pool in the atrium at its centre. The original internal layout was flexible, and in addition to consulting rooms and a laboratory there was a licensed café, a theatre, library, nursery, changing rooms, meeting rooms, pool tables and workrooms. The architect and Royal Academician Trevor Dannatt (1920–2021), who moved to Talfourd Road in 1989, recalled that it was one of the four modern buildings that he was sent to study as a trainee architect in the 1930s.

The potentially sinister interest of the 1930s in "social hygiene" can be found in Dr Pearse's explanation of the purpose of the Centre, at a time before a National Health Service existed. Membership was exclusively by family unit, paying a shilling a week, which is more than it sounds. Members had to undertake a compulsory annual "health overhaul", described as "an attempt to estimate the physical efficiency of the family and all its members, and their capability for: – (i) individual life; (ii) family life; (iii) social life". The language recalls the title of the nudist magazine *Health and Efficiency*, launched in 1900, when eugenics and concerns about racial fitness entered public discourse.

When it came to social activities, however, this Brave New World encouraged as much self-service and self-organisation as possible. Members were made to feel responsible for their own health, and for organising their own entertainments and activities. The aim was to attract 2,000 families, roughly 7,500 individuals. It had only reached half that target by the time war broke out in 1939, and the building was requisitioned as a munitions factory. It re-opened in 1946, but its ethos did not suit the National Health Service created in 1948. People could now get their health overhauls for free, and it closed for good in 1950. The building was taken over as an adult education and leisure centre by Southwark Council, but when adult education ceased to be a local authority responsibility Southwark sold the building. In 1999 it was converted into flats, no longer a community asset, but a privatised and gated space, an intended public good passed into private hands.

Although Peckham had experienced the war from the air in World War I, with 10 people killed and 23 injured on the corner of Calmington Road and Albany Road in Camberwell in the last zeppelin raid on London in October 1917, World War II brought lasting change. The railways and docks meant that Peckham came under serious bombardment from 1940 onwards (Figure 2.9). The Kings Arms on Peckham Rye was destroyed by a direct hit, with ten dead. The rear of Jones and Higgins was hit in 1943, and its clock tower damaged. Of the 40,104 houses in the Borough of Camberwell, which included Peckham, only 403 houses escaped damage. Churches, pubs, shops and factories were lost. The beautifully coloured bomb damage maps produced by the London County Council show North Peckham and east of Rye Lane badly hit. Although the docks themselves could not move, skilled people and their industries could, with consequences for the post-war period. In 1944 ominous circles began to appear on the LCC's maps, indicating the fall of first

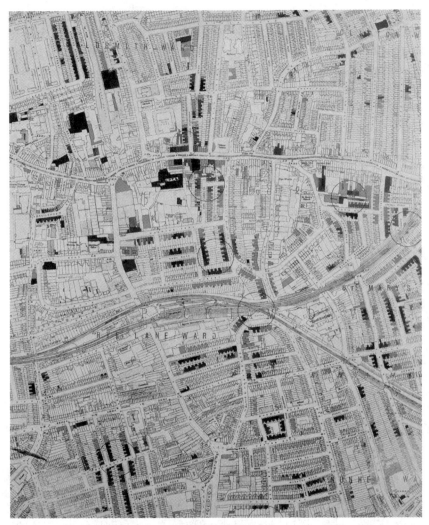

Figure 2.9 Bomb and rocket damage, 1939–1945. The circles represent V1 and V2 damage; darkest areas show total destruction.

V1 and then V2 rockets. On 22 June 1944, 24 people, mainly women, died when a V1 hit Savage's corset factory on the corner of Nunhead Lane and Peckham Rye. In all, ten V1s and two V2s struck the area.

Clearing bomb damage – such as the demolition of the Peckham Rye bandstand by a landmine – was one of the tasks assigned to Italian prisoners of war who were housed in huts on the Rye following the Italian surrender in 1943. (German POWs were also held on the Rye during World War I.) German POWs and Polish refugees followed later. The Peckham Rye POW camp was no *Stalag*; it was lightly wired and lightly guarded, and the Italians were sent out to work. At least one, who worked at Hartley's Jam Factory, impregnated a local woman, whose informal memoir suggests he was fondly remembered. The last of the huts, which later served as sports facilities, was only demolished in 2018.

The damage done by war created opportunities for Peckham, by knocking down inadequate houses, but as the next chapter shows, there is a question whether "planning" may not have been as destructive of place and community as bombing. The mutual interaction of industrial and demographic decline, post-war austerity, and, once the Welfare State had been brought into being, the sense of social exhaustion that pervaded the 1950s meant that Peckham appeared to have little to offer, beyond being a place where one just happened to live.

In 1966 the urban historian Ian Nairn took a melancholy and somewhat romantic view of what he called "the cockney kingdom" of South London. But he still managed to find signs of life in Rye Lane.

Now that the East End has been gutted by bombs and the wrong sort of rebuilding, Rye Lane is one of the few Cockney streets left inside the county of London. Cockney life has gone outside instead – to Mitcham or Slough or Romford, where the pressure of kind people trying to live your life for you is not so strong. But Rye Lane must always have been one of the best. It is on an old road, hence narrow and with a few bends in it, and unquenchable vitality has pulsed through it for ninety years. It is not only the Victorian detail that is full of life, but the jazz modern and the day-glo'd window displays. Everything fits except timidity, and a Rye Lane shopfront of 1933 matches a Rye Lane shopfront better than either of their prototypes. In the same way the display on a coster's barrow, a supermarket and a jeweller's shop are all part of the same family. It is not a dying family; in fact with luck it is a forecast, not a relic.

Nairn's optimism has been justified by newcomers who have remade Rye Lane as an exotic location, but in mid-century such streets had almost nothing to recommend them; they were as dull as Charles Booth had described them, and as ordinary and average as the human subjects of the Peckham Experiment.

In 1960 the architectural historian Sir John Summerson wrote off the area and its inhabitants in a snobbish summary.

A village in the middle ages, a semi-rural resort of well-to do professional men in the eighteenth century, and which in the nineteenth century became completely built up as a lower middle-class suburb. Sixty or eighty years ago the name of Camberwell [he includes Peckham] stood for the uttermost depth of social mediocrity. More recently it has stood not even for that; it has stood for absolutely nothing, a forgotten shapeless tract of London – from the air, just a part of the interminable London carpet and a part with no decipherable pattern.

Summerson depicts a settled milieu, recovering from the disruption of war, and now confronted by de-industrialisation, with a homogeneous population in terms of class and race, but on the edge of change. It sounds a dull place, yet in that same year, 1960, Muriel Spark, who had been living since 1955 in a bedsit at 13 Baldwin Crescent, close to Camberwell Green, published her novel *The Ballad of Peckham Rye*.

At first, this close description of lower-middle-class life, a very ordinary world of high teas, saving up for marriage, work in the typing pool at the local nylons factory, walks on the common, nights out at the pub and the dance hall, seems intended to confirm Summerson's patronising dismissal. But Spark's attention to topography and social geography – "there are classes within classes in Peckham" – reveals another, subterranean, life, emblematised by the excavation of an ancient tunnel below the nunnery that once existed near Meeting House Lane.

The "Ballad" of the novel's title hints at older ways of telling stories, of a survival from Peckham Fair, of unofficial, ordinary but individual and independent life. Spark's protagonist, Dougal Douglas, like her a Scot, is a crookbacked outsider, a devil-like shapeshifter, who through the pretence of "research into the real Peckham" disrupts the lives of those with whom he comes into contact. There are fights, a broken engagement, a murder, and eventually Douglas moves on, to upset others elsewhere.

Yet the novel ends on an epiphany. Not for Douglas, but for one of the characters whose assumptions he has disturbed. Spark's final words are:

It was a sunny day for November, and, as he drove swiftly past the Rye, he saw the children playing there and the women coming home from work with their shopping-bags, the Rye for an instant looking like a cloud of green and gold, the people seeming to ride upon it, as you might say there was another world than this.

William Blake was not the only one to have visions of another world on Peckham Rye. The mean streets of this forgotten, shapeless tract of London have stories to tell.

Sources

The opening of this chapter owes a great deal to my friend Tom Phillips. I also refer to his *Words and Texts*, introduced by Huston Paschal (Thames & Hudson, 1992). He was interviewed by Philip Dodd for "Free Thinking", BBC Radio 3, 25 May 2017. In 2015 Jake Auerbach, another denizen of Talfourd Road, made a documentary, *20 Sites n Years*, available on DVD (Jake Auerbach Films). Some of the images made for the *20 Sites* project are reproduced in Chris Scales, *Peckham Streets: A Photographic History* (The Peckham Society, 2017). *South London Dreaming* is the latest of a number of walk-works that Phillips has created. For theories on how spaces are "made", see Henri Lefebvre's *The Production of Space* (1974; English translation Blackwell, 1991).

My principal source for the history of 19th-century Peckham is H.J. Dyos, *Victorian Suburb: A Study of the Growth of Camberwell* (Leicester University Press, 3rd impression, 1973), to which should be added Mary Boast, *The Story of Camberwell* (Southwark neighbourhood history no. 1, 1996). Peckham has a number of distinguished local historians, J.D. Beasley being one. Among his works are: *The Story of Peckham* (Southwark Council, 2nd edition, 1983); *Building Together: The Story of Peckham Methodist Church* (Peckham Methodist Church, 1985); *The Story of Peckham and Nunhead* (Southwark neighbourhood history no. 3, 2nd edition, 1999); *Peckham and Nunhead Through Time* (Amberley, 2009). In 2017 the Peckham Society published Chris Scales's *Peckham's Streets: A Photographic History*; *The Peckham Society News* has also been helpful. Tim Charlesworth's *The Architecture of Peckham* was published by Chener Books in 1988. I have drawn on Derek Kinrade's *People and Places of Peckham's Past: A Selected Series of Short Articles* (privately published, 2016) and his *More People and Places of Peckham's Past* (privately published, 2020), as well as Peckham People's History, *The Times of our Lives: Growing Up in the Southwark Area 1900-1945* (Peckham Publishing Project, 1983). I have also used the resources of the Southwark Local History Library and Archive.

William Blake's vision is recorded in G.E. Bentley's *Blake Records* (Yale University Press, 2nd edition, 2004). Ruskin is quoted from his autobiography, *Praeterita*, vol. 35 of *The Complete Works of John Ruskin* (Library Edition) (George Allen, 1908). See also James Dearden's *John Ruskin's Camberwell* (1990; revised edition Guild of St George, 2020).

William Rossiter is quoted from Giles Waterfield's catalogue *Art for the People: Culture in the Slums of Late Victorian Britain* (Dulwich Picture Gallery, 1994), as is Mary Watts. Charles Booth's *Life and Labour of the People in London* (17 vols, 1902–1903; reprinted by Augustus M. Killey, 1969), has been enhanced by the reprint of all Booth's maps as *Charles Booth's London Poverty Maps* (London School of Economics and Thames & Hudson, 2019). I am indebted to Derek Kinrade for information about the earliest known Peckham Theatre.

The Peckham Settlement is recorded by Jennifer Stephens in *The Peckham Settlement 1896–2000: A Story of Poverty, Privilege, Pioneering and Partnership* (Stephens Press, 2002). *The Peckham Experiment: A Study in the Living Structure of Society* by Innes H. Pearse and Lucy H. Crocker was published by Allen and Unwin in 1943. The legacy of the Peckham Experiment and its wider context is discussed in Philip Cornford's *Realising Health: The Peckham Experiment, its Descendants and the Spirit of Hygia* (Cambridge Scholars, 2020). David Goodway has contributed an interesting paper on the Peckham Experiment's social principles to the online History & Policy network, "Anarchism and the Welfare State: the Peckham Health Centre", May 2007. I am grateful to the late Trevor Dannatt and Anne Dannatt for their recollections of Peckham.

The figure for war damage to Camberwell's housing is given by Tim Charlesworth in his *Architecture of Peckham* (Chener Books, 1988). In 2015 Thames & Hudson published Laurence Ward's edition of *The London County Council Bomb Damage Maps 1939–1945*. They are also available online. Ian Nairn is quoted from *Nairn's London* (Penguin Books, 1966). John Summerson's hostile comments appear in his essay "Urban Forms", in *The Historian and the City*, ed. Oscar Handin (MIT Press, 1963). Muriel Spark's *The Ballad of Peckham Rye* was published by Macmillan in 1960; there is a current edition by Polygon (2017). Jan Gorak has published an interesting commentary: "Angels, Dancers, Mermaids: The Hidden History of Peckham in Muriel Spark's *The Ballad of Peckham Rye*", *The Scottish Literary Review* 6, no. 1, 2014.

Figure 3.1 Peckham Road Memorial: Trotters Independent Trading Co in their Robin Reliant.

3

Only Fools and Housing, 1900–1990

Rodney: "Why do you want to buy it?"
Del-Boy: "So we can sell it!"

"Yuppy Love", *Only Fools and Horses*, 8 January 1989

British humour finds certain London place names inherently funny: East Cheam (*Hancock's Half Hour*), Balham (Peter Sellers), Neasden (*Private Eye*). In 1981 Peckham joined the list. On 8 October, BBC1 transmitted the first episode of *Only Fools and Horses*. Peckham became the setting for the gloriously comic adventures of the Trotter family, who work absurdly hard to prove that only fools and horses work. The series ran to 67 episodes, of which no fewer than 13 were transmitted in the absolute prime time of Christmas Day, the last one in 2003. Peckham became a bit of a joke. The reality was different.

The entire series was written by one man, John Sullivan (1946–2011). The Trotter family – the name plays on the old term for a rag-and-bone man, "totter" – was a three-character elaboration on the format of Galton and Simpson's father-versus-son comedy *Steptoe and Son* (1962–1964, 1970–1974). In its first series Lennard Pearce took the senior role as a crusty grandfather; David Jason played his grandson Derek – better known as "Del-Boy" – a fly ex-Mod, and a younger version of Arthur Daley in *Minder* (1979–1994). The elaboration was that Del-Boy has a younger brother, played by Nicholas Lyndhurst, of whom Del is fiercely protective. Rodney is 13 years his junior and, as it would turn out, only his half-brother. As the series progressed, this dysfunctional masculine household, living in a council flat on the 12th floor of the 26-storey Nelson Mandela House on Peckham's fictitious Nyerere Estate, was expanded and feminised by the introduction of

Tessa Peake-Jones as Raquel, Del-Boy's future wife, and Gwyneth Strong as Cassandra, a troubled and conflicted partner to Rodney. At what was expected to be the end of the series in 1996 the Trotters became accidental millionaires, but the series was so popular that three more Christmas specials returned them to their urban roots.

During the preparation of the fourth series in 1984 the sudden death of Lennard Pearce meant that an "Uncle Albert", played by Buster Merryfield, had to be substituted for Grandad in order to maintain the Trotters' wobbly triangular relationship, comically symbolised by their bright-yellow three-wheeled Robin Reliant van (Figure 3.1). David Jason as Del-Boy, with his flash clothes, cheap gold jewellery, cigars, and exotic cocktails, was the shiny lynchpin of the series, set off against the much taller Rodney. Del-Boy is the instigator; Grandad/Uncle Albert is the sardonic critic, accomplice, and disruptor of events; Rodney is the lugubrious but aspirational former art student and fall-guy in many of his brother's scams. Del-Boy is a "fly-pitcher", an unlicensed market trader working out of a suitcase, with Rodney as lookout. Behind Del-Boy's 1960s past as a Mod stand the figures of the strutting peacock Teddy Boys of the Elephant and Castle of the 1950s, and behind them the spivs of World War II, flashily dressed and dealing in black-market goods, probably pilfered from Bermondsey docks. Neither strictly legal nor strictly illegal, the business activities of TIT Co – Trotters' Independent Traders, "New York-Paris-Peckham" – represent a cheerful, but profound, working-class resistance to all forms of authority.

The author of the series, John Sullivan, was a South Londoner, born in Balham, southwest of Peckham. He left school at 15 and spent another 15 years in low-paid jobs, including second-hand car dealing, before he joined the BBC as a sceneshifter. Once inside Television Centre the camaraderie of the bar of the BBC Club meant that he was able to persuade producers to read his scripts. His breakthrough came with *Citizen Smith* (1977–1980), set in Tooting, though his next project was cancelled. A master of comic dialogue and a great plotter of farce, Sullivan, who coined the term "ethnic English", wanted to bring a greater reality to the portrayal of South London, and, as the Trotter family expanded, he was able to bring in broader themes of personal relationships and affective moments of pathos.

Sullivan wrote Del-Boy as a working-class Thatcherite – and Derek does indeed show his colours by exercising his right to buy his council flat, a policy introduced by Mrs Thatcher in 1980, only so as to be able to sell it at a profit. He is a proto-neoliberal, doing everything he can to avoid contact with the state, which he regards as a nuisance. The song over the closing titles, "Hooky Street" – a slang phrase referring to the sale of stolen goods – contains the immortal lines: "No income tax, no VAT / No money back, no guarantee". Ironically, when the Trotters do become millionaires, they lose everything again in the deregulated money markets that followed Mrs Thatcher's Big Bang.

Today, a facsimile of the Trotters' van is proudly parked outside the Best Western Hotel, Peckham – the former headquarters of the Amalgamated Union of Engineering Workers in the Peckham Road. But not a foot of film was shot in Peckham, throughout the entire series. The street market of the opening titles is in Islington, and Nelson Mandela House was in fact Harlech Tower on the Bollo Road Estate in South Acton, now demolished. The Trotters' tower block did not acquire a name until the fourth series in 1985. Local authorities had begun a policy of giving "positive" names to streets and buildings following the Brixton riots of 1981. In 1988 filming moved to Bristol, and Whitemead House, Duckmoor Road, Aston took over. The official reason for not filming exteriors in Peckham was that it was too far from the BBC's headquarters in West London, but it is equally possible that by 1981 the actual tower blocks of North Peckham had become too dangerous to work in. Having grown up there as an angry, illiterate teenager, the ex-SAS writer Andy McNab recalls: "Despite what Only Fools and Horses would have you believe, Peckham was never full of Del-Boy cheeky chappies, having a laugh on the market then going off to drink cocktails in the pub. It was full of unemployment, drugs, guns and mindless vandalism."

In 1994 the historian Roy Porter wrote in the introduction to his *London: A Social History*, "South London has gained a mean reputation for drug-dealing, racial violence, gangland crime and contract killing." In 1996 the American Embassy "red-flagged" Peckham, Brixton, and Lewisham, telling tourists to avoid them at all costs. Nissan once tried to promote a new car as "Tough enough for the streets of Peckham". This is a different movie to the jolly scenes of *Only Fools and Horses*, although echoes of this other world can be heard in the series. But the unregulated territory south of the Thames had been known for its brothels, bear fights, gaming dens, and general lawlessness since the Middle Ages. No wonder Shakespeare worked south of the river. In the 18th century, stagecoach travellers to Peckham needed an escort to see them through a particularly footpad-prone part of the route from the Old Kent Road to Peckham High Street.

So-called "Cockney" South London is a long way from the sound of Bow Bells in Cheapside in the City – to have been born within their hearing is the strict definition of a Cockney – but it has long enjoyed a tradition of working-class entrepreneurialism and the sort of contempt for authority shown by the Trotter family. It is wrong to smear a whole district because of the activities of individuals, but the area's reputation for criminality could be because it housed a lot of criminals. Another working-class family, the Richardsons, became one of the most famous gangs of the post-war period.

The childhood of Charlie Richardson and his younger brother Eddie, like that of another celebrated South London criminal, Freddie Foreman, was badly disrupted by World War II, which meant absent fathers, bombing, unhappy evacuation to hostile places, insecurity, a general lack of authority, and the need to fend for oneself. Brought up above a sweet shop in Wyndham Road, Camberwell, Charlie Richardson's first conviction was for stealing lead at the age of 14. In 1950, aged 16, he went into partnership with an uncle to set up a scrapyard in Peckford Place, Brixton. Scrapyards are ideal for all forms of illicit dealings, and Peckford Scrap Metal Works expanded its operations to a second yard off Addington Square in North Peckham. In his memoirs, Richardson recalls this as "a prosperous period, almost legal". His brother Eddie, meanwhile, was fighting his way up the local tribal hierarchy to become "King of the Teds". After National Service, mainly spent in military prison, where he first met the East End's Kray twins, Charlie Richardson moved into running drinking and gambling clubs. This time, "they were a bit illegal". When the government legalised high street gambling in 1960 it turned out that the people best qualified to run it were those who had experience in the previously illegal trade.

The career of Freddie Foreman, born in Sheepcote Lane, Battersea in 1932, took a similar path. At the age of 18, in his own words, he became "a full time thief", and went into partnership with his older brother George. Illegal drinking clubs were followed by legal betting shops. His most successful was in Nunhead Lane, where, he claimed, the comedian Ronnie Corbett was a regular punter.

As affluence overgrew austerity in the early 1960s, the pleasure-ground of London's West End became a battlefield for rival gangs supplying protection, prostitution, drugs, and gambling machines. Reggie Kray, with his homosexual and psychotic twin Ronnie, and their younger brother Charlie, had the East End sewn up, but expansion west brought them into conflict with the Richardsons and other gangs. Richardson received a hostile visit from the Krays at a drinking club he ran above a scrap yard in New Church Road, SE5. A shotgun was fired into the ceiling, but the police arrived, and the Krays withdrew. In the view of the cultural critic Dick Hebdige, the Krays, seduced by Swinging London, played out the media myth of being gangsters, whereas Richardson preferred (compare Del-Boy Trotter) to be seen as an entrepreneur.

Like all good businessmen in the entrepreneurial spirit that put the Great in Great Britain, we sought to minimize our investment and maximise our returns. We did not have the wealth and manpower (or the lack of morality) to travel the world and steal from starving colonials, so we confined our efforts to the home front.

Entrepreneurial business methods meant menace and murder. Things came to a sudden head in 1966 when it seemed that a Manchester-based gang was about to take over a club that the Richardsons also wanted to control, Mr Smith's in Catford, southeast of Peckham. A bloody affray left one man dead and Eddie Richardson wounded.

This, and the consequent police attention, should have been sufficient to remove the threat to the Krays of competition from the Richardsons, but the very next day Ronnie Kray walked into the Blind Beggar pub in Whitechapel and shot dead George Cornell, a former associate who had switched his loyalty to the Richardsons. This made things complicated for Freddie Foreman, who in spite of being a South Londoner was an ally of the Krays, and carried out certain services, such as the disposal of dead bodies. He had not been at the Mr Smith's fracas, but he helped to sort things afterwards, on this and other occasions. As a result, he was caught up in the wave of arrests and trials that saw Charlie Richardson sentenced in 1967 to 25 years in prison, and the Krays to 30 years in 1969. At his joint trial with the

Krays Freddie Foreman got ten years for disposing of the body of Jack the Hat, killed by Reggie Kray in 1967.

Although the removal of these major figures quietened South London for a time, family and territorial interests were still in play. Freddie Foreman's elder brother George was still free and enjoying the profits of a number of enterprises in Peckham, including a minicab firm and the café next door, and what he liked to call a "shush club" – an illegal drinking and gambling den – down the street. The Foremans also had an interest in the club and casino at 211 Balham High Street. In *Only Fools* Del-Boy plays and loses at the "One Eleven" Casino, which has a certain resonance, as do a couple of worried references to "the Driscoll Brothers" and the problems they might give the Trotters.

In real life, as the young artist George Rowlett, who stayed on in Peckham after graduating from Camberwell Art School in 1965, was to discover, Foreman family interests included the scrapyard that lay between the two lines of railway arches that extend east from Peckham Rye Station (the space is currently a scaffolder's yard, but there are enterprising plans for it to become part of a linear park, "The Coal Line", in the manner of New York's Highline). In 1970 Rowlett had acquitted himself well in a fight in the Camberwell Art School pub, the Walmer Castle, for reasons that will be explored later. The fight was observed by George Foreman, and Rowlett, needing to support himself and his family, accepted Foreman's offer of a job at the scrapyard. There, he graduated from sorting bales of rags and waste paper, metals and general junk to learning the tricks of the trade and buying scrap. This was a full-time job, cash-in-hand, but he was able to carry on painting, which seemed to be appreciated by his employers, along with his connections with Peckham's Black community.

By 1971, however, it became apparent that a Kray-associated outpost in a Richardson manor was not going to last. Rowlett was advised to leave his job – "as things were going to get heavy". The Foreman scrapyard business retreated to the safer territory of Bermondsey, and since 1974 the site has been occupied by D&R Scaffolding. Rowlett, by no stretch of the imagination a Del-Boy, was merely one individual caught in the rich subcultural life of Peckham. But his hands-on experience does confirm the generalisation made by the business-minded Charlie Richardson.

The most lucrative, powerful and extensive protection racket ever to exist was administered by the Metropolitan Police. As I got older, and became involved in more and more dealings, I made regular payments to the police. It was a sort of taxation on crime.

Rowlett witnessed regular Saturday-morning visits to the yard from the local police, based in Meeting-House Lane, to receive their pay-offs. They got their come-uppance, however; a young man from a criminal family, known as "Rubber", who had dropped out of Goldsmiths College, was called over by police in their car. Rubber was handed a stick of gelignite. Now that his fingerprints were on it, he was offered the choice of paying them off at £200 a week, or becoming an informer. Instead, he went to the newspapers and, after a sting, the Peckham nick was cleared out. In *Only Fools and Horses* series 7, Del-Boy is visited by the corrupt Chief Inspector Slater (played with sinister villainy by Jim Broadbent). Slater is a local boy-turned-policeman who in in the past has fitted up Del-Boy and all his mates, but this time he undergoes a comic humiliation.

Only Fools and Horses did not set out to glamorise the tower blocks of its imaginary Peckham, yet, as in Ealing Studios' *Passport to Pimlico*, the tenacity of its characters in the face of authority, and their laughter in the face of difficulty, may have brought some solace to the actual tenants of the grim social housing in North Peckham, an area which would become known as the Five Estates. During the long run of *Only Fools*, London was losing population and employment, and gaining deep pockets of social deprivation. To make matters worse, the abolition of the Greater London Council in 1986 meant that there was no central planning authority or leadership for one of the greatest cities in the world. By the 1990s, wrote Roy Porter, London was suffering "from a hardening of the arteries".

Crime and violence aside, in the eyes of many families, much of the capital – notably run-down inner-city districts such as Walworth, Peckham, Hoxton, Dalston and Tower Hamlets – appear decaying and dangerous, an undesirable environment for bringing up children.

Gentrification would begin to change all that.

The problem for working-class and lower-middle-class districts such as Peckham, apart from simply making ends meet, was housing. In 1866 the Labouring Classes Dwellings Act made it possible for local authorities to buy land and build houses for the said classes, but the take-up was slow until after 1900, when a consolidated version of an 1890 Housing Act empowered local authorities to build new houses to replace dwellings lost through much-needed slum clearance schemes. In 1919 the House and Town Planning Act transformed policy by requiring all local authorities to provide social housing. The Greater London Council's predecessor, the London County Council, which had acquired supervening planning powers in 1900, began to build its distinctive bald, brick, balconied four- or five-storey and lift-less blocks of flats across South London. The decaying streets of North Peckham were in obvious need of renewal – which would mean, in effect, hygienic destruction. In 1937 the LCC opened the Sumner Estate, north of Peckham High Street and west of the Peckham branch of the Surrey Canal. Sumner became the first of the Five Estates, a deliberately sinister branding created in the 1990s that reflected the ways in which the problems of social housing in North Peckham had become acute.

Until the Metropolitan Borough of Southwark was formed by combining the boroughs of Camberwell, Southwark, and Bermondsey in 1965, the London County Council took the lead in housing provision, while local housing policy depended on the political complexion of the respective boroughs. In the 1930s ratepayer interests dominated in Camberwell and Southwark, which meant that very little public housing was built. In 1945, in line with the country as a whole, the LCC, Camberwell, Southwark, and Bermondsey became Labour-controlled, and all faced the problems of reconstruction in the wake of serious bomb damage combined with five years of total neglect (Figure 2.9). Metal prefabs sprouted where bombs and rockets blasted spaces in Costa Street, Anstey Road, Raul Road, and Dundas Road, and some of them survived into the 21st century. The prefab once at 22 Bellenden Road lives on as part of the collection of the Imperial War Museum.

Between 1945 and 1965, 50% of new housing in London was built by the LCC, 42% by London boroughs, and only 7% by private enterprise. The figures for the three Southwark boroughs were: LCC, 11,006; Southwark, 9,362; private sector, 1,901. At the same time, the amount of publicly owned housing stock was increased by "municipalisation"; councils bought out private landlords who had been squeezed by the effects of rent control, or compulsorily purchased buildings judged unfit for habitation. In Southwark this meant that by the 1970s more than 65% of housing was council-owned, against a London average of 35% (though Tower Hamlets was at 82%). In North Peckham the LCC added nine blocks to the Sumner Estate, while further north, on the same side of the canal, the Willowbrook Estate was laid out, anchored by a point block completed in 1964 (and since demolished (Figure 5.6)). The architectural critic Iain Nairn approved of the work of the Camberwell Borough Architects Department, especially some of London's first tower blocks at Sceaux Gardens, behind Camberwell School of Art, and the Denes, further east, where Peckham High Street meets the Queen's Road, later demolished.

After the immediate surge of building post-war, and the Conservative government's housing drive, in the early 1960s construction fell to its lowest level since 1939, but in 1965 the situation was changed by the replacement of the LCC by the Greater London Council, and the merger of Southwark, Camberwell, and Bermondsey into the Metropolitan Borough of Southwark. The new local authority had greater planning powers, more money, and, faced with severe housing need, became the most active building borough in London. It announced plans to redevelop approximately 500 acres of bad housing, but this could not be done all at once, and as Southwark took over the construction of the Aylesbury Estate at the Elephant and Castle (later adding the Heygate Estate) and began work on the North Peckham and Camden Estates west of the Willowbrook and Sumner Estates, planning blight struck areas that would have to wait their turn. The GLC began work on the Gloucester Grove Estate, north of the Southwark redevelopments, and facing Burgess Park, created after post-war slum clearance and the closure of the Surrey Canal. It won an award when it opened in 1976.

By the time all these schemes came to fruition in the early 1980s, North Peckham had been transformed. But not in a good way. The change of perception was summed up by a director of housing in 1995: "It was a good thing to get a council flat in the 1970s. Now you have to be desperate." As early as 1968 Southwark's Development Department had identified up to 30 "problem estates", but by the 1980s the problem seemed to be universal. In a report for the Rowntree Foundation, *Swimming against the Tide*, Anne Power and Rebecca Tunstall wrote that by 1979 there were "shocking conditions" in the worst estates.

Figure 3.2 North Peckham in the 1990s, looking north towards Burgess Park. Gloucester Grove Estate runs along the edge of the park, distinguished by its castle-like access towers. Grid-like North Peckham Estate is immediately south and Willowbrook is to the east. Camden, with its sloping roofs, is below North Peckham, the older Sumner Estate to the East.

Dirty, chaotic, impoverished, vandalised, hard-to-let, unrepaired islands of neglect. Boarded-up properties, a massive exodus of tenants, very few, if any trained staff, low demand and no contact between tenants and landlords, made the estates unpopular, vulnerable and sometimes out of control.

The problem was economic, social, architectural, and – essentially – political; Conservative politicians, national and local, believed that individual homeownership was the foundation of a sound society, and that social housing should only be provided for the inadequate and the most in need. Labour politicians had no objections to homeownership but recognised that the private sector could not answer all the housing needs of the working class. Social housing was a necessary provision to guarantee the sound society the Conservatives also wished for.

In neither case were the tenants of social housing considered as active agents, with their own lives, values, and views. For Conservatives, they were a problem; for Labour, these were "their" people, voters to be paternally managed and shepherded into the polling booths. Councillors could influence decisions as to who got a home. Following the swings of the political pendulum, successive Housing Acts and government policies shifted the emphasis between improving living conditions generally, through slum clearance and rebuilding, and providing the minimum for those most in need.

However much they aspired to realise the social and aesthetic ideals of modernism, architects' solutions to the problem were constrained by cost imperatives. Land shortage and population pressure in South London made it difficult to create the "garden" estates with individual houses that British cultural tradition prefers. Flats, point blocks, and high-rises had to be part of the mix, and in spite of the partial collapse of Ronan Point in Newham in 1968, large-scale systems-building prevailed. Although the new Camden and North Peckham Estates were not considered particularly high-rise (Figure 3.2), the street patterns and informal networks that previously existed in these neighbourhoods were eradicated. People lost their landmarks, not just geographically, but socially and psychologically. It was hoped that new connections would be made by the "streets in the sky" that separated people from traffic, but the two and a half miles of walkways created by the deck access design of North Peckham had an alienating effect; the new estates and their tenants were cut off from the rest of the city. At the same time, social amenities and places for children to play were skimped on, or badly sited. Long-term, regardless of who was in political control, technical problems with these new buildings and the need to keep them in good repair put serious financial pressure on their landlords, the local authorities.

These problems were exposed by the recession of the 1970s, causing unemployment and social distress on the one hand, and a decline in maintenance on the other. The hostility of Mrs Thatcher's 1979 Conservative government towards council housing swung the pendulum towards provision by not-for-profit Housing Associations. Construction and maintenance budgets fell by almost half, while council rents trebled (as did housing benefit paid out). Southwark's ability to borrow capital for housing was cut by 60%, and maintenance almost stopped, generating a backlog of £90 million by 1987.

The Thatcherite "Right to Buy" one's council-rented property, enshrined in the 1980 Housing Act, was no solution. There were large discounts on the actual value of the properties, and the money raised went to the Treasury to pay off government debts, not to provide replacement housing. By 1994 a quarter of the national social housing stock had been sold off, but flats, as opposed to houses, were much harder to dispose of, and even harder on the big estates, where the 20% of housing stock officially described as "difficult to let" was concentrated; 60% of Southwark's social properties were flats.

As the urban historian John Boughton has commented in his study *Municipal Dreams*, the Right to Buy had a divisive and destructive effect: "it fed a powerful and damaging narrative that held, to put it crudely, that council housing was for losers". But this was only one factor in the combination of architectural arrogance, poor maintenance, unemployment rates three times the national average, many single-parent families, and a disproportionate number of children and young people with little to do. One third of young people were committing a crime before the age of 18. North Peckham was becoming a no-go area. The poet and filmmaker Caleb Femi – who on separate occasions was stabbed and shot while living on the North Peckham Estate – has described how "police would chase you up to a certain point, but it was so interlinked and complicated that you would have to live there to know how to get around. They would stop at the edge, and only come in to clean up after things had happened." The arrival of heroin in the mid-1980s, shortly followed by crack cocaine, made matters even worse; "it completely destroyed the neighbourhood", recalls another former resident, Russell Newell. In *Swimming against the Tide* Anne Power and Rebecca Tunstall identified the longest-lasting and most deep-seated problem created by these "problem estates": the social stigma of having to live there.

In 1981 riots occurred in neighbouring Brixton, in the words of Lord Scarman's subsequent report "the like of which had not been previously seen this century in Britain" – which were repeated in 1985 and 2011 – and showed that the "losers", whether Black or White, were not passive. The riots focused official minds on the growing problems in the estates, especially in North Peckham, where there had been trouble in 1981. Southwark took an unusual approach to changing its social mix by tolerating squatting (in 1988, 1,600 Southwark Council properties were squatted), but the squatters proved a source of crime. Art students and schoolteachers were encouraged with short-life tenancies to move into the North Peckham estates, but the newcomers did not last long. Former Camberwell art student Gregor Muir recalls:

Everything was scorched and blackened, including parked cars, bins and shop fronts. A discarded mattress lay propped up against an industrial wheelie bin in a burnt-out shed. The walkways were in permanent darkness, adding to the very real sense of danger. Students at Camberwell who were allocated flats on the estate had to gang up most evenings just to defend themselves from muggers on the journey home. At night, it was truly terrifying.

It was believed that former long-term patients of the near-by Maudsley Hospital were being rehoused as part of "Care in the Community".

In 1987 the journalist Robert Chesshyre described the North Peckham Estate as "Eleven thousand of the least desirable homes in the country", where *no one* had exercised the Right to Buy, and £5 million was owed in rent. The estate and its neighbours were rife with drug use, raddled with squatters, rigid with racial tension, and avoided by a frightened and corrupt police force. King's College Hospital was dealing with seven stab victims a day. Chesshyre observed: "a few streets away from the gentrified terraces, there was a world where the Queen's writ ran but fitfully".

This was not the wacky world of Nelson Mandela House or the Nyerere Estate. Chesshyre commented: "violence and the fear of violence are ever present in North Peckham, like muzak in a department store". The local vicar said of his parish of 8,000: "Life is empty of everything, there is no pattern to it; there is nothing to do, no point to anything. There is lethargy and apathy."

Figure 3.3 Russell Newell, *Night.* North Peckham Estate, 1984.

The stress that social housing was under is shown by the way that in 1975 the Southwark Community Development Project, which ran from 1969 to 1978, could publish a study with the bald title, *Housing the Poor? Council Housing in Southwark 1925–1975*. Community Development Projects were a failed attempt by the Home Office to relieve the pressure on local authority social services by persuading communities to take more responsibility for themselves – a ground-upwards idea; £5 million was spent nationally through the government's Urban Programme on 12 selected areas, of which Southwark's Newington ward was one. The "action" teams were paired with academic researchers, but there was stiff resistance from local councillors and Southwark bureaucrats to the intervention. The result, in the words of the first team of academics from Brunel University, who gave up in frustration in 1972, was "a Tower of Babel".

Although the Southwark Community Development Project concentrated on the northern ward of Newington – a triangle running south from the Elephant and Castle and framed by the Walworth and Kennington Park Roads (Figure 5.2) – its reports give an insight into the way an inner-London borough worked at this time. They show that one of the motivations for the government's Urban Programme was to answer Enoch Powell's profoundly influential and deeply racist "rivers of blood" speech of April 1968, which set back the hope of harmonious community relations as brutally as the White attacks on Black citizens in Notting Hill had done in 1958. Yet there was a desire to repress this anxiety. *Housing the Poor*'s thorough account makes absolutely no mention of race or ethnicities. It would not be until the national census of 1991 that direct questions would be asked about ethnicities, even though racial discrimination in housing (and everywhere else) had been an issue since the emblematic arrival of the *Empire Windrush* from the West Indies on 22 June 1948. They were by no means the first arrivals. Harold Moody (1882–1947) had established the first Black civil rights movement in Britain, the League of Coloured Peoples, in Peckham in 1931.

Brixton, in neighbouring Lambeth, and near the former deep air-raid shelters where some of the *Windrush* arrivals were first able to stay, became a centre of Caribbean settlement. Other *Windrush* passengers went to a hostel in Gordon Road, Peckham. Sam King, a *Windrush* arrival, returning after wartime service in the RAF, became a Bellenden ward councillor between 1982 and 1986, and Southwark's first Black mayor. The popularity of

South London increased after the riots in Notting Hill in 1958 dramatised the prevalent hostility that immigrants faced. The government began to address the most overt forms of discrimination, but the Commonwealth Immigrants Act of 1962, which ended the automatic right of Commonwealth citizens to live and work in Britain, was itself discriminatory. There was a rush to beat the deadline for arrivals; those in the UK could continue to bring in wives and family and felt reluctant to leave in case they could nor re-enter. Whereas many had intended to spend only a few years and go home, those who had made it to Britain settled, no longer as temporary migrants, but immigrants. The unintended consequences for the "*Windrush* generation" have been harshly felt since 2018; more than 15,000 innocent people without documentation have become victims of the "hostile environment" created by the 2015 Conservative government. Many lost their livelihoods, the right to work, and access to the health service; some were deported to islands not seen since childhood – or ever.

The post-war arrivals had to wait until the Race Relations Act of 1965 before discrimination on the grounds of colour, race, or national or ethnic origins became a civil offence, and it was not until 1968 that the Act was extended to cover private landlords. The need for more legislation was confirmed in 1965 by a report for the government from a committee on housing in Greater London chaired by the distinguished lawyer Sir Milner Holland. This was a response to the moral panic set off by revelations about the activities of a slum landlord, Peter Rachman, that had come out as part of the Profumo/ Christine Keeler scandal of 1963. The report concentrated on public and private rented housing and revealed that in the 1950s there were 43,000 slum dwellings in London. Patronisingly, the report described "coloured people" as "cheerful people, and given to much singing, to playing radiograms and holding parties", but revealed that they were discriminated against not only by private landlords, where they had to pay higher rents, but also when they tried to become tenants of council housing, where there appeared to be an unofficial quota of around 5%. As a result, they preferred to buy private properties, often of poor quality, and had little choice but to overcrowd them. There were plenty of such houses in Peckham.

In 1967 the Institute of Race Relations, which came into being as an independent charity in the same year as the Notting Hill riots in 1958, published the first ever study of local government housing policy, Elizabeth Burney's

Housing on Trial: A Study of Immigrants and Local Government. The introduction by E.J. Rose, director of the Survey of Race Relations in Britain, accurately warned:

The next ten years will decide the course of race relations in this country for several generations. By far the most critical influence will be the nature of housing available to coloured families, for this will determine the future pattern of settlement, the development of social relations, the type of schooling offered to the children, and finally the jobs for which they will be able to qualify.

Events have proved Rose correct. The report concluded: "there is absolutely no question that racial prejudice plays an influential role in the property market."

Landlords, estate agents, and building societies were all responsible, but so were the "investigators" or "visitors" employed by local authorities to assess the suitability of potential tenants, sometimes with patronage links to councillors. They were capable of comments such as: "although she is coloured she does seem very clean". These attitudes ensured that people of colour were at first rare on council estates, on average 5% nationally. When they were housed, often as a result of slum clearance, they were offered "patched" houses, or put on what were considered the worst estates. The change of Southwark's re-housing policy from giving priority to "established" residents (usually White) to those most in need (usually Black) created local tension. The report noted the emergence of "twilight areas" as a euphemism and commented of the term "ghettoes": "what began as a mere metaphor is taken seriously as a sociological description". This is in spite of the fact that people of colour were a minority of the population, rarely more than 10% in a few inner-London wards – some of which were in North Peckham. As slum clearance moved more people from private housing, however, and a second and third generation of once immigrant families began to grow up in Britain, North Peckham began to match the fashionable new sociological description.

When the painter George Rowlett arrived at Camberwell School of Art in 1962 he was appalled by the level of racism in the twilight zones of Peckham. Cards in shop windows advertising rooms to let warned: No Dogs, No Blacks, No Irish. He, his wife, and a newborn son found two rooms in a house next door to the Norfolk House Constitutional Club in Queen's Road: "The place was crawling with bedbugs. I didn't know what they were." The house was owned by a racist Pole, who had arrived at the end of the war. (It is forgotten that Poles, displaced by war, often deportees from the Soviet Union, were also passengers on the *Empire Windrush*.) Other tenants were West Indians, chiefly Jamaican, some of whom had served in the RAF during the war, and whose wives worked as nurses. Though "intensely patriotic, they were treated abysmally by the police". The Peckham police were notorious. The writer Stephen Bourne recalls that, growing up on a Peckham housing estate, "if we saw a policeman, we didn't ask him the time, we just ran for it".

In 1964 Rowlett moved a mile or so south, to two rooms and a kitchen in Fenwick Road, an area where, he noted: "most of the Whites had gone" (population maps confirm this). His relations with the Black community became closer after his first marriage broke down, and he met his future second wife, who was half-Nigerian. Hostile remarks by White racists when the courting couple were drinking in the Walmer Castle led to the fight observed by George Foreman, and the job at Foreman's scrapyard.

By the time Rowlett left Peckham for Rotherhithe in 1989, he thought Peckham an even more violent place than when he arrived in 1962. In 1972 his second marriage also broke up, and he and his son by his second wife moved to a commune in Gordon Road, where he found the atmosphere both middle-class and oppressive. The theory of holding all property in common proved fascistic. After time in nearby Brockley, where his landlady repaired her fence with some of his best paintings, in 1973 he found shelter in the former School House of St Luke's Primary School at 161A Sumner Road, north of Peckham High Street. The school had been opened in 1847 by Camden Schools, an offshoot of the Camden Chapel in Peckham Road (following war damage the Camden Chapel was demolished in 1952). The School House was being used as a base for an adventure playground, and when the school itself closed down, he was able to stay on as a protected tenant. But trouble started when the Sojourner Truth Youth Association (STYA), a local Black community group named after a heroine of the American Emancipation movement, squatted the school buildings, and then set about forcing him out. After the Diocesan Board sold the buildings to Southwark Council, and the council passed them on to STYA, an eviction notice led him eventually to be rehoused in Rotherhithe.

Rowlett was not sorry to go. North Peckham was being fought over by rival groups: West Africans competing with West Indians, Vietnamese boat people – refugees resettled after the Vietnam War at the end of the 1970s – Glaswegians, and Travellers who had moved into the Surrey Canal area after the Peckham Branch had been closed in 1972. (Peckham has three Traveller sites.) Some locals took to referring to the area as "Peck-Narm". 'Narm became a regular usage, as in Caleb Femi's spoken-word film *We Are The Children of the 'Narm*. All were struggling for space in some of the worst living conditions in London.

In *Lovers and Strangers*, her study of post-war immigration, Clair Wills points out that among these competing groups, the idea of an "Afro-Caribbean community" was itself a product of the pressures on new arrivals in Britain. This awareness developed in the two- to three-week sea voyage to Britain, where migrants from very different islands, with distinctive cultures, would meet for the first time. Wills quotes the writer George Lamming: "Most West Indians of my generation were born in England." Wills comments: "They were born in their twenties, to a new collective consciousness of themselves as Caribbean, and as Black, and these new political identities were to shape the immigrant experience in years to come." New cultural identities that evolved in parallel to the political experience of being in Britain would also shape the place they had landed in.

The most portable vessel of cultural identity is song. This is especially true if a slave past had forbidden access to reading and writing. Among those to arrive on the *Empire Windrush* was Trinidadian Aldwyn Roberts, better known as Lord Kitchener, who on landing sang "London is the Place for Me" for the benefit of Pathé News. The "Mother Country" he sang about would prove less "comfortable" and the English far less "sociable" than the rhymes in his song. He and fellow passengers Lord Beginner and Lord Woodbine brought with them their island's taste for topical calypso. Lord Beginner's "Cricket, Lovely Cricket" celebrated an important psychological victory when the West Indies beat England at Lords in 1950.

The independent record label Melodisc, founded in 1949 to licence American jazz and folk recordings, started to record Black artists in Britain, and formed a subsidiary, Blue Beat, which became a conduit for calypso, and its successor, ska. There was an important trade in recordings from the

Caribbean that influenced British-based artists who found work in West End night clubs, and in the network of lesser clubs and shebeens that became established in London and other cities. According to the Indian writer Dilip Hero, "at one time there were fifty basement clubs in South London managed and/or owned by West Indians. However, they could not establish public dance halls of their own."

By the time the magazine *Black Music* was launched in 1973 – in itself a sign of the growth of the form – South London's most popular club was Mr Bees at 43 Peckham High Street – it later went by the names of the Bouncing Ball, Chicago, and Kisses – from which grew the pirate radio station Kiss, one of up to 100 illegal Black music stations, and which in 1990 became the legitimate Kiss FM. Once known as Central Hall, the building had begun life as a mission hall in 1884, taken over in 1908 by "The Church of Strangers" run by the Rev. Ernest Thorn, who liked to preach while wearing a suit of armour. In 1910 Thorn sublet the hall as a cinema and concert hall. In 1932, however, it was acquired by Express Dairies, which opened a shop on the ground floor with restaurants above. Postwar, it once more served as a music venue, under various names, and in the early 1970s it became known for reggae. The as-yet-unrecognised Bob Marley and the Wailers played there on their first London visit in 1973. It also grew its own talent. The entrepreneurial resident DJ, Admiral Ken, ran Friday-night talent competitions. Jamaican-born, but Brixton-based, Glen Sloley won so often for his "talk over" of dub records that he was given a recording contract.

Although the acceptably cheerful rhythms of calypso could be heard on the BBC – the now embarrassingly titled *Serenade in Sepia* transferred from radio to television in 1948 – and the Anglo-Caribbean Island Records had a ska hit with "My Boy Lollipop" in 1964 (recorded in London with British session musicians), it was a constant complaint in *Black Music* magazine that the BBC was reluctant to play West Indian music, especially reggae, a form developing in Jamaica through the 1960s. Excluded from White British culture by racism, poverty, and poor housing and education, second-generation West Indians reached back for their cultural identity. Reggae was particularly appropriate; before Jamaica achieved independence in 1962 it was regarded as subversive because of its pagan roots in African drumming, and its association with a slave past and a working-class present. Rastafarianism reached further to Africa, appropriating Bible narratives to draw a parallel with the Babylonian captivity of the Israelites. As Dick Hebdige commented, Rastafarianism sought to turn "negritude into a positive sign".

As with other subcultures that Hebdige describes, a positive sense of identity came at a price. The chiaroscuro of reggae, sung in an increasingly dense Jamaican patois that asserted linguistic independence from the vocabulary of pop, and the association with the dreadlocks and sacramental attitude to ganja of Rastafarianism kept such music off the airwaves and out of the mainstream. Island Records broke through in 1975 with Bob Marley and the Wailers, only for Marley to be criticised for his success. The "otherness" of reggae and American soul appealed to similarly alienated White working-class youth, and attempts were made to deploy reggae in the Rock against Racism campaigns at the end of the 1970s, but it remained an essentially Caribbean medium. There was also a dark side. Britain imported not only the music of Jamaica, but the political and territorial conflicts of the island. Music had a strong association with politics, reflected in the intense rivalries of competing sound systems that were the public faces of local economic and political power.

DJs challenged and insulted their competitors, and "battles" between rival MCs and sound systems established a performance tradition that, as we shall see, continues with grime and drill music in the 21st century. Behind the scenes producers were ruthless, and the threat of violence between rival crews was ever present. This imported tension is vivid in Franco Rosso's film *Babylon*, released in November 1980 (and therefore anticipating the Brixton riots), starring Brinsley Forde from the British group Aswad. As *Babylon* shows, a north–south London rivalry, not unlike that of the criminal underworld, soured the club scene. Similarly, a shot fired in the Bouncing Ball on Peckham High Street opens the 1992 Channel 4-produced *We The Ragamuffin*, filmed on Peckham's Camden Estate.

The 30-minute *We The Ragamuffin* (Figure 3.4) is a remarkable record of life in North Peckham, not least because so many of its locations have since been demolished. It is a view from the inside, for it was part of Channel 4's remit to give local communities their own voice. (This did not stop Channel 4 insisting on the rich local patois being shown with subtitles, much to its creator's annoyance.) The driving force behind it was Russell Newell, Peckham-born in 1965 to an English mother and Jamaican father,

Only Fools and Housing, 1900–1990 | 57

Figure 3.4 Poster promoting *We The Ragamuffin*, 1992 (image credit: courtesy Julian Henriques).

who had left school at the age of 15 with no qualifications but with a passion for photography. This led to a job as a photographer and writer on Britain's first Black national newspaper, the *West Indian World*. Keen to move on from photography, he worked with the director Julian Henriques to secure a £225,000 commission from Channel 4 for a semi-improvised comedy-drama, set to "ragamuffin", a gentler British musical form of Jamaican dancehall.

In and around North Peckham, including a sound studio at the Sojourner Truth Youth Association (source of such trouble for George Rowlett), the local community closes ranks to see off two bumbling gunmen seeking to threaten the film's hero, "sing-jay" Buckey Ranks. Ranks was a late replacement for Newell's original lead, who had been arrested. All the cast were local, and some quite hard – as Newell reflects. But they were telling their own stories.

We The Ragamuffin premiered at the Bouncing Ball, where it was partly shot. Clubs are ephemeral institutions; the Ram Jam, opened in Brixton in 1966 as an offshoot of the Flamingo in Soho, closed by the end of the decade because of its dangerous atmosphere. Peckham's Bouncing Ball, under successive names, suffered a similar fate. Crime was always near the surface. In 1982 Neil Fraser, aka "The Mad Professor", made Peckham a key centre for recording reggae when he set up Ariwa Studios at 42 Gautry Road, but moved out of Peckham in 1986 after thieves completely stripped out his equipment. In 1977 the reggae specialist shop Dub Vendor Records had suffered a similar fate when it briefly opened a branch in the Peckham Rye Station arcade.

In 1979 Dick Hebdige could claim that "Reggae does seem to have at last broken through", but added a prophetic warning.

Little has changed in the Black community in Britain in the last twenty years. Housing still tends to be bad and in the late 1970s, as unemployment soars, even the menial jobs are hard to come by. But the mood amongst some Black British youth has changed. They have become more angry and bitter. As relations with the police have got steadily worse over the past few years, the reggae theme of "tribal war in Babylon" has come to seem more and more relevant.

Reggae established itself as an authentic form in Britain – as for instance in the work of the Brixton poet Linton Kwesi Johnson, a sociology graduate of Goldsmiths College – but the confidence it gave re-enforced the very real sense of oppression, as can be heard in Johnson's work. The most successful West Indian cultural import, the Notting Hill Carnival, ended in violence in 1976, 1977, and 1978. The combination of a worsening economic situation and the heavy-handed use by the police of the "sus" law that was, in effect, arbitrary arrest, meant it was only a matter of time before there was real trouble.

This duly occurred in Brixton in April 1981 when, already riled by the deaths of 13 young black people in a fire at New Cross in January, a mixed crowd of Black and White youth attacked the police, who had been running a stop-and-search operation. (There are many possible poetic meanings to be found in its code name, "Operation Swamp".) Among the rioters was a 16-year-old Russell Newell, who was beaten up by the police, charged with arson, and put on probation.

In July there were similar riots in Southall, Toxteth, Moss Side, and the West Midlands. (Bristol's St Paul's district had rioted in 1980.) On 28 September 1985, Brixton exploded again, following the shooting of the mother of a suspect by the police. On 30 September trouble spread to Peckham, with a shop at 103 Peckham High Street and a carpet warehouse set on fire. One of Peckham's oldest high street businesses, Wilson's Cycles, had its windows smashed. A week later it was the turn of the Broadwater Farm Estate in Tottenham, where a police officer died.

Reflecting on these frightening events, Robert Chesshyre wrote that another post-war assumption had finally been buried. This was:

The hope and expectation that Black Britons, the children and grand-children of the motivated, hard-working and God-fearing West Indians, and the White children of what had been the slums would become fully integrated citizens sharing the opportunities of their fellow Britons.

While the post-war generation of Black migrants had endured their cold reception out of necessity and a misplaced faith in the "Mother Country", their children, born British, were less accepting of their oppressed status; they were treated either as a dangerous problem or as pitiable victims. They wanted respect, and agency, but the authorities were reluctant to give them much of either. The Reverend Graham Dorriman, whose parish included the by now notorious North Peckham Estate, told Chesshyre in 1987 that his Black parishioners were denied real power: "because those in authority were frightened what they might do with it ... One way of compensating was to seek power in other ways."

One of these ways was laughter. Here, an accommodation could be reached between the oppressed and the oppressor, albeit on an imaginary level. Just as *Only Fools and Horses* articulated the unspoken pains of the White working class, and their resistance to authority, the arrival of Channel 4 television in 1982, with a remit to bring fresh and different voices into British homes, created opportunities for the next-generation, British-born, Caribbean community to at least hint at what it thought.

Stephen Bourne's study *Black in the British Frame: Black Experience in British Film and Television* (2001) shows that Black actors, writers, directors, and entertainers have never been absent from the British music hall, stage, or screen, although "British television has systematically failed Black audiences". As early as 1956 BBC television engaged with issues of racism in John Elliot's *A Man from the Sun*, starring Errol John as a Jamaican carpenter: "You're a British citizen in Jamaica, but here you are a coloured man." In 1959 Basil Dearden's film *Sapphire* responded to the Notting Hill Gate riots, but straight-talking would not often be heard again until the Channel 4 adaptation of Caryll Philips's *The Final Passage* in 1996. Errol John got a rare screen credit as a Black writer for the television version of his Royal Court play *Moon on a Rainbow Shawl* for ITV in 1960. (John was finally able to direct the play himself at Stratford East in 1985.) Lloyd Reckford, who had appeared in Ted Willis's ITV drama *Hot Summer Night* in 1959, became the first Black film director to have his work shown by the BBC, albeit with an only 12-minute drama, *Ten Bob In Winter*, in 1963. It was not until 1975 that Horace Ové directed the first Black British feature film, *Pressure*. Trinidad-born Ové became the centre of an international network of writers and artists, with a significant career in film and television, contributing episodes to BBC2's *Empire Road* – described as the first Black *Coronation Street* (1978, 1979) – created by the Guyanese writer Michael Abbensetts.

Coronation Street had its first Black character in 1963, but when they did appear there, and in other soaps, Black actors were given minor roles and minor plot lines. Fortunately, there were no regular Black characters to be on the receiving end of Alf Garnett's bigoted tirades in *Till Death Us Do*

Part between 1965 and 1975, but Rudolph Walker had to listen to plenty of "nig-nog" and "Sambo" from Jack Smethurst in ITV's *Love Thy Neighbour* (1972–1976) – a "reactionary sitcom" according to Stephen Bourne – based on the premise of a Black and a White family living as neighbours. In 1976–1977 *The Fosters*, the first sitcom to have an entirely Black cast, based on an American format, *Good Times*, brought together the actors Norman Beaton and Carmen Munroe, who would go on to star as husband and wife in *Desmond's*.

Desmond's was different. Although commitment to Black drama appeared to be shrinking in the 1980s, Channel 4's commissioning model created new opportunities for independent programme-makers. Its first sitcom, *No Problem!* (1983–1988) was also the first all-British Black comedy, though its focus on laughs was a disappointment for those hoping to see at least some reflection of reality. In 1984 one of its co-writers, Farrukh Dhondy, moved on to become a commissioning editor at Channel 4, where he forged an alliance with *No Problem!*'s producer Humphrey Barclay. That year, Barclay asked a young writer, Trix Worrell, to a meeting.

Born in Saint Lucia in 1960, Worrell arrived in South London as a five-year-old. He joined the youth theatre company of the Albany Theatre in Deptford, where he met Martin Stellman, a former alternative-theatre actor working there, who went on to the National Film School. White himself, Stellman was acutely aware of the racial oppression: "The racism was institutionalised. There was a lot of tension around." Stellman recalls the activities of the Metropolitan Police's Special Patrol Group in Peckham: "past 11.30 at night you were taking your life into your hands". The National Front was active, and Chapter 88 burnt down the original Albany Theatre. Writer of the 1979 film *Quadrophenia*, Stellman had been nursing a project with the director Franco Rosso (a graduate of Camberwell Art School) that in 1980 became the feature film *Babylon*, which as we saw captures the tensions of the times and the oppression of the police.

Trix Worrell won an Arts Council traineeship at the Albany and his first play, *School's Out*, was produced at the Royal Court in 1980, before he too went to the National Film School. In 1984 his Channel 4 drama *Just Like Mohicans* explored the strain that was beginning to be felt between first- and second-generation West Indians. In 1989 he wrote, and Stellman directed, the feature film *For Queen and Country*, about a disillusioned Falklands veteran, played by Denzel Washington. As had been the case with Sidney Poitier in *To Sir With Love* in 1967, and other projects, it was felt necessary to have an American star to secure the finance for the film.

Worrell has recounted that while travelling on the bus to his meeting with Humphrey Barclay he had no ideas, but then the bus passed a barber's shop, the Fair Deal in Queen's Road, Peckham. He saw the staff looking out of the window, ogling the passing girls, their customers unattended. From this grew the idea for *Desmond's*, a Peckham barber's shop that would be the ideal location for a family comedy that brought together the local community. This time the location – for the exteriors, at least – really was Peckham: Lloyd's Barbers at 204 Bellenden Road (Figure 3.5). Lloyd and his partner Fergie had been there for 30 years, and only changed the shop name to "Desmond's" after the success of the show. Like many such barber shops, Lloyd's/Desmond's was a community hub, a meeting point for an informal savings club or credit union known as a "su-su" or pardner system, and a source of support for Black taxi drivers learning "the knowledge". The television series brought it such celebrity that the American boxer Mohamed Ali is said to have insisted on getting his hair cut there. In 2000 – an index of gentrification – it became a picture-framers and in 2019, converted into a one-bedroom flat, went on the market for £425,000.

Figure 3.5   Norman Beaton and Carmen Monroe outside 204 Bellenden Road.

What made *Desmond's* unusual was the effort made by Humphrey Barclay to use not only Black writers – and, necessarily, actors – but also production crew. This significant empowerment of Black voices extended to the audience for the studio recordings of the show. Their audibly jeering responses, when Mrs Thatcher or *The Sun* newspaper are mentioned, make their allegiances clear. Norman Beaton, the show's lead, has said that *Desmond's* gave the cast and crew a sense of agency they had not had before: "it shows how we (that is, Black people) have moved on from just being passive, to be socially mobile".

Beaton was well qualified to lead the cast. Born in Guyana in 1934, he made his way into acting via calypso, teaching in Liverpool, playwriting, minor West End roles, and establishing the Black Theatre of Brixton in 1975. As we have seen, *Empire Road* gave him a television presence, but his most celebrated role is that of the captain of a Black South London cricket team in Caryl Phillips's *Playing Away*, directed by Horace Ové for Channel 4 in 1987. Also born in Guyana, Carmen Monroe, playing Desmond's wife Shirley, had a similar career via theatre and parts in *General Hospital* and *The Persuaders* to *The Fosters*. As far as she was concerned, *Desmond's* was "about real people".

Desmond's ran for 71 episodes from January 1989 to December 1994, reaching up to 5 million viewers, followed by a less-successful spin-off, *Porkpie*, featuring Ram Jam Holder, with two seasons during 1995–1996. The cast was deliberately chosen as pan-Caribbean, a community formed by migration, with White friends and a White assistant barber. With obvious irony a visiting Jamaican Auntie calls them "you English people". She warns of the disappointment felt by those who went home: "the West Indies have changed". The cast includes a Gambian, who regards himself as superior because of his non-slave heritage. This was a nod to the real tensions that existed between African and Caribbean, as the Ghanaian actor Gyearbuor Asante, who played him, has acknowledged: "when I was a kid, there were always conflicts between Africans and West Indians, and it was mega in Peckham, I can tell you". Caleb Femi recalls that as a young boy, "It was not cool to be Nigerian. You had to be Caribbean, you had to be Jamaican, that's what it meant to be Black British. So I guess you do your best to lose your accent, but with that you lose the language. I lost everything."

One of the key conflicts driving the comedy is that between Desmond Ambrose and his eldest son Michael (Geff Francis). Desmond, who arrived in Britain as a musician but has hung up his trumpet in the barber's shop, holds to traditional patriarchal ways of talking and feeling. His be-suited son uses Received Pronunciation, works in a bank, and has a Filofax and plenty of ambition for the future. In 1987 the social historian Paul Gilroy, author of *There Ain't No Black in the Union Jack*, had complained that no Black situation comedies seemed "able to portray inter-generational relations between Black characters or show their experiences over time", whereas "an equivalent programme centered on a White family in which notions of locality and 'ethnicity' play a similar role – *Only Fools and Horses* – builds its humour out of the tensions between generations". In Gilroy's view, "the logics of racist discourse militate against the possibility of making British Blackness visible in a family or an inter-generational group". In other words, Black Britons could not be, in Carmen Monroe's words, "real people".

Almost in response, *Desmond's* showed good-humouredly that it was possible to extract comedy from Desmond's difficulties with a yuppie son challenging him for position, from a larky adolescent daughter, and from a son of school age who speaks almost entirely in rap. The programme clearly articulated one deep-seated inter-generational conflict: between the *Windrush* generation (the ship features in the opening titles) and the second and third that followed, who were born in Britain. A long-running theme is Desmond's desire to retire, to "go home" to Guyana, and build a house with his savings. Shirley Desmond has a moving speech in the first episode in series 2, written by Trix Worrell.

None of us when we came to England wanted to die here, least of all Desmond. I know he is not going to die yet, but now he want to go home so that he can. I can't ... there is nothing out there for me anymore. My life, my family, my whole existence is here.

Tragically, at the end of 1994 Norman Beaton, who thanks to his drinking was in poor health, did return to Guyana, and suddenly died there, on 13 December. The programme could not continue without him. The last (pre-recorded) episode of series 6 went out six days later.

Sitcoms are not sociology, but *Desmond's* did give voice and agency to an oppressed community. Reflecting on the series in 2019, Trix Worrell said:

I didn't write *Desmond's* for Black people. I wrote it for White people so they could see how Black people really are. At that time, the negative press about muggings and shootings was all we seemed to get. I was fed up with it.

Worrell created his own story; laughter voiced his complaints less dangerously than did riots. Not that laughter was a complete solution. As Worrell said in 2016, "Being Black in a minority situation in a dominant culture, you have to laugh. Otherwise you are going to cry."

Sources

I am very grateful to my friend George Rowlett for his contribution to this chapter. *Only Fools and Horses* speaks for itself, with all episodes available online; Richard Webber and John Sullivan collaborated on *The Complete A-Z of Only Fools and Horses* (Orion, 2002). Andy McNab is quoted from *The Guardian*, 24 June 2019. Roy Porter's *London: A Social History* was published by Hamish Hamilton in 1994 and he is quoted from the same text later; I have also drawn on Gareth Stedman-Jones, *Outcast London: A Study in the Relationship between Classes in Victorian London* (1971; reprint Verso, 2013). Charlie Richardson wrote *My Manor: An Autobiography* with Bob Long (Pan Books, 1992), quoted here, and followed it up with *Charlie Richardson: The Last Gangster* (Arrow, 2014). I also consulted Gary Robson, *Class, Criminality and Embodied Consciousness: Charlie Richardson and a South East London Habitus* (Centre for Urban Community Research, Goldsmiths, 1997). Freddie Forman published *Brown Bread Fred: The Autobiography of the Godfather of British Crime* (John Blake, 2007). The Krays are the subject of John Pearson's *The Profession of Violence: The Rise and Fall of the Kray Twins* (1972; new edition Harper Collins, 1995). Dick Hebdige wrote "The Kray Twins: A Study of a System of Closure", stencilled occasional paper no. 21 for the Birmingham University Centre for Contemporary Cultural Studies studio, in 1974.

My leading source on housing is John Boughton's *Municipal Dreams: The Rise and Fall of Council Housing* (Verso, 2018); he also has a very useful blog of the same name. The director of housing is quoted from Anne Power and Rebecca Tunstall's *Swimming Against The Tide: Polarisation or Progress on 20 Most Unpopular Council Estates* (Rowntree Foundation, 1995). Anne Power is the author of *Estates on the Edge: The Social Consequences of Mass Housing in Northern Europe* (Macmillan, 1999). Caleb Femi is quoted from a profile *in The Peckham Peculiar*, no. 9, June 2015.

Penguin published Lord Scarman's *The Scarman Report: The Brixton Disorders, 10-12 April 1981* in 1982. Gregor Muir wrote *Lucky Kunst: The Rise and Fall of Young British Art* (Aurum, 2007). Robert Chesshyre published *The Return of the Native Reporter* (Penguin, 1988). Neil McIntosh is the author of *Housing the Poor?* (London Southwark Community Development Project, 1975); Stephen Hatch, Enid Fox, and Charles Legg wrote *Research and Reform: The Case of the Southwark Community Development Project 1969-72* for the Urban Deprivation Unit (Home Office, 1977). Alan David, Neil McIntosh, and Jane Williams wrote *The Management of Deprivation: Final Report of Southwark Community Development Project* (Polytechnic of South London, 1978). Elizabeth Burney wrote *Housing on Trial: A Study of Immigrants and Local Government* (Institute of Race Relations and Oxford University Press, 1967). I also consulted Sheila Patterson, *Immigration and Race Relations in Britain 1960-67* (Institute of Race Relations and Oxford University Press, 1968). Caleb Femi's spoken-word-film *We Are The Children of the 'Narm* is produced by the SXWKS (SixWeeks) collective and can be found on the web.

Clair Willis's *Lovers and Strangers: An Immigrant History of Post-war Britain* was published by Penguin in 2017. Dick Hebdige is quoted from his *Subculture: The Meaning of Style* (Methuen, 1979), and then later from his *Cut'n'Mix: Culture, Identity and Caribbean Music* (Comedia/Methuen 1987). Franco Rosso's *Babylon* (1980) was re-released in 2019 by the National Film Finance Corporation. The film's writer Martin Stellman gave me a very helpful interview. *We The Ragamuffin* (Channel 4, 1992) can be found on YouTube. Russell Newell and Julian Henriques also gave me insightful interviews. Stephen Bourne's *Black in the British Frame: Black Experience in British Film and Television* was published by Continuum in 2001; he also wrote *The Black Presence in Southwark since 1600* for Southwark Council in 2005, which identifies a number of local heroes. I also consulted Jim Pines (ed.), *Black and White in Colour: Black People in British Television since 1936* (British Film Institute, 1992). I am grateful to Charmaine Brown of Greenwich University for information about Lloyd's/Desmond's. Humphrey Barclay told me that although *Desmond's* had a mixed production crew, the successor series *Porkpie* had an all-Black creative and production team. Norman Beaton and

Carmen Monroe are quoted from *Black and White in Colour*, as is Gyearbuor Asante. Trix Worrell gave a public interview at the British Film Institute on 21 December 2016; his further (closing) comment was printed *in The Guardian*, 4 January 2019. Paul Gilroy's *There Ain't No Black in the Union Jack: The Cultural Politics of Race and Nation* was published by Hutchinson in 1987.

Figure 4.1 Camberwell School of Arts and Crafts and South London Gallery, 1915. The Gallery entrance is on the right (image credit: courtesy South London Gallery).

# 4

Only Artists: Peckham Painters (and Others), 1891–2000

"We don't have students here, we only have artists."

Jon Thompson on teaching art at Goldsmiths

At the end of the 19th century Peckham benefitted from two acts of philanthropy that had a long-lasting influence on its character. In 1891 the Goldsmiths' Livery Company took over the former Royal Naval School at New Cross, Deptford, a mile or so to the east of Queen's Road, where it opened the Goldsmiths' Technical and Recreative College. That same year, the South London Fine Art Gallery opened at the Camberwell end of the Peckham Road. On a grand scale, the two centres of creativity that grew from these locations shaped the direction of British art; close-up, they contributed to the area's special flavour.

The South London Fine Art Gallery later dropped the "Fine", and then the unfortunate resulting acronym SLAG, to become the South London Gallery, now modishly shortened to SLG. The institution developed out of the South London Working Men's College, founded in 1868, and, following the example of the London Working Men's College founded in Bloomsbury in 1854, was a pioneer in working-class adult education. It had a peripatetic South London existence, arriving in 1887 at a former glass warehouse at 207 Camberwell Road, by which time it was also offering a free library and picture gallery, the first educational centre of its kind in South London. The College's founder, William Rossiter, had good contacts in the art world, among them with G.F. Watts and Edward Burne-Jones, whose wife Georgiana became closely involved in the gallery's administration. In 1887 she persuaded the president of the Royal Academy, Lord Leighton, to become the gallery's president.

Leighton was a strong supporter of the project, and had a hard time persuading Rossiter to relinquish his very personal interest in what he saw as a future "National Gallery of South London".

In 1889 Rossiter bought, and moved into, Portland House at 63 Peckham Road, behind which he built a library, lecture hall, and the present gallery. Dedicated to bringing art and education to the working class, the gallery was the only one in London open on a Sunday. The local clergy thought this a very bad idea. An inlaid floor by the designer and illustrator Walter Crane (1845–1915) in the main gallery declared: "The source of life is the art of a people." In keeping with this sentiment, and in honour of one of Camberwell's most celebrated residents, in 1902 the main gallery was named the Ruskin Gallery and a small group of his drawings was acquired. Ruskin, who had founded his own museum for the benefit of working-class people in Sheffield, had died in 1900; in 1907 his links with the area were further celebrated when the London County Council, together with the boroughs of Camberwell, Lambeth, and Southwark, combined to create Ruskin Park, opposite his former home at 163 Denmark Hill (both his Camberwell homes have since been demolished). The Ruskin Gallery appears to have lost that name after the building was taken over for government use during World War I.

The Peckham Road gallery was free, open in the evenings, and child-friendly, showing works by its artistic supporters, including members of its council. This was the basis of a small collection of late Victorian works, subsequently added to over the years, with renewed energy in the 1950s. But in spite of support from leading figures in the London art world, money was a problem, and in 1896, partly thanks to Georgiana Burne-Jones's efforts, the "South London Art Gallery and Institute" was transferred to the public control of the Camberwell Vestry, the first of a succession of local authorities, the current one being Southwark. Although council-funded and run, the gallery has anomalously retained charitable status. In 1898 the appearance and situation of the South London Gallery was radically changed by the construction of what was to become the Camberwell School of Arts and Crafts (Figure 4.1).

Paid for by the philanthropist Passmore Edwards, who had already helped with extensions to the Gallery, the design by Maurice B. Adams integrated the two institutions behind a single imposing façade that gave South London one of its grander public buildings. But although at first the headmaster of the school was also director of the gallery, that was almost as far as integration went. The main entrance was exclusive to the new "Technical Institute", while the Gallery had a smaller entrance to its right. Administratively and financially, the two institutions remained separate. The Gallery continued under local borough control, but the School was run by the recently created London County Council; later, it was run by the Inner London Education Authority and eventually became part of the University of the Arts, London.

Camberwell School of Arts and Crafts expanded rapidly, doubling to 400 students in its first three years, with new painting and drawing studios opening in 1913. Though painting and drawing classes were provided, the emphasis was on teaching practical design: pottery, printing, textiles, and metal work, rather than fine art. Gilbert Spencer, brother of the better-known Stanley Spencer, was a pre-World War I student, and returned to teach there as head of painting between 1950 and 1957. David Jones, artist and writer, attended at the age of 14 in 1909, and returned after war service in 1919, when the school re-opened. In 1920 it established a small Fine Art department, the same year that it set up a Junior Art School, starting at age 13, which generated a supply of students for the main school until its closure in 1958.

Camberwell began to acquire its reputation as an art school, as opposed to a craft and technical college, with the appointment of the Scottish painter William Johnstone (1897–1981) in 1938. At that time there were as many as 900 students, the majority of them printers on day-release, and only about 30 full-time art students. Johnstone described Camberwell as "a district well known for its printers, its music hall artists and its 'petermen'" – meaning safe-blowers. His cosmopolitan experience in Paris and the United States caused him to set an important precedent by engaging practising painters to teach. He wrote: "I taught, not as an art teacher, but as an artist", a sentiment later also expressed by a leading teacher at Goldsmiths. He brought in a version of the Basic Design course developed at the Bauhaus in Germany, led by the head of the junior school, Albert Halliwell. Johnstone claimed: "the battle for a change in the whole of art teaching in Britain was fought and won at Camberwell, 1938–39".

The outbreak of a real war in 1939 made it difficult to consolidate this claimed victory, but the revolution in post-war British art teaching has one of its roots here. Both the junior and senior schools were temporarily evacuated, to Chipstead and Nottingham respectively, and the South London Gallery was used for the distribution of ration cards. It suffered severe bomb damage in 1941, losing the lecture hall, (replaced in 2010 by a Clore Education Centre). The Gallery did not open again until 1949, but the school – which had deep cellars – gradually re-opened after the end of the Blitz in 1941. In 1942 Kenneth Clark, director of the National Gallery, recommended Victor Pasmore, who had served a prison sentence as a conscientious objector and whom he was supporting financially, for a teaching post. He was joined by two leading lights of the wartime neo-romantic school, Michael Ayrton and John Minton. Johnstone did not consider Ayrton a good teacher and he left in 1944, but Minton, gay and independently wealthy, became a popular figure, teaching illustration, composition, and perspective and animating the school's fancy-dress balls and parties. His close friend Keith Vaughan joined him to teach illustration until 1948. Camberwell would retain its reputation for parties well into the 1980s.

In spite of bomb damage, the school filled up rapidly after the war, with many students studying on ex-servicemen's grants. Conditions were austere. The canteen food was terrible and the studios over-crowded with students trying to keep warm in army greatcoats and RAF flying boots. The artist Gillian Ayres (Figure 4.2) recalled: "It was poor, very poor. People didn't always have socks and shoes, they drank out of jam jars." Drawing materials were rationed to one quarter-sheet of imperial paper per day, and both sides had to be covered before a fresh one was issued. Some students took to living in the attics, feeding themselves from the still-lives, herrings included, set up by part-time students. But there was time for amateur theatricals, cricket matches with Goldsmiths College, and fancy-dress themed balls. Three cafés opened up to accommodate the 1,600 registered students. The nearby Victorian pub the Walmer Castle – later wrecked by fires in 2004 and 2009 – held art shows for students and staff regulars (Figure 4.2). In 2013 the nearby Peckham Pelican arts café took up the tradition.

As professional artists were gradually released from wartime duties such as designing camouflage, Johnstone took the opportunity to bring together former members of the pre-war Euston Road School, who had sought to inject a fresh note of social realism into British painting. Victor Pasmore was joined by Lawrence Gowing, Claude Rogers, and the dominating William Coldstream, who had learned from Walter Sickert. Johnstone

Figure 4.2 A Camberwell show at the Walmer Castle, 1948. Gillian Ayres is in the white blouse; Henry Mundy is on her left looking up at one of his paintings. Anthony Eyton, an ex-army student and later Camberwell teacher and RA, stands on the right (image credit: courtesy of the Estate of Gillian Ayres).

found Gowing business-like, Rogers pleasant but lazy, and had increasing difficulties with Coldstream. The writer Colin MacInnes, who had studied at the Euston Road School before wartime service in military intelligence, became a part-time art history lecturer in 1946. Two refugees, the painter Martin Bloch and the sculptor Karl Vogel, introduced a more expressive European sensibility into the increasingly severe, objective, "point-to-point" drawing style imposed by Coldstream, who became head of painting in 1948, the year that Leonard Daniels (1909–1998) arrived from Leeds College of Art to take over as principal.

Daniels found "a distinguished but ill-assorted staff", and set out drastically to reduce the number of subjects taught. True to its 19th-century origins, vocational craft courses were as important to the school as fine art, but Daniels set out to make drawing key to textiles, graphics, and ceramics: "Drawing was everywhere the basis of our study. Other approaches were possible and exemplified in the work of some staff and many students, but basically we were concerned with aspects of reality from our study of the visible world." The visible world of Peckham was gritty and grey, and seems to have influenced the artists' vision; the colourful free spirit of abstraction was not favoured in either painting or sculpture.

Jon Thompson, who had had an indifferent training at St Martin's and the Royal Academy Schools in the 1950s before attending the British School in Rome and a brief flowering as a Pop painter, and who went on to revolutionise art teaching at Goldsmiths in the 1970s, surely has Camberwell in mind when he writes:

The British post-war art schools, especially the London ones, taught a form of painting which combined the Euston Road's total misunderstanding of Cezanne with a strong tradition of painting reportage stemming from the painters of the Camden Town School, most particularly the later work of Walter Richard Sickert. This combination tended to produce a rather eccentric form of figurative painting, couched in the depictive language of mark-making derived from Impressionism and using an almost through-the-keyhole approach to the motif.

Coldstream left Camberwell in 1949 to become principal of the Slade School of Art, but the Euston Road influence lingered on into the 1960s and beyond, notably through the work of Euan Uglow, who as a student followed Coldstream to the Slade, before returning to teach at Camberwell part-time. Not everyone accepted Coldstream's approach; Gillian Ayres arrived in 1946 aged 16 and became a close friend of fellow student Howard Hodgkin. They formed a pocket of expressive colourists, along with the returned prisoner of war Terry Frost, and Henry Mundy (Figure 4.2), whom she married in 1951.

When the painter Robert Medley took over as head of fine art in 1958 he compared the place to "a motor car that was not firing on all cylinders", partly because Gilbert Spencer as head of painting had been out of touch with both staff and students. Medley decided to instil a greater intellectual rigour with a programme of colour and tonal exercises, bringing in the American Charles Howard, a now neglected figure who had shown at the International Surrealist Exhibition in London in 1938. He also asked Frank Auerbach to teach drawing as a challenge to the Coldstream style, with great success.

Art schools are never just about art. The school played a key role in the post-war revival of traditional jazz, a stomping, earthy style that went with the

Camberwell painting of the 1950s and the austerities of the times. George Webb's Dixielanders had launched what became known as "Peckham Pandemonium" in 1943. Trumpeter Humphrey Lyttleton spent a year at Camberwell from 1946, playing at the nearby jazz mecca, the Red Barn in Barnehurst, Bexleyheath, as well as at student dances. Saxophonist Wally Fawkes, like Lyttleton a cartoonist as well as jazzman, studied illustration, and played with George Webb at the Red Barn. Clarinettist Monty Sunshine returned to Camberwell after National Service in 1951. The future *Private Eye* cartoonist Barry Fantoni studied painting from 1953 to 1958, using the school's boiler house as a music room, and painting almost exclusively jazz subjects. Skiffle and pop musicians would follow. Syd Barrett, founder of Pink Floyd, arrived to study graphics in 1964. This musical life spread beyond the school; after the saxophonist Ronnie Scott opened his first club in Soho in 1959, the Walmer Castle became a popular Sunday session spot for musicians who had been playing at the club the night before. At this period Peckham's other jazz spot was the White Horse in Rye Lane, whose interior remains, to quote a *Time Out* review, "browner than your grandad's socks", but has DJs rather than art school bands.

Camberwell's confluence with a distinctly British tradition in visual art meant that it was well placed when the reforms to art teaching designed by their former head of painting William Coldstream came into force in 1962. These established a new Diploma in Art and Design (DipAD), which was treated as the equivalent to a university degree. This had the advantage for art school graduates who became school teachers that they qualified for higher salaries. Even more importantly, it gave art schools greater freedom, releasing them from a centralised examination system. Subject to government accreditation, they were able to devise and examine their own courses. Approval, however, required more academic content in the curriculum, which disadvantaged working-class, or simply educationally less conformist, applicants.

The DipAD established the practice by which students would do a preliminary general foundation course for a year, followed by a further three years, often at another school. There, students concentrated on fine art or sculpture, or print-making, graphics, textiles, or a number of specialisms, such as furniture design. Once a school established an approved course, students could attend from anywhere in the country, not just their own local authority district, which paid their fees. This gave London art schools an advantage in recruitment. By 1965 Camberwell's fine art student numbers were up to 90. In response to the requirement for more academic content in the course, Michael Podro was brought in to lead a new art history department. Another future influential figure in art history, T.J. Clark, also began his career there.

In the studios, Frank Auerbach became a star attraction. One of his early students was Tom Phillips. Phillips, who has described Auerbach as "the handsomest man in town", recalls that although he had studied art all his life, "Frank Auerbach opened the door to me as to what it really was: 'This is what it is all about. It's hard'." George Rowlett, who arrived a year after Phillips, joined him in Auerbach's evening life-classes in preference to studying print-making: "It was standing-room-only in his classes. We sneaked in with our sketchbooks and hoped we wouldn't be thrown out. Frank was always pushing people not to work like him. He was inspirational." In his second year Rowlett found Euan Uglow's tutorship equally inspiring: "I spent every moment in the life-class."

These proto School of London influences were tempered by the teaching of Charles Howard, who encouraged Phillips to explore the possibilities of abstraction and expressionism. Another of Auerbach's pupils was Sargy Mann, who came to the school in 1960, and joined the teaching staff at the end of the decade. He lived in Talfourd Road, and although he began to lose his eyesight in 1973, he continued to teach until 1988, and to paint, though blind, until his death in 2015.

In the 1960s Camberwell was regarded as one of the places to be. By 1968 it had eight separate departments, including a foundation course and art history. In addition to painting and sculpture it remained consistent with its history, and that of the local area, by teaching printing, graphic design, textiles, ceramics, and metalwork. Paper conservation was added in 1970. All this put pressure on space. Sculpture got a new building in 1953; painting moved out to Meeting House Lane between 1966 and 1971. In 1973 a large semi-brutalist block opened next door in the Peckham Road, in time for another change in art teaching with the introduction of BA degrees in 1974. Gregor Muir, today a curator, arrived in 1984 intending to spend three years studying painting.

This hot bed of creativity turned out to be an uninspired concrete block next to a petrol station on the Peckham Road ... Camberwell appealed to me. Not because it was believed to be the country's leading fine art painting course, but because the surrounding area – urban, grey and bleak – reminded me of Joy Division, whose music evoked perpetual melancholy. Situated on the margins of Central London, the area was populated by Afro-Caribbeans, Greeks, Irish and the English working classes.

The perils of gentrification had yet to reach Peckham.

Muir records that he began to lose interest in painting in his second year. It was an individual choice, but it points to a loss of energy in Camberwell as the independent spirit of art schools was gradually smothered by changes in higher-education policy. Personalities also count; Medley and Auerbach both moved on in 1965, Medley to look after his lifelong partner Rupert Doone, Auerbach to the Slade. The creative autonomy of art schools was brief. In the 1970s there was economic pressure to merge with larger units, by linking with polytechnics. From his studio in Talfourd Road, Tom Phillips, who had awarded a drawing prize every year "until the students stopped drawing", observed "the decline of the school into an adjunct of a polytechnic for, by 1992, it had lost its Fine Art Course". Camberwell had been celebrated for its courses in printed and woven textiles, but the textile department closed in 1983.

In 1986, driven by the Inner London Education Authority, Camberwell joined the London Institute, a federation of six London art schools that became the University of the Arts in 2004. In 1989 it changed its name to Camberwell College of Arts, with two schools: Applied and Graphic Arts, and Art History and Conservation. In 2000 Art History was renamed "professional development". Fine art was restored in 2004, but in 2011 Camberwell started to deliver foundation courses for 750 students, in partnership with Chelsea and Wimbledon art schools. The school was over-crowded, and, unofficially, at least 20% of foundation students were expected to drop out. By then the Walmer Castle and its trad jazz had gone. The ex-servicemen of the 1940s would not recognise the place.

The art teaching at Goldsmiths, three or so miles to the east, followed an opposite trajectory, benefitting from the unusual institutional position that Goldsmiths found itself in in the 1970s as the once independent art schools began to be absorbed into the larger polytechnic system. In 1904 the Goldsmiths' Livery Company gave the land and buildings of what had become known as the Goldsmiths' Institute to London University, but it did not become a full part of the university; it issued its own diplomas and concentrated on teacher training, the arts, and adult education. The Goldsmiths' Company had set up an art school, and continued to fund it after the handover, paying for new studios at the rear of the main building in 1907. The school placed more emphasis on fine art than was the case in the former government schools of design; its most distinguished alumnus before World War II appears to have been Graham Sutherland, who between 1921 and 1926 benefitted especially from the school's reputation for etching and engraving.

Like Camberwell, Goldsmiths was evacuated to Nottingham during the war; its main building was badly damaged by bombing, not re-opening fully until 1947, but there was some residual activity in Clifton Rise, Peckham. According to Lucian Freud's biographer William Feaver, in late 1943 the young Freud and his friend John Craxton were sent to improve their drawing at classes organised by a Goldsmiths teacher, the designer Clive Gardiner, on the recommendation of Graham Sutherland. That important patron of wartime art and literature Peter Watson offered to pay for their classes, but Freud and Craxton did not stay long.

In the post-war period Goldsmiths was part-funded by the Inner London Education Authority, which took over from the LCC, and partly by the Department of Education, but its ambition was to become a full college of London University, able to award its own degrees. While Goldsmiths as a whole was led by a warden, the art school had its own principal, as did drama and music. The main focus stayed on teacher training, and in the 1950s and early 1960s the art school was regarded as something of a backwater. The future fashion leader Mary Quant met her husband, Alexander Plunket Greene, there in the 1950s, while studying for an art teacher's diploma. He was supposed to be studying illustration, but rarely came in, living the life of an art student rather than actually being one. Quant wrote of Goldsmiths: "I realized that there are people who give their lives to pursuit of pleasure and indulgence of every kind in preference to work." She did not get her diploma, but was well prepared for the coming hedonism of the 1960s. Another early post-war drop-out was the art forger Tom Keating, who had picked up skills in restoration. Before moving to Cornwall in 1967 he ran a junkshop in Fenwick Road, Peckham, where he would produce convincing German Expressionists – painted in acrylic.

Bridget Riley studied at Goldsmiths from 1949 to 1952 before going on to the Royal College of Art, but did not emerge as an important Op artist until the early 1960s. By that time Goldsmiths was better known for its large music department, which developed courses in both jazz and popular music. In 1964 the avant-garde Fluxus group mounted a "Little Festival of New Music" where Robin Page performed his piece "Shouting a Plant to Death". Composers and musicians, like visual artists, could find part-time work in art schools. Cornelius Cardew, a former assistant to Karlheinz Stockhausen, taught part-time at Goldsmiths and at Morley College. According to Tom Phillips, himself also a composer and musician, the constitution for Cardew's improvisatory Scratch Orchestra (1969–1972) was drafted in his Grove Park garden, and Phillips took part in its performances. Phillips also worked with the composer Hugh Davies, another former assistant to Stockhausen, who

Figure 4.3   The Bonzo Dog Doo-Dah Band, circa 1964. Neil Innes is on the right.

set up Goldsmiths' Electronic Music Studios in 1968. On the lighter side, Goldsmiths lecturer Vernon Dudley Bowhay-Nowell and his lodger, fine art student Neil Innes, combined with jazzmen from St Martin's and the Royal College of Art to form the Bonzo Dog Doo-Dah Band in 1963, the epitome of an art school band, nostalgic, satirical, and surreal (Figure 4.3).

In 1963 the Robbins report on higher education encouraged a significant increase in national student numbers, and prepared the way for the conversion by 1992 of all polytechnics – of which most arts schools were becoming a part – into universities. Goldsmiths, which had 800 students in 1963, expanded to 2,500 by 1965, mostly in the arts and social sciences, where sociology encouraged critical thinking that contested the post-war consensus. Expansion placed a significant strain on accommodation and resources, just as a new and less deferential generation of students began to assert themselves. The mounting horrors of the Vietnam war were an international source of discontent; domestically, students began to challenge their institutions over student representation on committees, on the curriculum, and on who should teach it. When such demands were rebuffed, as at first they inevitably were, there were demonstrations and sit-ins, and then further protests at the disciplinary measures that followed.

By June 1968 student protests had affected 17 higher- and further-education institutions. The most celebrated case was at Hornsey College of Art in North London, where a long student occupation briefly turned into a siege. There, the authorities refused to negotiate with the students, with student expulsions and the sackings of part-time staff as the end result. The Hornsey students were in touch with their comrades at Goldsmiths, where a faction of self-styled Maoists, prominent among them the future manager of the Sex Pistols, Malcolm McClaren, were causing chaos in the art history department and elsewhere. As the largest teacher training establishment in the country, students felt particularly provoked by the government's decision in 1969 to freeze teachers' pay.

The warden of Goldsmiths, Ross Chesterman, took a different line to Hornsey; following his Quaker beliefs, he declined to confront the students, even when in 1970 the library was set on fire. Tensions were high in 1969, when Peter de Francia, a socialist-realist painter and Marxist art historian, took over as principal of the Art School. He attempted to impose discipline, but was mortified to discover that his radical credentials were dismissed as "Marxist Revisionism". Andrew Forge, head of painting, a graduate of Camberwell and the Slade, had a nervous breakdown, and resigned, moving to America. The vacancy this created was filled by one of the most remarkable art teachers Britain has seen.

When Jon Thompson arrived for his first day of work at Goldsmiths in January 1970, he was pursued down the corridor by students throwing copies of Chairman Mao's Little Red Book. But Thompson had a plan that was to prove far more revolutionary than the fantasies of his assailants. After early success as a pop artist with the Rowan Gallery, on his return from his Rome Scholarship in 1962 he had a crisis of confidence in pop painting and turned increasingly to teaching, first at Lancaster College of Art, then Leicester, and finally St Martin's, where he had spent four years in the 1950s under the old National Diploma of Design system. Following the Coldstream reforms, St Martin's, whose sculpture course with Anthony Caro had made the school famous, applied to the Council for National Art Awards for recognition of its foundation course under the new Diploma of Art and Design, but, to its surprise, it was turned down. In 1967 Thompson was invited to run the course with the aim of securing accreditation, and he began to put into practice his ideas on "student-centred" teaching, cross-disciplinary methods, and the introduction of critical thinking. But the old regime, under which individual teachers held sway in their studios, producing clones of themselves, proved resistant. When the opening at Goldsmiths came up, he took it.

On his second day at Goldsmiths, Thompson called a school meeting, held in the largest space available for the 200 or more students, known as the Elephant House, the name given by students in the education department to a lecture theatre that became an art gallery in 1981. Only one member of the staff, painter Peter Cresswell, was willing to face the turbulent students with him. Cresswell was to become Thompson's right-hand man. Shortly after Thompson had begun to make his pitch that in this school there would be no students, only artists, the Maoists began to prevaricate, but a student of Polish origin smashed a chair over Malcolm McLaren's head, and a brawl broke out. The quaintly named Beadles – Goldsmiths' security team, who had been kept in reserve by Thompson – cleared the room.

Thompson was unfazed by his reception, for he knew he had the full support of the warden, and the school was in such chaos that the situation could only improve. He began by doing what he could to change the staff, most of whom were over 50. About nine left in the first year. He limited all part-time teaching to a maximum of three days a week, which freed up space to bring in fresh minds. When he arrived, there was only one female member of staff, and she was on sick leave, and he determined to have an equal gender balance within four years. The radical feminist artists Mary Kelly – he had taught her at St Martin's – and Andrea Fisher, both American, joined the team, as did Helen Chadwick. At last Thompson was able to abolish the craft distinctions between painting and sculpture and newer disciplines such as film, where Peter Logan, brother of the flamboyant artist and designer Andrew Logan, and who had never actually made a film, was brought in. The future Oscar-winning director Steve McQueen, who arrived from Chelsea School of Art in 1990 as an abstract expressionist, would be a beneficiary of his teaching, switching entirely to film at the end of his first year.

Students could move freely between media, and decide their own courses, for there was no formal syllabus. Backed by warden Chesterman, and seemingly without much in the way of formal interviews or appointment procedures, by the end of the first academic year Thompson became head of the merged departments. When Peter de Francia left for the Royal College of Art in 1971 he took full charge. His professional presentation of the 1970 degree show impressed more traditional-minded teachers such as Basil Beattie and Bert Irwin; on his own authority, he selected the entire student intake for 1971. The Maoist movement evaporated and McLaren moved on.

The key to Thompson's approach was that art teaching was not "developmental" – that is to say, there were not certain skills, and by implication certain styles, that a student would progressively acquire until qualifying as "an artist".

As he had experienced at St Martin's, teaching in art schools tended to centre on especially charismatic tutors who could attract a group of students who would then reproduce the master's (almost inevitably male) style. Thompson broke up this fundamentally 19th-century studio system by assembling teaching groups from all three years that would be deliberately

Figure 4.4 Jon Thompson (1936–2016), circa 2012 (image credit: photo Andrew Webb, courtesy Andrew Reynolds Gallery, London).

re-formed on a yearly basis, and not allowed to settle. These groups were led by two tutors, who were not expected to agree, so that every discussion in the studio became a debate: "everything was being shared and challenged". In his view, teachers were not "messianic figures"; teaching took the form of open group seminars, and any student could approach any teacher for an individual tutorial. Furthermore, Thompson employed a number of what he called "artist philosophers" – John Tagg, Andrew Brighton, Yehuda Safran, Enrique Pardo, Carl Plackman, Trevor Pateman – who taught in the studios, and whose job it was to act as bridge between what was going on there and in the art history department.

It was characteristic of his approach that he closed the life-drawing room. This was not out of hostility to drawing, which he encouraged, but because he did not see it as an end in itself. Models were always available if students wanted them. There is a suggestion that this was also a gesture towards the strong feminist group in the school, by ending the male gaze on the female body, but Thompson has said more simply that he thought the life-room "boring".

Prominent among Thompson's appointments was the Irish-American painter and conceptual artist Michael Craig-Martin, whom he asked to take on a full-time job (that is, three days a week) in 1973. Craig-Martin recalls Goldsmiths at that time as "the stubborn underdog among the London art schools. It also had a reputation for being liberal to the point of chaotically free." He felt immediately at home: "Jon hired lots of other young artists around the same time, all my age or younger. His agenda was to renew art education completely. All of us signed up with enthusiasm – we were going to reinvent the British art school." The art dealer Maureen Paley, who would have a lot to do with the artists coming out of Goldsmiths, describes Craig-Martin's teaching in a way that encapsulates the whole approach of the school.

He gave students a sense of possibility, a sense that they could do anything, and when they talked to him he was able to teach by suggestion. Partly because his style or his manner of working was so diverse and so complex he would not really dictate a particular style.

Craig-Martin's student Glenn Brown recalls: "Painting wasn't taught. Philosophy was taught."

The sculptor Richard Wentworth, who had only graduated from the Royal College of Art in 1970, was taken on for two days a week in 1971, and was to prove as stimulating a teacher as Craig-Martin: "I never thought I had a job there. It was my education." Typical of his teaching methods was to urge a student to throw a piece of work out of the window, or to tell student Matt Collishaw that his paintings were OK, but not as interesting as a paint-spattered cigarette packet on the floor. The teaching staff grew to about 40, among them the mime artist Lindsay Kemp to work on performance, and the critic Peter Fuller, whose intense seminars later emerged as books. John Cage and Merce Cunningham had a week's residency; John Berger gave his last masterclass on photography there. Unlike many schools, there was a constant emphasis on what was going on in the outside world, not just in terms of practice, but in philosophy and critical theory. Audrey Walker, appointed head of textiles and embroidery in 1975, enthusiastically put Thompson's principles into practice in her department: "My whole approach to teaching was to put students first."

In 1978 connection with the outside world was made easier when the art school moved out of the main campus in New Cross. For several years it had been using additional studio space in a former dock building in Lower Road, Rotherhithe, where Thompson lived as caretaker, but government rationalisation of the teacher training sector meant that the redundant premises of St Gabriel's, an Anglican college opposite Myatt's Fields park in Camberwell, became available, and other properties were rented in the area. (Myatt's Fields park was the scene of a famous fight at a summer dance in the 1950s when Charlie Richardson's brother Eddie established himself as King of the Teds.) Renamed the Millard Building after a former principal, it had begun life as an Edwardian hospital – the writer Vera Brittain worked there as a nurse during World War I – and its architecture over three floors was particularly conducive to encounters on the stairs or in the garden outside. St Gabriel's former chapel became a library; Thompson had a small flat and studio in the building. In nearby Flodden Road a former gym provided first-year students with studios, and a building known as the Tower House became a space for more reclusive students. The move from New Cross, which included the textiles department and elements of art history, brought the students much closer by bus and tube to the public and commercial galleries of central London. The Millard Building produced an ideal space where creativity could flourish.

The move to Myatt's Fields coincided with the beginnings of an important shift in the economic and social space of the whole of London, and the art world moved eastwards with it. The recession of the early 1980s, combined with Mrs Thatcher's neoliberal refusal to bail out failing industries, emptied commercial properties such as shops and warehouses that could be taken over as studios, as living spaces, or could simply be squatted. In 1981 the London Docklands Development Corporation was established to take control of eight-and-a-half square miles of land, both sides of the Thames below Tower Bridge, free of normal planning constraints. While developers schemed the mercantile metropolis that would become Canary Wharf, they were willing to let out empty buildings such as the Tally Office that became Goldsmiths' temporary studios in Rotherhithe. The Thatcherite economy that emerged with the deregulation of the City – the so-called Big Bang of 1986 – created new money, some of which went into the market for contemporary art. In 1985 the advertising millionaire Charles Saatchi and his then wife Doris opened their private gallery in Boundary Road, Finchley. Appropriately, the building was a former workshop and warehouse. Jon Thompson immediately seized the opportunity to take his students to the opening show, with works by Cy Twombly, Brice Marden, Donald Judd, and Andy Warhol.

It is customary to refer to the generation of artists that emerged in the 1980s and 1990s as "Thatcher's children", but that is a misdescription. Beneficiaries of the welfare state and free education, they were socially egalitarian and open-minded when it came to race and gender. They were no respecters of tradition. When the conventional routes became blocked in terms of public patronage and job opportunities as a result of Thatcher's policies, they turned to more entrepreneurial ways of promoting their work. Goldsmiths students took the lead. The art historian Richard Shone describes them as:

Absolutely typical of the time – poor, enthusiastic, hardworking (with some noticeable periods of flunk, when the pool-table in the bar was more attractive than the studio). Most were from modest backgrounds outside London: they were quarrelsome, clannishly protective and socially rumbustious. They liked being at Goldsmiths.

In contrast to the more southern, middle-class atmosphere that predominated at Camberwell in its heyday, Goldsmiths benefitted from the northern, working-class elements in its intake, who shared a toughness – even aggression – and a liking for immediate gratification. In addition to the hedonism encouraged by not needing to have a job, there was a shared disrespect for authority, including the authority of the canon of fine art. A certain irreverent jokiness replaced Camberwell's painterly seriousness, for instance, Glenn Brown's painting *The Day the World Turned Auerbach* (1992), which satirised the doyen of Camberwell and the Slade by creating an illusion of Auerbach's rugged impasto on a totally flat, slick surface.

This sardonic wit was most evident in the cohort of Goldsmiths students who broke through with the "Freeze" exhibition of 1988, but Thompson's approach produced results well before that. Antony Gormley studied sculpture between 1974 and 1977 before completing his studies at the Slade. Richard Wentworth encouraged him and his wife, the artist Vicken Parsons, to buy a house in Talfourd Road, and he subsequently built a studio in Bellenden Road with Tom Phillips. Julian Opie, taught by Thompson's appointments Glen Baxter and Richard Wentworth, was taken up by the Lisson Gallery on his graduation in 1982; gallerist Nicola Jacobs took on Lisa Milroy, tutored by Tony Carter. Until then, it was unusual to find a gallery immediately, but now there was new money around. Opie's success was an encouragement to other Goldsmiths artists; it showed there was a market for their work. But while the Millard building was a hothouse of ideas in a mutually supporting community, life could be cold and lonely once you had left.

Partly to remedy this situation, in 1982 Thompson decided to launch a further degree to ease the transition into professional life. The traditional route was to go on to take an MA at the Slade, or the Royal College of Art, or to attend the Royal Academy Schools, but the Royal College of Art in particular did not seem to favour Goldsmiths graduates, and some who went there did not stay long. It may be that Goldsmiths students were already too "made" to interest the RCA. Technically, Goldsmiths was not allowed to award master of arts degrees, which were limited to only six art schools in the country, but when Chelsea got one of the coveted accreditations, Thompson was provoked into using Goldsmiths' status as an adult education institution to set up a two-year part-time MA degree. Students had to have their own studios outside the College, where they would receive a tutorial at least once a month, while doing group work two evenings a week. Glenn Brown, Mark Wallinger, Matthew Collings, Cathy de Monchaux, Simon Linke, Perry Roberts, and Yinka Shonibare were among those who took this route. Thompson could see that the conditions of patronage were shifting, and that the changes in higher education meant that it would no longer be possible to rely on part-time teaching while developing one's own practice. He felt no qualms about sending a taxi for the dealer Leslie Waddington to come down to the Millard Building and talk to the students about the realities of life as a professional artist.

Figure 4.5 Installing "Freeze", 1988. Left to right: Dominic Denis, Michael Landy, Steve Adamson, Angela Bulloch, Sarah Lucas. Foreground with back to us: Damien Hirst. At rear: Gary Hume, Matt Collishaw (image credit: Lala Meredith-Vula).

Conditions were ripe, then, when in the autumn of 1986 a particularly entrepreneurial working-class BA student arrived from Leeds. Damien Hirst had been unable to get a place at any of the London colleges at the start of the academic year, but when a vacancy unexpectedly occurred at Goldsmiths, Thompson took him on and became his tutor. Thanks to the group tutorial system, in 1988 Hirst was able to bring together 16 second-year students, third-year students, and recent graduates, to put together the shows known collectively as "Freeze" from August to November. By their end the young gallerist Karsten Schubert had taken on Michael Landy, Ian Davenport, and Gary Hume, and Hirst had made his name.

Following the example of Goldsmiths' temporary occupation of former Tally Offices in Rotherhithe, Hirst secured the use of an empty Port of London Authority building on the south side of the river in the Surrey Docks. It was not in the area controlled by the London Docklands Development Corporation, but the LDDC had decided to launch a cultural programme. Hirst and his unstoppable fundraiser, Goldsmith's sociology student Billee Sellman, had secured £10,000 in sponsorship from the Canary Wharf developers Olympia and York, but predictably had been turned down by the Arts Council and Greater London Arts. With only a few weeks to go before the show was due to open they ran out of money. On his first day in the job as the LDDC's arts administrator, John Kieffer came up with enough for "Freeze" to go ahead. Thompson provided letters assuring the LDDC and property owners of the students' *bona fides*. Hirst had a job part-time as a dog's-body at Anthony D'Offay's gallery and quietly borrowed his employer's invitation list. Responding to Thompson's teachings about the new economy for art, he produced a professional-looking catalogue with an essay by art history tutor Ian Jeffrey, and did his best to get visitors and press coverage for the show.

Although visitors were few (but thanks to Hirst's efforts, among them were important figures such as Tate director Nicholas Serota, Royal Academy exhibitions director Norman Rosenthal, and collector Charles Saatchi) and there was little press coverage, "Freeze" caught the moment. Hirst followed up in his third year by securing a former Peak Frean biscuit warehouse in Bermondsey, known as Building One. The project was backed by the LDDC, Rank Xerox, Saatchi and Saatchi, the Lisson Gallery, and Anthony D'Offay, but Hirst fell out with his partners (and housemates), Billee Sellman and fellow sociologist Carl Freedman, just as their first show, "Modern Medicine", featuring Hirst, opened in March 1990.

Helped by industrial recession, the era of warehouse culture was in full swing, though more people used them for ecstasy-fuelled raves rather than to see the work of a new generation of artists. By no means were all of them from Goldsmiths; in 1994 thanks to Charles Saatchi they collectively acquired their own brand name: Young British Artists.

The energy channelled by "Freeze" was felt throughout the London art scene. Soho revived as a social centre; Clerkenwell, Hoxton, and further parts of the East End where similar property conditions prevailed became better known for their artists than Peckham, which suffered from poor public transport and its reputation for criminality, although that did not stop artists taking advantage of lower property prices and empty commercial spaces. A new generation of dealers emerged, among them Jay Jopling, founder of White Cube, whose house in Shakespeare Road near Herne Hill made Goldsmiths a convenient hunting-ground for talent. A recession at the start of the 1990s helped to shift the terms of trade in favour of younger artists. Bankable senior artists became too expensive for first-time collectors, but the buzz around the rising generation attracted investors, who found them both fashionable and affordable. The long boom of the 1990s created plenty of surplus wealth; speculation on properties, commodities, and currencies proved a useful introduction to speculation in contemporary art.

Looked at from one point of view, what was consequential about the warehouse art of the 1980s and 1990s was not the quickfire, accessible mixture of minimalism and conceptualism developed at Goldsmiths, but its contribution to urban regeneration. This was certainly the case with the institution where, in a sense, Peckham's creative life had begun, the South London Gallery. Neglected by Southwark Council, in the 1980s it had to abandon the contemporary art collecting programme it had restarted in 1953, and in 1991 it closed for a time altogether. But as we will see, control of Southwark Council was moving from Old to New Labour, which saw the value that cultural assets could bring. A new leader of the council, Jeremy Fraser, was sympathetic to the expansionist enthusiasm of borough architect Fred Manson.

In 1992 David Thorp, once briefly a foundation student at Camberwell, who had returned from working as a painter and curator in Australia, was appointed gallery director. According to Thorp, "Manson saw that this bit of South London could become a cultural hub". On his return to England in 1986, Thorp had established a solid reputation as the founder-director of the Chisenhale Gallery in Bow, part of a complex of studios occupied by many artists who had moved on from the SPACE studios set up by Bridget Riley and Peter Sedgley in St Catherine's Dock in 1968. Thorp commented on his new appointment: "I can't tell you how stuffy and dowdy the place was when I arrived. The staff were old retainers. It was all brown hessian, and the gallery was dominated by a large clock, as though to tell visitors that their time there was up."

Southwark wanted the South London Gallery to play the pivotal role that the similarly long-established Whitechapel Art Gallery was playing in the cultural revival of the East End. Sadly, it did not quite provide the means. The £85,000 a year it gave in funding was a tenth of what the Whitechapel was getting. Thorp found himself at the bottom of Southwark's bureaucratic hierarchy – "I had no power, and money for just four salaries" – although he did have a direct line to Fred Manson. He had

Figure 4.6 South London Art Gallery: The Minky Manky Show, 1995. Tracey Emin's now-lost tent is on the right; behind it is a Hirst vitrine. Gilbert & George are on the left wall; in front of them are works by Sarah Lucas (image credit: courtesy South London Gallery).

to adapt to the realities of the new commercial world that treated culture as a useful commodity.

Thorp took down the clock, painted the gallery white, changed the lighting, and installed a sculpture by Ron Haselden outside as a marker of fresh life. His exhibition programme began in 1993 with a touring show by four women artists, Anya Gallaccio, Pat Kaufman, Cornelia Parker, and Pat Thornton, continuing in midsummer with two Goldsmiths tutors, Mona Hatoum and Andrea Fisher. Although the London Institute, now in charge of Camberwell School of Art, had designs on taking over the gallery, Camberwell students were not frequent visitors. Instead, Thorp set up a useful connection with students on Goldsmiths' MA in creative curating – the existence of such a course was in itself a sign of the times – who presented an exploration of aural art, "Sound Factory" in 1998, and an examination of art and urban renewal in "Non Place Urban Realm" in 1999.

In Thorp's words, "the show that changed our identity" came in 1995: "The Minky Manky Show" (Figure 4.6), curated by Damien Hirst's former collaborator at Building One, Carl Freedman, who would go on to run his own galleries in Shoreditch and Margate. The show was a provocative selection of Goldsmiths alumni – Hirst, Matt Collishaw, Sarah Lucas, Gary Hume – with the addition of the more senior Gilbert & George, and newcomers Critical Décor (David Pugh and Toby Morgan) and Stephen Pippen.

Later that year Thorp put on Gilbert & George's "Naked Shit Pictures". Some of these had proved too strong for the Serpentine Gallery or the Royal Academy to display, but when all 16 were shown together at the SLG they proved a turning point in the artists' critical reception – and further raised the gallery's profile.

Although she had already had a show at Jay Jopling's White Cube Gallery in 1993, Royal College of Art graduate Tracey Emin was the discovery of the "Minky Manky Show". Freedman had met her at the "shop" she had run with Sarah Lucas in Bethnal Green and they travelled together in America in 1994. Emin attributes Freedman's provocation to the creation of her celebrated embroidered tent, *Everyone I Have Ever Slept With 1963–1995*, for the show (Figure 4.6). In 1997 Thorp invited her to follow up with a solo show at the SLG, "I need Art like I need God". This was one of three Thorp put on in collaboration with Jay Jopling, the others being Mark Quinn in 1996 and Gavin Turk in 1998. He was less happy in 1997 when he showed Anslem Kieffer in association with Anthony D'Offay, but it was a coup to have Kieffer working in the gallery. Julian Schnabel followed in 1999, Leon Golub in 2000, Barbara Kruger in 2001; "I wanted artists in Peckham to be able to walk down the road and see world class art." A "Peckham Open" at the end of 1995 showed there was no shortage of local artists ready to submit their work. Thorp gave solo shows to local Black artists Zarina Bhimji, a Goldsmiths graduate, and the late Donald Rodney, but not because of their ethnicity or because they were local: "we showed more BAME artists than other galleries, but this was not a box-ticking exercise".

In 2001 Thorp moved on to become curator of contemporary projects at the Henry Moore Foundation. His successor was Margot Heller, who remains in charge. She saw the gallery through a refurbishment in 2003. In 2007 there was an unexpected windfall from the decision by Kennedy's Sausages to give up its factory on the opposite side of Peckham Road. The plan, as usual, was to build flats, but the site included what had been London's first purpose-built fire station, a handsome Grade II-listed building from 1867. As we will explore further in Chapter 10, in 2011 the artist Raqib

Shaw intervened to buy the site for his studio, including the semi-derelict fire station, and in 2015 he quietly leased it to the SLG for 99 years on a peppercorn rent. With help from the Heritage Lottery Fund and Southwark Council, since 2018 it has become an important extension to the gallery. In keeping with the gallery's original foundation in 1891, the SLG chiefly concentrates on its role as a centre for education.

Thorp's programme in Peckham prepared the way for the defining event of the period: "Sensation" at the Royal Academy in September 1987, containing 110 works by 44 artists, all drawn from Charles Saatchi's collection. Of them, 21 were Goldsmiths graduates, which is a remarkable tribute to the teaching they received there. But Sam Taylor Wood, and Gillian Wearing – whose 1994 video *Dancing in Peckham* shows her solitarily bopping without music among the apparently unconcerned shoppers in Peckham's Aylesham Centre – were among the last to graduate from the BA course under Thompson's leadership quickly to make their mark; Jane and Louise Wilson completed their MAs in 1992, the year Thompson stepped down.

Goldsmiths sustained its energy, but Thompson's "community of artists talking and working together", which had generated such creativity for more than 20 years, had begun to disperse. Richard Wentworth left in 1987, Michael Craig-Martin in 1988 – though they both kept a friendly eye on former students. In 1998 the Millard Building was given up and the artists returned to the main campus in New Cross, Deptford (Figure 4.7). Jon Thompson's departure was unhappy. In 1988 Goldsmiths had at last become a full college of London University, and in 1990 received its Royal Charter. The college wanted to promote Thompson, now a "Reader", to a full professorship, but the Slade – part of University College London – blocked the move, seemingly on the grounds that it would give Goldsmiths art school equal status to that of the Slade. When Goldsmiths failed to fight his corner, Thompson resigned.

This may help to explain Thompson's view, expressed in 1999: "I think that it has almost always been true, that the enemies of art are in the art schools, and mostly they have been running them, and they will go on running them I suspect." For him, Britain's art schools had flourished for about ten years between the 1970s and 1980s, after they had secured creative autonomy from central government, and before they began to

Figure 4.7 The entrance to the Millard Building, on the day the Goldsmiths arts department moved out in 1998 (image credit: Lala Meredith-Vula).

be sucked first into the polytechnic and then the university system. He dismissed London's University of the Arts, the merger of six colleges that had begun life as the London Institute, as "a Micky-Mouse institution".

He was also dismissive of the success of some of his students. In his view, "the high point was before the Damien Hirst generation". "Freeze" had produced a critical reaction in the school, with an anti-"Freeze" pamphlet in circulation, and some students attending seminars in fur coats. He thought the 1997 "Sensation" show "ersatz", a manufactured cultural moment. Yet, however unwelcome, a cultural moment it was. Thompson's verdict in 2001 was:

What had started off as a radical, artist centred initiative set to bypass both the gallery system and the orthodoxies of the middle-class cultural establishment, by the mid-1990s had drifted into a new kind of commercially focussed, commodity-oriented conservatism. For the most part, the new generation of British artists had succumbed entirely to the heady blandishments of the galleries and surrendered themselves to the institutions of the state, to be used jingoistically in the promotion of the economically revitalized new Britain.

Whether they liked it or not, the artists and designers of Camberwell and Goldsmiths played a significant part in imagining this new Britain, and the South London Gallery had pioneered their work. The number of artists hoping to make a living from their art multiplied, and they spread out across neglected parts of London in search of somewhere to live and work, bringing new life with them. As the century turned, economic revitalisation began the transformation of Peckham.

Sources

The epigraph is taken from Jon Thompson, as quoted in Elizabeth Fullerton's *Artrage!: The Story of the BritArt Revolution* (Thames & Hudson, 2016), which I have also drawn on for the account of the rise of the Young British Artists later in the chapter. The early history of the South London Gallery is given by Nicola Smith in her contribution to Giles Waterfield's *Art for the People: Culture in the Slums of Late Victorian Britain*, the catalogue of an exhibition at the Dulwich Picture Gallery in 1994. The gallery also features in Mary Boast, *The Story of Camberwell* (London Borough of Southwark Neighbourhood History No.1 1996). The SLG's helpful archivist Lucy Inglis gave me full access to the SLG's archives.

Sources for the account of the Camberwell School of Art are William Johnstone's *Points in Time: An Autobiography* (Barrie & Jenkins, 1980); Nigel Llewelyn (ed.), *The London Art Schools: Reforming the Art World 1960 to Now* (Tate, 2015); Leonard Daniels, *Camberwell School of Arts and Crafts* (LCC, 1948); Robert Medley, *Drawn from Life: A Memoir* (Faber & Faber, 1983). Gillian Ayres is quoted from Martin Gayford, *Modernists and Mavericks: Bacon, Freud, Hockney and the London Painters* (Thames & Hudson, 2018). Jon Thompson is quoted from *The Collected Writings of Jon Thompson* (Ridinghouse, 2011), which are also cited later in the chapter. George Rowlett gave me an invaluable interview, already used in Chapter 2. Gregor Muir's *Lucky Kunst: The Rise and Fall of Young British Art* (Aurum, 2009), quoted here, builds up the picture of Brit Art. Tom Phillips on the later Camberwell Art School is quoted from *Works and Texts* (Thames & Hudson, 1992).

William Feaver's *The Lives of Lucian Freud: Youth 1922-1968* was published by Bloomsbury in 2019. He kindly answered my detailed enquiries about Goldsmiths during the war. Mary Quant is quoted from *Quant by Quant* (Cassell, 1966). I am grateful to Tim Hilton for drawing my attention to Mary Quant. Apart from general reference sources, the account of Goldsmiths following Jon Thompson's arrival in 1970 is based on the interviews he gave to Cathy Courtney between 2011 and 2014 (he died in 2016) for the British Library's sound archive project *National Life Stories: Artists Lives*, together with his *Collected Writings*, mentioned earlier. The 1960s atmosphere at Goldsmiths is captured in the text and photographs of David Boucher, *The Way We Were: Photographic Reflections of Student Life at Goldsmiths College in the late Sixties* (2012; reprint DB Publications, 2019). I thank Tim Crook for information on Goldsmiths Elephant House, and other details of Goldsmiths history. Michael Craig Martin describes his involvement with Goldsmiths in *On Being An Artist* (Art Books Publishing, 2015). Maureen Paley is quoted from *Technique Anglaise: Current Trends in British Art*, ed. Andrew Renton and Liam Gillick (Thames & Hudson, 1991). Glenn Brown is quoted from *The Guardian*, 4 January 2018. Richard Wentworth gave me interviews, contacts, much help, and encouragement; the Collishaw story comes from *The Sunday Times*, 14 May 2017. Audrey Walker is quoted from her obituary in *The Guardian*, 17 February 2021.

Richard Shone is quoted from his essay in the catalogue to *Sensation: Young British Artists from the Saatchi College* at the Royal Academy, 1997. The catalogue contains useful biographical information. John Kieffer told me the story of Hirst's fundraising for "Freeze". A critical account of the rise of the Young British Artists is told in Julian Stallabrass, *High Art Lite: The Rise and Fall of Young British Art* (Verso, 1999; revised and expanded, 2006). David Thorp gave a lecture on the South London Art Gallery in April 2000, now in the SLG archive, and gave me a generous interview.

Figure 5.1 Russell Newell, *Shadows*, North Peckham Estate Walkway, 1984.

5

"We Are Trying To Build a Bit of Ordinary London": Politics and Planning, 1965–2000

"Peckham is a crucible for a set of forces. If you can see the future coming, do what you can to help it."

John McTernan, former councillor for Southwark's Bellenden ward

On the afternoon of Monday, 27 November 2000, ten-year-old Damilola Taylor was chased by youths on his way home to the North Peckham Estate from the recently opened Peckham Library. He was a newcomer, having arrived with his family from Nigeria that August. He made friends, among them his neighbour, the future broadcaster Yinka Bokinni. But that day he offended someone, or simply was in the wrong place at the wrong time. He took refuge in a stairwell, bleeding to death. A broken bottle had cut an artery in his leg. In 2006 – after three trials – two brothers, who had been 12 and 13 in 2000, were convicted of his manslaughter.

Such cruel deaths have become all too familiar in London, but something about the boy's youth, his engaging photograph, the reluctance of witnesses to come forward, and the time the police took to secure a conviction made this a particularly grim case. It did no good to Peckham.

In 2000 Southwark was the ninth-most deprived borough in England and Wales. Of its 21 electoral wards, 15 were in the band defining the most deprived 10%. Southwark Council was also the largest social landlord in London, with 59,000 properties, 90% of them flats and maisonettes. At a time when councils were being encouraged to reduce their responsibilities for social housing, 55% of housing in the borough was still in the public sector, when the London average was 27%. Some wards with a high density of social housing, including where Taylor lived, had a Black or Minority Ethnic population of over 50%. This was partly the result of the 1973 Land

Compensation Act and the 1977 Housing (Homeless Persons) Act, which meant that those formerly housed in the worst and most overcrowded private rented sector – many of whom, for reasons that were given in Chapter 3, also happened not to be White – gained priority in the allocation of social housing.

The unintended consequence was reinforcement of the ghetto-like atmosphere of places like the North Peckham Estate: "a scary place, like a maze, with lots of dead space", as former resident Russell Newell remembers it (Figure 5.1). The under-employment and casualisation seen in the 19th century had returned to South London, even as plutocracy emerged elsewhere in the capital. Southwark had London's highest crime rate. In 2000 Southwark Council's education department was judged to be so poorly run that the Department for Education ordered that its management responsibilities be handed over to a private company. The company failed to turn the situation round, and withdrew from the five-year contract in 2003. Another private company was hired.

It may be that there was some perverse romantic thrill to be derived from the J.G. Ballard-like dystopia represented by the North Peckham Estate – if you didn't live there. Russell Newell says, however, that it could feel different on the inside: "I know the area has been portrayed negatively in the press and popular culture but for many of us living there that was/is not the experience. Even back then it was a friendly and close knit but poor community often overshadowed by tragic events (eg Damilola Taylor)." The irony of Damilola Taylor's death was that it came towards the end of a programme of renewal, signified by the library from which the boy had set out, and the demolition in 2001 of the place where he died.

When the Metropolitan Borough of Southwark was created in 1965 out of the former boroughs of Southwark, Bermondsey, and Camberwell, the geographic shape that emerged resembled that of a Christmas stocking, hanging open from the southern banks of the Thames between Southwark Cathedral and the Surrey Docks, its toe filled by Dulwich. But a planner such as Fred Manson, who became borough architect in 1986, likes to think of it in terms of a dumb-bell. There was economic opportunity in the north, as the riverside began to recover from post-industrial blight and the docklands were redeveloped on both sides of the river; in the south there was suburban comfort and security. But in between lay problematic Peckham. Beginning in

Figure 5.2   Southwark wards, 2002–2018.

the late 1980s, Peckham experienced two processes of change. One was official: "regeneration". The other was unofficial: "gentrification".

The fundamental purpose of urban regeneration is economic: to revive commercial activity, raise land and property values, and increase returns to the state through taxation that can be directed to improving health and education. Finance may come from the state, but for preference the funding will come from private capital, including global capital returning a profit to whatever tax shelter it can find. From this process is presumed to flow the possibility of social revival, of inclusion where there has been exclusion, of social harmony where there has been complete dysfunction. Properly managed, regeneration will also bring benefits in terms of the natural as well as the social environment. But in practice the social gains from regeneration have been less obvious than the consequences of economic change, which have emphasised rather than reduced the inequalities that regeneration is assumed to address. Public regeneration produces private profit. The architectural historian Ben Campkin has written: "although regeneration is frequently justified in terms of fostering 'mixed-use', 'diverse', 'creative' and 'biodiverse' neighbourhoods, it often appears to remove – in spontaneous, informal, community- and citizen-led manifestations – precisely the qualities and activities it claims to engender".

As I have already argued, regeneration and gentrification are not opposites, but present the polarities of urban development and change. Regeneration clears neighbourhoods; gentrification can be more subtle. Unlike the enforced changes of regeneration schemes, rundown areas, largely occupied by the working class, are gradually taken over by middle-class homeowners and businesses, and the former occupants are dispersed. Yet although the results of compulsory purchase, demolition, and rebuilding can be part of the mix, gentrification also involves the voluntary exchange of property. People who chose to sell or leave a property may do so because they find living there unbearable, but they may also wish to capitalise on their asset. Buyers will be attracted to an area by price, by geography, and by its perceived potential as a place to live.

Gentrification is cultural, in that it is the result of many individual decisions and so appears to be more organic. By rehabilitating a neighbourhood and its housing stock in preference to wholesale demolition and reconstruction, it brings its own forms of social and environmental improvement. But it is still an economic process, driven by capital, and there are winners and losers. Both regeneration and gentrification are shaped by national policy decisions and local political developments. Both raise the question of how much agency the people who experience these processes have in their lives. Both provoke forms of resistance.

Improvements to Peckham were proposed as soon as Southwark Borough Council came into being in 1965. Because of Camberwell's greater size, former Camberwell councillors at first dominated the new merged borough, so it is no surprise that a draft town centre plan for Rye Lane was quickly launched in 1966. As well as the permanent search for increased rateable value, it reflected the concerns of the time: office-building, traffic management, and shopping. Rye Lane was losing its sheen as "the Golden Mile". One of the first moves was to drain and fill in the Peckham branch of the Surrey Canal in 1972. It has become a green lane, popular with kamikaze cyclists, but now that waterside developments are so fashionable this was a mistake, even if the area was in a rough state of dereliction. Several former Camberwell councillors lost their seats in the 1968 local elections, and from then until 1982 the new Southwark Council was led by John O'Grady, a prominent member of the "Bermondsey Mafia", who dominated the former borough's local politics. A retired councillor described them to me as "ruthless". Their power base was the old dockland communities and trade unions, and they kept a distinctly paternalist Old Labour hold on the council, controlling access to housing and not welcoming immigrants. Southwark's director of housing until 1986, John O'Brien, had joined from Bermondsey and maintained a firm grip on the estates.

In spite of Labour's long-established domination of the borough's parliamentary constituencies, it showed little interest in increasing party membership, so that by the close of the 1960s the local constituency parties were virtually moribund. As a report by the Home Office's Urban Deprivation Unit on the "inglorious" failure of the Newington Community Development Project commented in 1977: "Municipal politics in Southwark revolve around what happens inside the Labour Party and the ruling Labour Group in the Council." A former councillor described Southwark to me as "a brutal place, politically", where departments and their heads closely guarded their fiefdoms.

It was typical of the Bermondsey Mafia's municipal ambitions that much energy was spent on plans to build a new, multi-million-pound town hall, bang in the middle of the dumb-bell, where Labour electoral power was greatest. Its proposed site shifted from the north end of Rye Lane, then to the east side, and finally to the north side of Peckham High Street, where it was intended to take advantage of a Greater London Council plan to make a four-lane highway of the high street. Peckham's clogged, village-scale arteries have always been a problem, and there had been an attempt to solve it with widening in the 1880s.

These plans were resisted by a pressure group inspired by the Civic Trust, typical of the many that were springing up all over the country in response to the "modernisation" of town centres and the destruction of old buildings and streetscapes. Chaired by the journalist Bob Smyth, who lived in King's Grove, the Peckham Society was formed in October 1975, following a campaign to defend an elegant late-Georgian terrace off Asylum Road where demolition had already begun as part of wider "slum clearance".

Clifton Crescent was saved, but the town hall and high street widening plans presented an even greater challenge.

Eileen Conn, a senior civil servant who had bought a house in Nutbrook Street in 1973 and was secretary to the Peckham Society, formed the Peckham Action Group to lead resistance to the scheme. Some Society members had felt the proposed name, the "Peckham Society Action Group", was too provocative. They were clearly unprepared for the determination that Conn has shown in the planning battles since then. Tyneside-born in 1941, and brought up in an Evangelical Protestant sect, she left school at 16 and joined the civil service in a junior clerical role. After moving to London, however, she attended night school and went up to Oxford at the age of 25. On graduation, she returned to the civil service, this time in Whitehall. She has used her professional experience, working on government organisation and management, and in developing systems of corporate responsibility, to become a protector of Peckham's past and future, and a defender of Peckham's varied communities.

Russell Newell, a photographer involved through his mother's work with Harriet Harman, who would become Peckham's MP in 1982, recalls the Peckham Action Group as remarkably plural and classless. It was also inventive. This being the moment of punk, PAG member Peter Bibby persuaded a local avowedly Trotskyist pop group, Crisis, to make a protest record, "No Town Hall", on the PAG's own label, which it played from the back of a lorry at a protest march from the Elephant and Castle. (The DJ John Peel gave it some airtime.) Eileen Conn found an unexpected ally in a Conservative councillor, Toby Eckersley, a passionate believer in the property rights of those who would be expropriated by the council's scheme. There was also support from the militant New Left, and Conn recalls the unusual sight of both left and right taking part in the same protest: "somehow I was able to keep the whole political spectrum together".

Punk and local politics may have done the trick, for neither the town hall nor the road widening came to pass. The Bermondsey Mafia's grip on the council began to weaken. However, in preparation for the second town hall scheme (abandoned in 1976) the council bought and demolished a row of houses in Moncrieff Street, on the east side of Rye Lane. As he describes in his memoir, *Inside Out*, the abandoned rubble became an adventure playground for Rick Atkinson and his chums on Raul Road, before he moved on to nicking lead, minor drug dealing, and prison. The site was taken over by Sainsbury's, which wanted to replace its classic 1931 shop in Rye Lane, the last in the chain to have counter service, with a superstore. In 1977 it applied for planning permission to build a brutalist concrete monolith, topped by a ten-storey car park for 700 cars, to be operated by the council. The Peckham Action Group campaigned for a public enquiry, but this time the council prevailed, and the building opened in 1982. Set back from Rye Lane, but completely inappropriate in scale, it was sometimes known as the Peckham Mountain because of its hulking bulk. According to a local councillor it was believed to have the highest level of shoplifting in the country.

Figure 5.3 Sainsbury's, 1982 (image credit: © The Sainsbury Archive, Museum of London Docklands).

The council's deal with Sainsbury's, which committed the firm to staying for a minimum of ten years, chimed with the new approach that local authorities were being forced to take as the Thatcher government bore down on local authority budgets and encouraged commercial development. Preparation for widening the high street had created opportunities on its north side: 1.6 hectares at the former end of the Peckham branch of the Surrey Canal. In 1990 the developers Flaxyard submitted plans for a £100-million, six-storey mixed development in the standard developers' formula of offices, retail, and leisure. The proposed glass-enveloped building bore a resemblance to the Centre Pompidou in Paris, and so became known as the Peckham Pomp. The recession of the early 1990s killed off the plan, although some buildings were demolished. The site was grassed over, and became known as Flaxyard. In 2014 council proposals to develop the site caused fresh conflict.

The "Golden Mile" continued to tarnish as chain stores gave way to smaller ethnic enterprises. Holdron's, whose *moderne* glazed roof to its arcade was rediscovered only in 2016 (Figure 9.3), closed as early as 1949, having been taken over successively by Selfridges and John Lewis. In the 1990s it was a Blockbuster Video store, before gradually becoming a bazaar-like warren of lettings and sublettings. Most of the site of the once mighty Jones and Higgins was cleared after closure in 1980, rebuilt in 1986 as the banal Aylesham shopping centre, which expanded in the 1990s to take over a former 1950s bus garage at its rear. Its only architectural distinction was an artwork of inlaid metal tiles featuring birds, made by students at Camberwell Art School. The 1894 Jones and Higgins tower (Figure 2.4), remodelled after bomb damage and shorn of its pinnacles, remained as a mute landmark, its clock stopped at 7.35.

The estates that Southwark and the Greater London Council had completed in the 1970s were decaying badly. So was the quality of life on them and their surrounding streets. High levels of youth unemployment contributed to the riots of 1981 and 1985. In 1985 the Conservative government established its Urban Housing Unit, which in 1987 produced an Estate Action Plan. This sounded better than it was, for the funds made available were taken from the already existing housing budget, reducing investment elsewhere. Southwark put together a successful bid for £40 million for help with its North Peckham

Project, launched in 1987 (Figure 3.2); 1,200 homes were refurbished; some money went on adding pitched roofs to the 1960s Willowbrook Estate, which was otherwise in not too bad a condition, but a major change was made to the North Peckham Estate, where second-storey walkways were removed so that flats could be accessed directly from ground level. Some front and rear gardens were created and the parking blocks (where few risked actually parking their cars) were repurposed.

While these changes got under way, in 1988 a different threat to the centre of Peckham appeared in the mainly privately owned Warwick Gardens area to the west. Warwick Gardens had opened as a park next to the rail line in 1963, using the space created by bomb damage, close to what would become Peckham's first conservation area, established around Holly Grove in 1971, and later extended. British Rail proposed that the high-speed link to the Channel Tunnel, on which work had begun that year, would run along the rail route through Peckham and Nunhead, with a tunnel under Blenheim Grove and a "sub-surface junction" at Warwick Gardens. British Rail offered to buy all the houses in a 240-metre-wide corridor along the route, and acquired 170 homes, with the effect that the Gardens, the conservation area, and a long swathe of properties were blighted.

The Peckham Society had not taken part in the Sainsbury's campaign. Bob Smyth stepped down as chairman when he became a councillor in 1978, succeeded by a local artist, Bob Wollacott, who from his home in Nunhead made a great success of the Friends of Nunhead Cemetery. But, as is sometimes the case with voluntary bodies, the Peckham Society's energies flowed and ebbed. In 1982 Eileen Conn withdrew for a time from local activities because of her position in the civil service, but returned in 1986 as the Society's representative on the new Southwark Police and Community Consultative Group, set up following the 1981 Brixton riots. She served as chair from 1993 to 1996, achieving its independence from the council.

In February 1988 local historian John Beasley, editor of the Peckham Society's news sheet, reported it was bankrupt, but the new threat produced two fresh campaign groups: PEARL – Peckham and Environs Against the Rail Link, led by another local historian, Dereck Kinrade – and NARL – Nunhead Against the Rail Link. This was a largely middle-class protest from affected householders, but the "Sink the Link" campaign made its appearance in *Desmond's*, for lead-character Porkpie's flat was under threat. Guerrilla tree-planting, banners proclaiming "You Are Now Entering A British Rail Devastation Zone", and claims that Warwick Gardens had been a plague pit made little impression. In 1991, however, the Department of the Environment decided that the line would take a different route, and the plan was abandoned. House prices recovered.

Peckham could thank politician Michael Heseltine for the change of route, for he had returned as a minister under the government formed by John Major after Mrs Thatcher's resignation in 1990. Earlier, Heseltine had set up the London Docklands Development Corporation (taking control of areas of Bermondsey from Southwark) and championed the regeneration of Liverpool following the riots there. In 1991 he signalled a change in the government's attitude to local councils by launching the City Challenge, which was intended to revive local economies through a partnership between national and local government, businesses, and the education and training sector. This was followed in 1994 by the far more ambitious Single Regeneration Budget, which brought together up to 20 different government initiatives into a single scheme, with the intention of not only improving local environments and infrastructure, but supporting local economies and tackling social exclusion and crime.

This change in government policy coincided with a significant shift in Southwark politics. Nearly half the working population were now in office or other non-manual occupations, and as the borough became more middle-class the younger incomers reflected the social values of a post-1968 generation. As we have seen, resistance to plans for the town hall had come from across the political spectrum, including from among Labour Party members, "the new urban Left". The phrase is from Sue Goss, who became a Southwark councillor in 1982, at a time of turmoil in the local party. She records that in the face of the council's attitude:

The burgeoning community groups, the new voluntary workers and professionals interpreted this as the Council refusing to listen to anyone but themselves. To them, the Labour councillors represented a virtually dynastic group, patronising and paternalistic in their insistence that they knew best and could be trusted to act on behalf of the people.

What this meant, according to Goss, was that the old guard in the council was "*for* offices, *against* the homeless; *for* young married couples, *against* ethnic minorities; *for* the traditional community and *against* community groups".

Matters came to a head in November 1981 when the gay rights campaigner Peter Tatchell, who had become secretary of the Bermondsey Constituency Labour Party, was selected as parliamentary candidate to succeed the constituency's very Old Labour MP, Bob Mellish. Deeply offended, council leader John O'Grady stood against Tatchell in the subsequent 1983 election, fighting a poisonous campaign as "Real Bermondsey Labour". Labour split, and Bermondsey was won by the Social Democratic and Liberal Party candidate, Simon Hughes. O'Grady was expelled from the Labour Party. Although Labour continued to control Southwark, in 1986 for the first time it lost ward seats to a local alliance of the Liberal and Social Democratic Parties, who later merged as the Liberal Democrats.

O'Grady's successor as council leader was Alan Davis, who had worked as a social worker on the Newington Community Development Project and was an opponent of O'Grady. He had to preside over a fractious group of councillors, some of whom sympathised with the radical values of the new cultural and gender politics that, for instance, at the behest of the newly formed Women's Committee, meant a ban on having an official Carnival Queen. Davis was replaced – "dumped", in the words of one former councillor – in 1984 by a former member of the old guard, Tony Ritchie, who it was felt could be influenced by the left and centre. Councillors wanted to fight the Tory government, but showed an alarming tendency to (quite literally) fight among themselves. The political battle-ground was the government's introduction of rate-capping in 1984. In 1985 Southwark deferred setting a rate, at the risk of its councillors being disbarred. Council house building had stopped, and Southwark's planning ambitions were further moderated when the former Peckham Society chair Bob Smyth became deputy Labour leader in 1982, and the architect Nick Snow became deputy chair of the planning committee. Snow, prompted to stand as a councillor following his key membership of the Peckham Action Group, pioneered the practice of holding planning meetings in the areas affected by planning applications.

The Liberal/SDP success in the 1986 ward elections produced a further change in Southwark politics. Several New Left councillors of 1982 moved on; other councillors were expelled in the following years. Tony Ritchie stepped down as leader in 1986, but remained a councillor as well as serving on the London Fire Brigade authority, where his expenses were challenged. Ritchie was old-style, with close links to the public-service trade unions in Southwark, and he remained a force until he was suspended in 2004 for irregularities in the awarding of council tenancies.

Ritchie's successor as leader in 1986, Anne Matthews, was from the New Left, a former carpenter by trade, gay, and not part of the boozy world of Ritchie and his union friends. She was a hard-working council leader, and after the rate-capping row recognised the futility of directly confronting the government, seeing the need to cut expenditure and improve council services. This was especially true in the large and bureaucratic housing department. There was a long-standing overhang from the earlier building programme, with debt charges, millions owing in rent arrears, and problems with squatters. In 1981 Southwark had compounded its difficulties by voluntarily taking over the housing stock of the Greater London Council, so that 68% of residents were council tenants, although Southwark lacked the management skills to care for them properly. The direct-labour force had powerful unions; favouritism and racism influenced the allocation of tenancies.

Having already deployed rate-capping to narrow the room for manoeuvre of local councils, in 1988 the Conservative government reinforced its policy of prising social housing from local authority control with a new Housing and Planning Act, which set up a series of pilot Housing Action Trusts. These were intended to restore the very worst estates in the country, and then hand them over either to private landlords or to the not-for-profit housing associations that had become popular with the government in the 1980s. North Peckham and Gloucester Grove estates were nominated as Housing Action Trust areas, but the change would have to be agreed to in a vote by a majority of the residents. The most likely new landlords, housing associations, were not bound by the Homeless Persons Act that required councils to find housing for those who most needed it, and association tenancies did not allow people to pass on their tenancies to their children. This, plus the entirely reasonable fear that housing association rents would be higher, meant that after a vigorous campaign, in October 1990 the occupants of the two estates voted emphatically against the scheme.

After Mrs Thatcher's departure in 1990 the Conservative government began to take a less confrontational attitude to local councils. But in the 1990 ward elections Southwark Labour continued to lose to the Liberal Democrats, who were gaining strength in the north of the borough. Anne Matthews was succeeded as leader by Oxford-educated Sally Keeble, a former journalist who had worked as a press officer for the Labour Party and then the GMB union. In 1993 she stood down in favour of Jeremy Fraser, ahead of the 1994 ward elections. These brought in more fresh faces, but the Liberals continued to gain wards. As we saw in the case of the South London Gallery, Fraser favoured cultural investment. He encouraged co-operation with developers and was happy to see the south bank of the Thames redeveloped, unlike his New Left predecessors. Southwark was on a new path.

In 1994 the council was restructured, with the creation of the more powerful role of executive councillor for leaders of realigned departments. The American-born Fred Manson, appointed in 1986, was promoted from borough architect to acting director of development in 1990, and in 1994 became director of regeneration and environment, with responsibility for planning, public health and property. Manson was a pragmatic believer in social engineering, with no objections to gentrification. Like Fraser and his successor as leader from 1997 to 2000, Niall Duffy, Manson was convinced that culture could play a significant role in urban regeneration. He enthusiastically supported Southwark's decision to facilitate, and partly fund, the conversion of the redundant Bankside Power Station into Tate Modern, which opened in 2000. (At one time Manson suggested building the new Tate in the centre of Peckham.) He was also responsible for getting new ferry services running on the river and promoting the Millennium Bridge which, with Tate Modern, was catalytic in the redevelopment of the south bank of the Thames.

Now that Southwark had dropped its ideological objections to office-building along the river, the north end of the dumb-bell was proving its commercial potential, but there was much work to be done in Peckham. Plans for a town hall might have come to nothing, but the area between the filled-in canal, now a linear park, and the junction of Peckham High Street and Rye Lane, with Peckham Hill Street running north, was ripe for development, as Flaxyards had shown (this was the proposed site for the new Tate). The idea was to create social space in the form of a town square, between the canal head and the High Street. In 1992 £1 million was secured

Figure 5.4 The Peckham Arch, with the Peckham Library behind (before the construction of Mountview Academy of Theatre Arts). Peckham Pulse is on the left and the City can be seen on the skyline (image credit: Benedict O'Looney).

from the Department of the Environment. Work began with demolition of a group of 18th-century buildings on the High Street to create a site for the Peckham Arch (Figure 5.3), an open, canvas-roofed structure with a light sculpture by Ron Haselden, whose work had re-opened the revived South London Gallery. It was intended as a symbol of the new world that was coming, though some councillors feared it might become a conveniently central location for gang fights. In 2019 the arch was menaced by demolition because the council wanted part of the site for housing; it survived, but is still expected to be replaced by development.

The innocent arch was followed in 1998 by the £10-million health and leisure centre Peckham Pulse, designed by Southwark's Building Design Service. Its function was supposedly an echo of the Pioneer Health Centre in St Mary's Road – at that very moment in the process of becoming a gated community of yuppie flats – but certainly does not function in the same way. The jewel in the town square, however, was the new library (Figures 5.3 and 5.4). Manson recalls of this time: "there was an optimism, there was a belief that something was going to happen". A sign of the times was the choice of

Figure 5.5 Peckham Library with Mountview Academy of Theatre Arts to the left, in 2021.

designer, the radical post-modern artist-architect Will Alsop, a runner-up in the competition to build the Centre Pompidou who had made his name in 1994 with the municipal offices on stilts in Marseille, known from their colour as Le Grand Bleu.

Colour also features strongly in Peckham Library's exterior, with bright red and yellow glass on the north face, and a green-blue patinated copper covering on the rest. The extraordinary inverted-L-shape profile of the building (L for library) derives from Alsop's decision to lift the reading areas (complete with internal bean-like pods) above the traffic, and create a sheltered open public space beneath. Because of the engineering challenges of this unusual structure, Alsop had to insert his signature stilts to support the massive overhang. The roof is topped by a cheeky orange beret and the free-standing word "LIBRARY", which appears to have been lifted from a drawing by David Hockney. (In 2005 Alsop went further, with a 30-tonne steel "scribble" on the top of his new visual arts department for Goldsmiths.)

The old library in the North Peckham Civic Centre, on the corner of the Old Kent Road and Peckham Park Road, was closed, and the centre became the home of the Everlasting Open Arms Ministries. Opened in 1966, it has a striking external mural by Adam Kossoski, but although the mural is now listed, there are plans to replace the building with a 30-storey tower as part of the redevelopment of the Old Kent Road. The new library cost £5 million to build, and won the Stirling Prize for architecture. When it opened in 2000 it was an immediate success, and proved very popular with young people, among them Damilola Taylor.

£1.5 million of the cost of the library came from the government's Single Regeneration Budget, set up in 1994, and which became a turning point for Peckham. To qualify, Southwark assembled the Peckham Partnership, an alliance of the council, the developers Countryside Properties, the builders Laing's, half-a-dozen housing associations, tenants' associations from the affected estates, and representatives from the voluntary sector, plus the Metropolitan Police. Although the council took the lead, the various interested parties elected representatives to the Peckham Partnership Forum, which in turn elected the membership of the Peckham Partnership Board. There was not always agreement, especially within and between the tenants' associations, as to how to proceed. For the duration of the scheme, which ended in 2002, the partnership worked with the Government's Office for London, and, after the change of government in 1997 to Labour, with the London Development Agency.

For every £1 of central government money, the partnership was expected to find £4. The theory was that the scheme would be in part self-financing; land values would rise as areas were cleared for redevelopment and developers would move in, providing finance for the next phase. This followed Conservative economic thinking, and Conservative ideological thinking as well: hostility to council housing, a desire to reduce population density, and a desire to alter the social mix by bringing in more middle-class householders. For those already there, redevelopment meant relocation. The inhuman term "decanting" was used for the process by which tenants were moved out of their existing homes, usually to temporary accommodation, on the understanding that they would be able to return to new or improved premises. This took time and a lot of negotiation, and the maths did not add up.

Southwark won the largest Single Regeneration Budget grant in the country: £60 million. The council contributed a further £47 million, other public sources £37 million, and private investment £79.6 million. It is estimated that in total £290 million was spent, of which £180 million went on housing. Although the town square, Peckham Pulse, and the library were included in the scheme, the main focus was on the estates in the (since abolished) Liddle ward (Figures 3.2 and 5.6). As told in Chapter 3, they were collectively branded as the Five Estates – Camden, Sumner, Willowbrook, North Peckham, and Gloucester Grove.

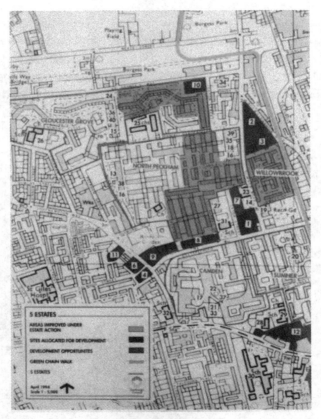

Figure 5.6 Redevelopment plan for the five estates, 1994. The darker the area, the more intense the intended redevelopment.

Responsibility for them was taken from the housing department and put in the hands of the borough planner, Malcolm Smith. They had different histories, different demographics, and were in different conditions, but Southwark emphasised the overall figures for unemployment and social deprivation in order to strengthen the Peckham Partnership's case. The number of housing units would be reduced from 4,532; 3,203 homes would be demolished and 2,019 new homes built, 70% with gardens. That meant significant change in ownership patterns; 625 homes would be privately owned, including those acquired under the Right to Buy; 915 would be managed by housing associations; 2,154 would be managed by Southwark Council. As a result local authority tenancies fell from 99% to 61.5%.

While the Willowbrook and Gloucester Grove estates were mainly refurbished, most of Sumner, all of Camden, and half of North Peckham came down, replaced by a generic mixture of terraced housing and medium-rise blocks. The architects responsible for master-planning the project explained: "The intention was to have a mixed tenure neighbourhood and

Figure 5.7   The new North Peckham: Leyland Court, council-built for private ownership, 2021.

make it possible for people to want to buy private property in an area that was not popular. We are not trying to build a new estate, we are trying to build a bit of ordinary London." This sounds like a recreation of the mediocrity of Sir John Summerson's "interminable London carpet", but according to Fred Manson, "it changed the dynamic dramatically. Previously, 80% of people would leave. Then, 80% wanted to stay."

Except they could not all stay. The reduction in the overall number of homes meant that some 2,000 people had been "decanted" who would have nowhere to return to. Nobody seems to know what happened to them, a point forcibly made by Luna Glücksberg in her 2013 study, "Wasting the Inner City", a doctoral thesis for Goldsmiths. Glücksberg had set out intending simply to investigate how people living in inner-city housing disposed of their rubbish, but, coinciding as it did with the Five Estates process, it turned out to be a fascinating anthropological study of regeneration – and covert gentrification. As an inhabitant of Peckham herself, she was concerned to counter the negative, journalistic perceptions of the area such as we have seen from Robert Chesshyre and Gregor Muir, in the popular response to the Damilola Taylor case, and indeed in the council's own presentation of the Five Estates. She also noted that "residents' views were routinely, one may even argue institutionally, ignored and misrepresented". The unexpressed metaphor of her thesis on waste disposal is that it was the people themselves who were being treated as rubbish.

It was difficult to shake the impression that what was going on could also be seen as a generalized wastage of the area and its inhabitants. By this I mean that their homes were being demolished, they were told to move away and, by and large a new affluent middle class was moved into the new homes built where the old estates stood.

Glücksberg found at least one Southwark councillor, who had served on the Peckham Partnership Board, who agreed with her, saying:

In the process communities were destroyed, a number of local facilities that did exist were taken out as part of the regeneration, with the understanding that they were going to be replaced, new. And that wasn't always the case.

There was the same skimping on communal facilities that happened with the original 1970s estates. Another problem was that there were almost no single-bedroom or bedsit flats in the new build. The Right to Buy had complicated the mix of tenancies in a block, and some people refused the alternative accommodation offered. This slowed the whole decanting process down, while others had to assert their "right to return" through the courts.

Mathematically, it was not possible for all to return, these people becoming a problem that appears to have been transferred into thin air – although they may have rematerialised during the Peckham riots of 2011. Glücksberg does not deny that the Five Estates programme achieved its aim in altering the social mix (as gentrification does) but she questions whether the intended social and economic benefits, in terms of education and employment, were achieved in the way intended.

It is not the established residents of the area whose education or health has improved, or who have suddenly found new or better jobs: it is new, different people who have better health, education and jobs who have moved into new and better housing.

No one begrudges people good health, jobs, education, and housing, but there does seem to be something missing from the equation here. The architecture of the Five Estates, and by extension their inhabitants, was being blamed for failings caused by structural economic and social conditions beyond local control, and which are the responsibility of national government. Glücksberg cites another, more positive councillor who believes the process has "changed the area massively, it's made it much much better, is a much more pleasant, visually, area, it feels safer, and in some ways I think … a lot more interesting than it used to be". But it may be significant that in 2002, just as the Peckham Partnership programme was drawing to a close, Labour lost control of the council. Its majority had been falling for some time, then in 2002 the Liberal Democrats won 30 council seats, the Conservatives 5, and Labour 28.

A council scrutiny review of the Five Estates Programme concluded that there had been significant failures in the community aspects of the programme. As a result £3 million was awarded to help set up the Greater Peckham Alliance to bring community representatives together to help improve Peckham from a community perspective. The process was managed by a new unit in the office of the council's chief executive, the Peckham Programme, led by Southwark's most senior Black officer, Russell Profitt. Eileen Conn, who as we shall see had formed a Bellenden

Residents Group in 2002, was invited to join the Greater Peckham Alliance, which made her and others aware of proposals for Rye Lane and the area around Rye Lane Station. Profitt facilitated the formation of a Rye Lane and Station Action Group, which led, again as we shall see, to the restoration of the station's hidden top-floor waiting room (Figures 8.6 and 8.7) and further developments.

Southwark's regeneration schemes continued, as did opposition. In 1999 the occupants of the Aylesbury Estate in Walworth (described as a slum on the day it opened in 1975) rejected a transfer to a housing association. In 2002 they rejected a partial demolition and refurbishment, but under Liberal Democrat control the council decided to go ahead, and in 2005 demolition was ordered, which began in 2009. Despite the vigorous protests articulated by the bloggers of Southwark Notes, the neighbouring Heygate Estate followed in 2011, the Elephant and Castle shopping centre in 2020. In 2010 control of Southwark returned to Labour; under leader Peter John, Southwark Council continued to know best.

Sources

In October 2020 Channel 4 broadcast Yinka Bokinni's documentary *Damilola: The Boy Next Door* about her friendship with Damilola, which sought to combat some of the negative perceptions of the North Peckham Estate, but did not engage with the mindset of those responsible for his death. A participant in the programme, Cornelius Walker, whose family moved from the estate after the killing, has become a filmmaker; his documentary *Black Sheep* was nominated for an Oscar in 2019.

Eileen Conn, who has been a key source for this study, was profiled in *The Peckham Peculiar* 31, February/March 2019. Russell Newell is quoted from an interview he gave me, and subsequent correspondence.

Ben Campkin is quoted from the introduction to his *Remaking London: Decline and Regeneration in Urban Culture* (I.B. Tauris, 2013). Harold Carter's *Life and Death of Old Labour: Collective Action and Social Cohesion in Sheffield and Southwark 1945–1997* (Oxford, 2005) is an invaluable guide to Southwark politics, as is Sue Goss's *Local Labour and Local Government: A Study of Changing Interests, Politics and Policy in Southwark from 1919 to 1982* (Edinburgh University Press, 1988). I have also been guided by interviews with John D. Johnson, Fred Manson, and John McTernan. Rick Atkinson's *Inside Out: You Can Take the Boy Out of Peckham...* was published by Xlibris in 2010.

For an overview of housing policy I continue to draw on John Boughton's *Municipal Dreams* (Verso, 2018) and the three parts of his coverage of the Five Estates for his "Municipal Dreams in Housing London" blog in October 2016. The planner who supplies the title for this chapter is quoted in Boughton's *Municipal Dreams*. Luna Glücksberg's "Wasting the Inner City: Waste, Value and Anthropology on the Estates", her PhD thesis for Goldsmiths, is available online. The description of the Aylesbury Estate as a slum comes from Neil McIntosh's *Housing the Poor? Council Housing in Southwark 1925–1975*

(Southwark Community Development Project, 1975). The Aylesbury and Heygate Estates are discussed in the "Sink Estate Spectacle" in Ben Campkin's *Remaking London* (I.B.Tauris, 2013). The Southwark Notes website (southwarknotes.wordpress.com) takes a very jaundiced view of Southwark Council's actions, gentrification, and just about everything else.

Figure 6.1 Tom Phillips, *We Love Peckham*, Bellenden Road mural, in 2021.

6

An Elective Montmartre: Renewal, 1990–2010

"Artists are such a lively group of people and they have so much to offer, that it's a shame this sort of thing doesn't happen more often."

Antony Gormley on the Bellenden Renewal programme

The transformation of North Peckham and the town square, together with the burgeoning developments stimulated by the success of Tate Modern, may have attracted most attention in Southwark, but at the same time that other, slower, and subtler process of urban change was taking place, for which the pejorative term is gentrification.

In London the driver is the rise in house prices seen in the 1980s and 1990s, and which has hardly slackened, for homeownership is now embedded in the national consciousness as the signifier of prosperity and, more importantly, security. Some gentrifiers have been unable to acquire property in the inner city, or in its more affluent suburban areas, but there is also an element of cultural choice in preferring to rehabilitate property rather than retreat to the outer suburbs.

The process begins with an area where property is relatively cheap and the tide of local commercial and industrial activity has gone out, as happened to Peckham after the 1950s, but which has not yet sunk to the point of utter dereliction and economic desolation, when, as we saw in the last chapter, planned regeneration appears to be the only answer. Southwark's working-class industrial base had collapsed by the 1970s, but there was sufficient economic activity in London to prevent local breakdown. Unable to afford anything else, discriminated against in social housing and by the property market, immigrants are often the first to see the opportunity, and move in. This at first makes the area even more unpopular, but gentrification begins when people young enough and enterprising enough to spot the possibilities of an otherwise rundown area take an interest.

This wave is not looking for profit; rather, it is simply looking for somewhere to live and work, although no one undertakes rehabilitation projects in order to make a loss. But once these generally middle-class immigrants have established themselves, then the services they require in terms of shops, restaurants, transport, and eventually health, education, and security, follow. Property developers see what is going on, there is refurbishment and new building, house prices continue to rise, and the transfer of the area from working-class to middle-class occupation continues. Public resources follow, yet somehow the "buzz" that attracted people in the first place fades. Some first-movers in this process find that they themselves have to move on. Gentrification does by stealth what policies such as the Single Regeneration Budget did by fiat.

It has long been recognised that, like migrants, artists are prime movers. In London the process known in America as "loft-living" began as far back as 1968 when Bridget Riley and Philip Sedgley got permission to convert a warehouse in St Katherine's Dock, hard by the Tower of London, into studios. Similar temporary arrangements spread to Wapping, Bermondsey, and Clerkenwell. The East End has always accommodated artists, but now whole streets were taken over. These were houses, supposedly awaiting demolition, that might otherwise have been squatted, plus commercial buildings left vacant by the vicissitudes of the property market. Like the more sober art dealer Jay Jopling, the former Camberwell foundation course student Joshua Compston (1970–1996) was one of the arts entrepreneurs who spotted the opportunities and led the East End revels of a Young British Bohemia in the 1990s. By 2000 Hoxton, Shoreditch, and Hackney were fashionable addresses for those working in the newly labelled creative industries. When a group of local artists set up the Southwark Arts Forum in 1987 they identified more than 1,000 living in the borough.

Peckham's unofficial gentrification started later than north of the river, partly because its transport links were poor, but it had long housed artists thanks to the presence of its art schools. Tom Phillips and Antony Gormley, neighbours in Talfourd Road, combined forces to build a new studio hidden behind a tall blank gate at 153 Bellenden Road, completed in 1988. It was a first commission for the architect Eric Parry, who has since gone on to projects such as the Stock Exchange and the East London Olympic Village. One of the labourers on the studio was Damien Hirst. Other Bellenden Road artists were John Latham (subject of the next chapter), Goldsmiths graduate and "Freeze" participant Ian Davenport, and the ceramicist and artist Jaqueline Poncelet, wife of the sculptor Richard Deacon. In 1990 a group of artists and ceramicists who had known each other at the Central School of Arts and Crafts (before its merger with Saint Martin's School of Art) moved

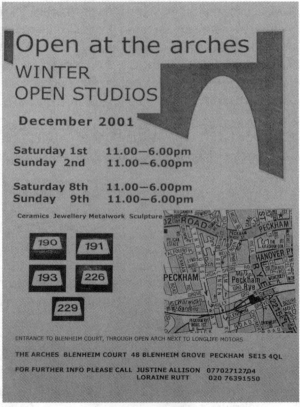

Figure 6.2   Flyer for the first Blenheim Arches Open Day, 2001 (image credit: courtesy of Jane Muir).

into some of the railway arches at Blenheim Court, sharing the space with motor mechanics' shops, as their successors still do. In 1997 they were joined by the ceramicist Jane Muir, graduate of Central and then the Royal College of Art, and she is still there. She remembers that the arches had been used by some dubious characters. Conditions were "pretty primitive, bitterly cold in the winter". The leaky arches are still cold in winter. Muir and her painter partner moved to Peckham, though they have since moved to Crystal Palace: "the work space was the most important thing". The arch artists formed an informal community, holding their first open day in 2001, now a regular feature of Peckham's cultural life (Figure 6.2).

In 1998 the architect Ken Taylor bought a former milk depot at King's Grove. He converted the building into three flats, but in partnership with the sculptor Julia Manheim created Peckham's first new gallery, The M^2 Gallery, so-called after the one-metre-square gallery window. The small-scale nature of defunct local industries had left a useful legacy, especially in the form of the Bussey factory (then known as the CIP Building) and the neighbouring warehouses south of the rail line in the Copeland Road Industrial Park. There were plenty of opportunities, if you were prepared to endure the downsides of squatting.

The area that had once been called the French Quarter was becoming, to use the writer Iain Sinclair's perceptive phrase, "an elective Montmartre".

The conditions for this to go further were ripe when Southwark Council launched another programme of renewal, aimed at private properties. This time the motive was not an alteration of the social mix, but an improvement to housing stock and the filling of empty properties. The 1989 Local Government and Housing Act had empowered local authorities to declare Renewal Areas within which the streetscape could be redesigned, social housing improved, and private owners encouraged to refurbish their properties with grants of up to £20,000 to cover 75% of the work to be done. The 1997 Labour government decided to go further by establishing a £900-million Neighbourhood Renewal Fund to be distributed over three years to 88 of the UK's most deprived boroughs. Certain criteria had to be met: 75% of the properties in the Renewal Area had to be privately owned, and of these a minimum of 75% had to be in a state of disrepair. At least 30% of the occupants had to be on a means-tested social benefit.

A Southwark Housing Department survey demonstrated that Peckham's Bellenden ward qualified easily; in an area bounded by Rye Lane and Peckham Rye on the east, East Dulwich Road, Goose Green, and Grove Vale as the southern border, and with the rail line running up from Dulwich to Peckham Rye closing the square to the west and north, the survey concluded there were 3,324 properties, of which 78% were privately owned and of which 84% were unfit or in need of repair; 34% of the inhabitants were on means-tested benefits. Further study showed that 67.6% of the population was White, and of the "ethnic" remainder about half were Caribbean, the rest a mixture of African, Irish, and small fractions of Indians, Pakistanis, Bangladeshis, and Chinese. The commercial centre of the area, such as it was, was Bellenden Road (Figure 6.3).

Beyond the significantly smaller financial scale of the project, there were two important differences between what was being done in North Peckham and here. The first was that the project was being run by Southwark's housing department, which was outside the Regeneration and Environment Department's remit. (According to Fred Manson, Michael Irvine, the director of housing, opposed Manson and would have nothing to do with him.) The second was that since the scheme involved private owners and members of housing associations, local people had to be properly consulted, and, given help, were able to specify the improvements to their own homes, though these would be carried out by the council. (Reciprocally, private owners would be contributing to the cost, and would have to repay their grants if they moved within five years.) So-called Group Repairs tackled major problems such as roofs in whole streets, bringing together in the process private, council, and housing association tenants and owner-occupiers.

The first streets to be made over – Nigel Road, Waghorn Street, Howden Street, Wingfield Street – had new pavements and lamp-posts and rebuilt front-garden walls in a uniform style marked by specially designed house numbers inset into the street fronts of the properties, but householders found internal works irksome and invasive. From this emerged the lighter and less expensive concept of "facelifts", which involved cleaning and repainting external frontages, new front paths, and rebuilding walls and railings, without inset numbers. Local businesses were similarly encouraged to contribute to the improvement of their buildings and streetscape. Prompted by Eileen

Conn, whose house was in the area, the housing officer responsible, Paddy O'Neil, organised a series of public meetings. The intention was to listen to local people's views; not surprisingly, since local artists were also vocal local residents, the meetings confirmed that they wanted as many local artists as possible to be involved.

Launched in 1997, with a time frame of ten years, the Bellenden Renewal Area Scheme began with a government grant of £5.2 million, and by its conclusion £12.4 million had gone into the scheme from various sources. The artist projects were managed by an experienced senior housing officer, Roger Young, who had worked in Birmingham before joining Southwark. In addition to a small staff of four, he brought in a consultant, Camilla Goddard, who had spent a year as an arts officer for Southwark, having previously worked as an arts officer in Lincolnshire, after graduate experience at Sotheby's and a degree in English and art history from Cambridge. Goddard was employed to work with the contributing artists, and assembled a database of some 60 local artists who might become involved. She and Roger Young got on well together; she recalls Young as "very enthusiastic. He had a way of making things happen." Others thought he had a tendency to overpromise. A Renewal Office was opened in a shop at 174 Bellenden Road; a scale model of the area was made so that locals could place cards on it with suggestions; barbecues were organised and a fair was held at Goose Green.

It was a principle that it was essential that there should be local ownership of the scheme, not just for local artists, but local people, and a steering group, the Residents Renewal Committee, was set up with its own art representative on the council's Renewal Area Board. The official line was that it is "important that artists work with residents and not consider themselves as working for the Council". This put a prudent distance between the council and any potential controversy. To secure a commission, artists had to take into account how residents thought and felt about a particular area, and consult them on their proposals. The emphasis was on the practical and the functional – railings, shop fronts, tree planting – rather than what Goddard calls "art for art's sake".

The process took some managing, as Goddard describes.

You are stuck between a slow, fearful, ambitious, bureaucratic Council on one side, and thoughtful, fearful, important, suspicious, enthusiastic individuals on the other: completely different animals with completely different ways of working.

An Elective Montmartre: Renewal, 1990–2010 | 129

Figure 6.3 Bellenden Road before, 1997 (image credit: courtesy of Camilla Goddard).

Figure 6.4 Bellenden Road after, 2021. Left to right: in 2021 a spruced-up Prince Albert Pub; "Odds and Ends" has become American artist Michael Petry's "Museum of Contemporary Art"; "Ossie Plumbing and Heating" has become the photographer's gallery "ECAD"; "Farmhouse" has become "Lovely House Restaurant".

This contrast in modalities and mentalities, further discussed in Chapter 10, is well illustrated by the case of Antony Gormley's bollards.

Gormley became involved as the result of attending a public meeting for local residents and, being a sculptor, came up with the need for bollards that would help to separate traffic and people. He was excited by the prospect of making something sculptural, but useful. Demonstrating a prototype, he said: "The art world is just a tiny, tiny little world, and this bollard is in a way, just another attempt to break out of it. Artists are such a lively group of people and they have so much to offer, that it's a shame this sort of thing doesn't happen more often." He produced four designs. They were unusual shapes,

Figure 6.5 Antony Gormley bollards, 2021. "The peg" is in the foreground. Left to right behind: "the egg", "the penis", and "the snowman".

but eminently practical because of their robustness, and the fact that, just like those contemporary sculptures that are intended to rust, they would never need repainting. Council members, however, found them too radical, and indeed "suggestive". It is difficult to imagine how a bollard could be suggestive, but then Gormley had named the designs "the penis", "the peg", "the snowman", and the "the egg".

It was decided that this commission could not go ahead, but local traders, possibly attracted by the potential for the very scandal that the council feared, decided to pay for them, and they have become one of the most distinctive (and effective) parts of the Bellenden Road streetscape. Sadly, a further Gormley project did not survive. Arts & Business (founded in 1976 as the Association for Business Sponsorship of the Arts, and part-funded by the government to stimulate collaboration between business sponsors and arts organisations) was a helpful early investor in the Bellenden scheme, putting up £280,000. It arranged a partnership with Thames Water for Gormley to design new manhole covers for the area, an ingenious design depicting the artist's feet in water. Prototypes were produced, but no sooner were they installed than they were stolen.

Sometimes a project went wrong for other reasons. The Slade-trained artist Emily Toscano-Heighton painted a striking Italian-themed mural for the interior of Chaz Hairdresser's on Bellenden Road, at a cost to Arts & Business of £2,200. On installation at the end of 2001 the mural went down well with customers, but in 2003 the owner decided to remodel his shop and, to the distress of the artist and the dismay of the Renewal Team, painted it out. Landscape artist Lucy Swan's long-term scheme to create a topiary project with new-planted yew trees outside Bellenden Old School, a community youth and education centre, has also disappeared, following the change of use of the building to become the new Belham School.

Heather Burrell designed exterior railings for the Victoria Inn (then called the Wishing Well) on the corner of Choumert Road that have survived – at the other end of the road Sokari Douglas Camp worked on the setting of the Choumert Road market. Burrell also designed (alongside Heather Moral) gates for All Saints Church in Blenheim Grove, and gates for the London Wildlife Trust Centre on Marsden Road. This had been created in 1989 out of an old council depot where, reputedly, Charlie Richardson had been in the habit of stashing stolen goods.

Although not asked to design for the scheme, the artist Clive Burton had a positive experience. A graduate of Ravensbourne College of Art and Design when it was sited in Bromley, Burton taught part-time at several London art schools, including Camberwell. In 1994 he bought the former Caribbean Palm Tree Restaurant at 157 Bellenden Road for use as a live-in studio, where he is still: "what you did then wasn't highly controlled".

"The area was run down, pretty dodgy", he says, but when Goddard and Young arrived, "we were very much consulted – in fact heavily encouraged". He was offered the chance to make over his frontage, but did not want to install the village-shop-style awnings that were being favoured. Instead, he was allowed to design a clean modern shop façade, and his own shiny metal railings, and used the shop as a gallery for a while. He recalls being expected to pay a small percentage of the cost, but does not think he was ever billed for it.

One of the most prolific contributors to the scheme was Tom Phillips, who created two of his characteristic *lettriste* pieces: "We Love Peckham" mosaics (Figure 5.1) above a "curiosity shop", Curios2Retro, and the facing Peckham

Figure 6.6 Tom Phillips, Arch for McDermott Grove Wildlife Garden, in 2020.

Experiment Restaurant, one of the new ventures – such as the Ganapati Indian restaurant – that were moving into what was becoming known as the "Bellenden Village". (Emblematically, Ganapati took over a truckers' café. In 2020 it survived in difficult conditions, but other places have changed hands.) Phillips also designed barcode mosaic pavement patterns, and an archway (Figure 6.6) and gates for another wildlife garden, created by local volunteers out of council-owned wasteland at McDermott Grove, off Costa Street.

The garden was supplied with benches by Adam Lowe, and entertaining sculptural sheep by Helen Harrison. Phillips's most unusual commission was to design the elegant white lamp-posts that add a distinctly modern note to otherwise architecturally undistinguished streets (Figure 6.10).

Figure 6.7   Lamp-post by Zandra Rhodes, with hawthorn blossoms, Goose Green, in 2021.

The fashion designer and Bermondsey resident Zandra Rhodes also contributed lamp-posts, this time in black, with quirky, twisted tops that she compared to liquorice sticks (Figure 6.7).

They are part of the thought-through makeover she gave to the shopping parade in East Dulwich Road, on Peckham's southern border. The designer's exoticism and love of pink was expressed in pink-and-black bollards (Figure 6.8), terra cotta pavements and a pink bus shelter, now sadly painted black. In the month of May, the hawthorn trees she had planted sprout pink blossom.

In the nearby open space of Goose Green, Jamaican sculptor Marcia Bennett Male applied her stone-carving and lettering skills to marking out its paths.

Figure 6.8   Zandra Rhodes bollard, Goose Green, in 2021.

Figure 6.9 Marcia Bennet Male, path marker, Goose Green, in 2021.

In all, some 30 artists, craftspeople, and designers worked on the project, memorialised in the pavement map by Loraine Butt outside the Petitou Café, a former butcher's shop in Choumert Road. Local residents benefitted from the improvements to their homes – though working with Southwark's sub-contracted labour force proved frustrating, to say the least. Some acquired inside lavatories for the first time, others central heating. The new pavements and new front walls to their properties improved the look of the terraces. There seems to have been general satisfaction, even if not every house or street benefitted – approximately 1,200 houses had been upgraded by 2005. Not everything went smoothly or according to plan, as we will see from John Latham's struggles to achieve his ambitions in the following chapter.

By 2002 the scheme was running into difficulties. In 2000 Southwark made an unsuccessful attempt to transfer all its housing stock to another social landlord, which caused considerable uncertainty for the housing department. There was a political hiatus in 2002 when Labour lost Southwark to Liberal Democrat minority control, after the Labour mayor of Southwark resigned in protest at his own party's policies. This coincided with a change in government policy that ended renewal grants for private properties. These uncertainties were reflected in the drying up of communication between Southwark and Bellenden area residents; the local newsletter stopped appearing. It seemed there was a lack of transparency about decisions both on repairs and artist commissions. The formal Bellenden Advisory Board, established in 1999 with 15 elected local representatives, ceased to function. In 2002 Bellenden ward was divided between new wards: South Camberwell to the west, and The Lane to the east (Figure 5.2). (North Peckham and Liddle wards also disappeared at this time.) It was suggested that the new Nunhead and Peckham Rye Community Council covering the area – an attempt to establish the equivalent of parish councils in urban areas – could take on a representative function, but the remit did not fit.

However much the council claimed credit for the level of local consultation, residents tended to find out what was going via the press, and had unhappy experiences with the work being done. As elsewhere, their response was to organise in self-defence, and in January 2002 the Bellenden Residents Group was formed, 350 members led by the indefatigable Eileen Conn. The group had no official status or financial support, but it became a useful pressure group, and a vent for some of the inevitable frustrations of such a long and complicated scheme.

There seem to have been a lot of unfulfilled promises, made to groups of residents in streets or individual residents or traders for their own properties. These promises led to people rearranging their lives to accommodate them, taking out loans and re-mortgaging, preparing for work which never happened, not hearing adequately what was happening, or suffering financial loss.

This submission to a Housing Scrutiny Committee set up by Southwark in 2004 in response to pressure from residents (the results of an earlier scrutiny were never published) reflects the frustrations felt, but it is difficult to disagree with the Scrutiny Committee's finding that, notwithstanding the problem of poor communications and insufficient manpower:

The Bellenden Renewal Scheme had significantly improved the look of the area. Properties, and entire streets, and many public areas are looking much brighter and revitalised. Shop fronts, many situated along Bellenden Road, have been revamped and a number of new businesses have moved into the area. New public artworks have appeared ... There has also been some limited success in bringing empty homes and shops back into use.

Southwark was pleased with the press coverage it received, and the awards, including the British Urban Regeneration Association Award in 2005. With the Bellenden project drawing to a close in 2007, it felt encouraged to launch two more renewal schemes, for East Peckham – principally the Queen's Road area – and Nunhead. The repair and refurbishment plans were on the same lines as Bellenden, but the Renewal Team's ideas for public art were significantly more ambitious; Damien Hirst was asked for designs for Nunhead station bridge, Tracey Emin for fluorescent signs on either side of the Queen's Road Bridge. Jeremy Deller produced a sculptural concept for the Queen's Road Station terrace; Chris Ofili proposed two mosaic designs for Queen's Road. Paul Smith would design a restored clock tower of a former steam bus garage for Nunhead. Dr Harold Moody (1882–1947) would be celebrated as a local hero for setting up the first Black civil rights movement in Britain in 1931, the League of Coloured Peoples, with a statue outside his former house at 164 Queen's Road. At Meeting House Lane – which in spite of its proximity to Peckham Police Station was notorious for its crack-houses, illegal gambling, and prostitution – would have a sculpture by Maggi Hambling, while the police station would have a tiled mural designed by the Turner Prize-winning artist Gillian Wearing, using images derived from another Turner Prize winner, Mark Wallinger.

    Most of these projects were outlined and priced by 2009, but the stock market crash of 2008, and the ensuing cuts to local authority budgets imposed by the 2010 coalition government, has left them as paper memorials to the age before austerity. The 1960s Wood Dene Estate on Queen's Road, sold by the council to a housing association and demolished in 2006, remained a vacant lot until 2020. Roger Young left the council. Camilla Goddard decided to become a bee-keeper.

    But not before they had achieved a project of lasting national importance.

Sources

Iain Sinclair's "elective Montmartre" appears in his *London Overground: A Day's Walk around the Ginger Line* (Hamish Hamilton, 2015). Jane Muir welcomed me to her studio in the Blenheim Court arches. The story of the Bellenden Renewal project, and the subsequent renewal plans for Queen's Road and Nunhead, uses information helpfully supplied by Roger Young and Camilla Goddard (who also gave me an interview), Southwark Council archives and publications, and the John Latham archive at Flat Time House. I am very grateful to Clive Burton for his account of the Bellenden Renewal project.

An Elective Montmartre: Renewal, 1990–2010 | 139

Figure 6.10 Bellenden Road, 2021, looking north, with a Gormley "penis" beneath a Phillips lamp-post.

Figure 7.1 210 Bellenden Road in 1986 (image credit: photo by John Latham © John Latham Foundation).

7

"Incidental Person": John Latham and Flat Time House, 1985–2021

"The problem is in the verbal medium – where it has drowned philosophies and faiths alike".
John Latham, 2 February 2000

In 1985 the artist John Latham moved into 210 Bellenden Road, part of what he called a "forlorn and desultory terrace" at the southern end of what is now the thriving route from East Dulwich to the junction of Peckham Road with Peckham High Street. The southern end was laid out between 1872 and 1874 by the British Land Company, which sold on building plots to individual builders at local auctions. Number 210 was the end building of a row of five houses with ground-floor shops, running up to number 200. Number 204 was Lloyd's barbershop (Figure 3.5), which would serve as the exterior for *Desmond's*. Next to the terrace came the parish buildings at the east end of the Victorian gothic church built by the United Methodists in 1884 to replace an earlier iron church, at the junction with Danby Street. It is now the Pentecostal Faith Chapel, frequented by the post-war Black community.

In 1985 the shopfront of 210 was boarded up; on the left, barn doors gave access to a side-passage just wide enough to bring in a car, and which in theory gave right-of-way to the backs of the other houses in the row. On the right, a street door led up to the two floors above. At the back of the house was an overgrown garden and a large shed, known as "the stables". Number 210, like its neighbour at 208, "Patricia Hair", had seen better days. The whole area was run down. Number 206 carried out motor repairs in the street. Cars were parked on the pavement, or quietly rusted in the gutters, their wheels up on bricks to avoid paying road tax.

Like other artists, Latham had come to Peckham in search of cheap space. He had previously lived in West London, an unwitting early artist-gentrifier of Holland Park, at 55 Norland Road, moving to 22 Portland Road, and then 5 Boscombe Road in Shepherd's Bush, which had begun to fall down. He lived apart from his wife and long-term collaborator, Barbara Stevini (1928–2020), but both moved to Peckham, she to Anstey Road, and Stevini remained a collaborator and frequent visitor. Number 210 had a rateable value of £670; the ground floor gave him a place to work and store things, with living quarters above the kitchen at the back of the house, accessed by a tight spiral staircase. He built a small glass-roofed studio beyond the back kitchen, adding a linking side passage. There were separate flats on the first and second floors, but he was short of money, and sold on the top floor. Although he had become something of a counter-cultural celebrity in the 1960s, thanks to his controversial sacking from part-time teaching at St Martin's School of Art, and his book-tower burnings as part of the Destruction in Art Symposium in 1966, by the 1980s his reputation and finances were at a low ebb. He had been suffering from poor health, and put a lot of energy into disputes with the Arts Council and government. Yet – in time – 210 Bellenden Road would become one of his most important works of art.

What time meant was a problem for Latham, and he wrestled with it all his life. Although his ideas and manner could appear divisive, his quest was to bring all things towards unity. His ambition was to realise a "universal order" through art. The world, he believed, was "an indivisible whole that is not a space-time entity". Latham had discovered this concept in the 1950s. Born in 1921 and educated at one of England's most intellectually distinguished public schools, Winchester, he served as commander of motor torpedo boats and a mine-sweeper during World War II, and was sunk twice. Demobbed, he used his ex-serviceman's grant to study painting at the Regent Street Polytechnic and Chelsea School of Art. He left Chelsea in 1950 without a diploma but married to Barbara Stevini, and they were to have three children. In 1948 he shared his first gallery show with the future critic and novelist John Berger. In 1954 he began to use a spray gun to make works in black paint (Figure 7.2), followed in 1958 by cutting and collaging second-hand books as sculptural material. Though this was the heyday of action painting, Latham's ideas were neither purely abstract nor simply expressive. Friendship with two married scientists, astronomer Clive Gregory and psychologist Anita Kohsen, who were also in search of a unified world theory, led to the formation in 1954 of the Institute for the Study of Mental Images, with Latham as honorary founder member. After Gregory died in 1964, Latham carried on the mission.

Latham's ideas about time and – in his view, its opposite – space were in constant evolution, and were generally greeted with complete bafflement. In 1984, however, just before moving into Bellenden Road, he produced an unusually accessible statement in the form of *Report of a Surveyor*, a book also presented as an art work for an exhibition in Eindhoven. Since he wished to bring the whole world to an understanding of its fundamental unity, the *Report* was addressed to the one man who could be said to have responsibility for the whole world, the secretary-general of the United Nations. The secretary-general's response is not recorded.

Latham's problem was that he was living in a different dimension to other people. Some might have said that unkindly, but it is meant seriously here. For practical purposes the ruling dimension of everyday life is the object-world of space, which he liked to abbreviate to just "S". Space is the dimension that is understood through the ordinary common sense of having to deal with material things. But there is the other dimension, of time – or, as he put it, "Time-and-Event based T". In T, objects are not fixed objects but, as we experience them continuously across time, constantly renewed events. Newtonian physics expressed the world in terms of objects in space; relativity theory expressed it in terms of energy and mass; and quantum mechanics expressed it in terms of "fields". Latham added consideration of the role of the observer in what was being seen. He described the relationship between the observer and what is observed as an "Event-Structure". Thus, because time is constantly moving, the world of apparently solid objects melts into a series of successively evolving events. These concepts are not easy to grasp, because the medium available for expressing them is language. And language is itself a linear object that imposes its own logic on the ideas to be conveyed. He wrote:

The transposition from object to event terms suggests that the problem of society lies within the medium of language itself and the way it imposes its dimensionality on the ordering process. Language is unable to tell the whole truth owing to the incongruity inherent in its framework.

Worse, for someone seeking unity, language was also a divisive medium, and had been ever since Plato established the structuring principles of philosophy. Latham was trapped by the very words he was obliged to use to frame his ideas: "If, to account for a sense of the fundamental I adopt the medium of words *and follow their conventional logic* [his italics], I defeat my purpose." To those living in the space dimension, "the Time-based tradition is romantic, and non-rational". Because language depends on objects – "that is to say nouns, named entities" – it is unable to handle the concept of objects as a stream of continuously happening events. T appeared to be non-rational, and to many so did its advocate, Latham.

But there was another way to express ideas, through art: "Art proposes wholes within which parts relate integrally." Art reverses the process of division, and, appropriately, Latham was in the habit of reversing language. Two of his early inventions, "Skoob" and "Noit", are, in the first instance, "books" spelt backwards, and in the second, "-tion", is the word-ending that turns verbs into nouns – actions into objects. The product of the interaction between the observer and the event – the Event-Structure – was art.

While much of Latham's ideas depend on bringing the different discourses of science and art together, he remained, first and foremost, an artist. But an artist of a very special type, who was prepared to compare himself, in an interview in 1968 with the critic Charles Harrison, to an engineer.

Change the point of vision and problems aren't solved so much as dissolved – you don't see them as problems any more perhaps. The artist's attitude is basically an engineer's but using information in the people context.

The artist Richard Hamilton compared Latham to that earlier Peckham visitor, William Blake.

Just as Blake was rigorous in his determination to use the new science of anatomy to represent his vision of creation, so Latham insists on the taut muscular equations that modern scientific methods require.

Latham was happy to associate himself with Blake: "T artists are sometimes called pejoratively emotive names but could it not be that Blake, Vincent [Van Gogh] and many others classified as romantics were profoundly concerned with the expression of an order in the whole?" Artists were driven by intuition.

Latham's gaunt appearance, piercing eyes, lank hair, and fierce Rasputin-like aspect may have suggested he was a visionary in the manner of Blake or Van Gogh; nonetheless, though he believed in the spiritual vocation of the artist, he preferred to use the humbler term "Incidental Person".

As well as language there was another divisive medium: money, a dimension in which Latham rarely moved. Just as language imposes its own structures on ideas, so money imposes its own values on art. It is "a form of authority" and the Incidental Person is bound to challenge it. Although Latham had sold work to the New York Museum of Modern Art and the Arts Council (which, he claimed, then never showed it), he made little money that way, or through teaching at St Martin's School of Art. After an earlier brush with the 1960s dealer John Kasmin, he was represented by the securely established Lisson Gallery, but (like many artists in relation to their dealers) he believed that its director, Nicholas Logsdail, was not good at pushing his work, and Logsdail did not appear interested in his cosmological ideas. In 2001, in his eightieth year, Latham's solicitor calculated that his income was below the poverty line: a state pension of £285.40 a month, plus rent from the shed in the garden and a room in his house, coming in all to about £4,800 a year. The purchaser of the top-floor flat discovered that Latham had no building insurance, and was forced to insure the whole building in order to protect her flat, hoping, almost certainly in vain, that he would be able to meet his share.

Latham accepted society's need to cling to the space dimension: "legal and administrative processes depend on it". As far as the art business was concerned, after the emergence of object-resistant conceptual art, artists became divided between those interested in:

A former, manageable conflux of marketed activity, and those for whom the markets are an irrelevance; (that is to say, not a determining factor in what constitutes art). Art institutions, including colleges, museums and dealer rings, appear to act in concert to maintain the former conveniences however.

In 1966, helped by one of his students at St Martin's, the sculptor Barry Flanagan, Latham challenged the authority of art schools and art critics by organising the chewing up and then distilling of pages from the American art critic Clement Greenberg's holy writ, *Art and Culture*. He lost his job as a result, but created a classic of conceptual art.

Latham and Steveni had, meanwhile, developed an alternative means to find practising artists both paid work and a way to make a social contribution: the Artist Placement Group. APG would engage with the S world by enabling Incidental Persons to work inside organisations – commercial businesses or government departments – not necessarily to 'make art', but by having an influence through their observations of, and presence in, these institutions. Initially supported by the Arts Council, APG got a number of adventurous and provocative artists, among them Garth Evans, Ian Breakwell, Barry Flanagan, Stuart Brisley, David Hall, Maurice Agis, and Ian McDonald Munro, into a number of unlikely institutions, such as British Airways, British Steel, and British Petroleum. But the problem of language, and the way it structures thought, was ever present.

The work of art uses a logic that discovers itself to the user through the assertion of freedom from other conventions and idiomatic uses. As everyone probably recognizes, this is the distinguishing feature of art and of invented language, and in easy contrast to the grammar, syntax and vocabulary of shared meanings implicit in the standardized forms of language, for example in administrative business.

By 1970 it was clear that the grammar, syntax, and vocabulary of the Arts Council and the language of APG no longer made sense to each other. The Arts Council withdrew its funding. The official reason was that the APG was "more interested in social engineering than with pure art" (a distinction Latham would not recognise), but a less evasive justification was given in 1982 by the Arts Council's secretary-general, Roy Shaw, in a letter to Andrew Faulds MP, when Latham was trying to take the Arts Council to the European Court of Human Rights. In Shaw's opinion, Latham was "either mad, or bad – or perhaps both". Latham's response in 1984 was: "The Arts Council is seen in the present circumstances as a permanent and perhaps intentional clearing house for the maintenance of a status quo, but with a passing reputation for supporting what the public interpret as clowning."

The struggle with the S world of authority, represented by the Arts Council, was not, however, a grubby argument about funding, or even cultural politics. The issue was much bigger than that. Money and language were instruments of power, and their power was a source of negative energy. There was "a conflict of authority and cataclysmic collision between opposing systems of belief as to its source". Having fought in the war, and living with the constant threat of nuclear annihilation, Latham was convinced of the profound significance of his argument.

The combination Language plus Money constitutes the media of governments, but the functioning is not understood. Language + Money function as the fission reactor of society, (the end reaction being ultimate fission).

In 1989 APG reconstituted itself as O+I, arguing that its idea of artist placements had been plagiarised. O+I stood for "Organisation plus Imagination", but it can also be read as a play on Latham's formulation of 0, standing for a "nonextended state" (that is to say, nothing, a vacuum – but also the universe before the start of time), and 1 for a unit of time "deriving

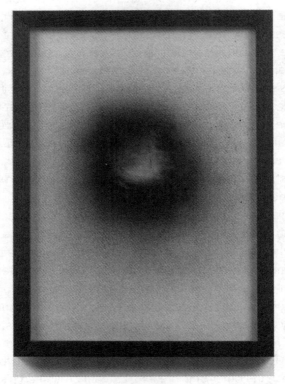

Figure 7.2 One-second drawing: John Latham, *Organism Somewhere*, 1980. (image credit: © John Latham Foundation).

Impulse (to extend) from State 0 and returning to State 0". Thus a "least-event", the shortest possible event to be more than nothing, could be notated as 01–10. The idea goes back to his time with the Institute for the Study of Mental Images, which in 1959 published a paper, "The 0 Structure: An Introduction to Psychophysical Cosmology". This proposed that the "0 Structure" was a basic unit, a micro-event. The visual manifestation of this idea was Latham's *One-Second Drawings*, a micro-event in the form of a short blast of black paint sprayed on a surface (Figure 7.2). 0 was a singularity that had the potential – "the impulse" – to become something, in other words, to become 1. The formulation 01–10 represents the movement from nothing to event: the "impulse", followed by the "discharge of impulse" with 0 marking the end of the event.

This was important in terms of Latham's interpretation of art history. In 1915 Einstein's theory of relativity had posited the existence of mass as a dimensionless point, a 0 (Stephen Hawking's 1983 theory of black holes added force to this idea); art had reached a similar point zero in 1951 with Rauschenberg's blank canvasses, *White Paintings*, followed in 1952 by John Cage's silent composition for piano, "4'33". From this point, the nominally objectless (but eventful) practice of conceptual art began. In the 1980s Latham turned to glass as a physical expression of point 0: "It's very hard, you can see through it, so it is not an object. In photographs, it's difficult to puzzle that there is anything there at all. But when you place a book through it, that is by contrast, very much like the extended world, like a person with a whole history that goes down the line."

01–10, glass and books, were to come together in a spectacular way at Bellenden Road, but Latham was still struggling with the concept of time. Or, rather, two concepts of time. Language had divided time; there was linear time, but there was also "omnipresent time", an a-temporal time that was "non-extended". It might be expressed as memory, or, as Latham put it: "a world which changes and a world which does not change". Modern physics had allowed a view of the world as "an insistently recurrent, accretive event" – which sounds very much like the "field" of quantum mechanics. To demonstrate the idea that time moves in two directions, the one linear, the other omnipresent, Latham presented historical time as horizontal, and omnipresent time as vertical. The physical realisation of this in 1972 was the *Time-Base Roller*, a motorised form of roller blind

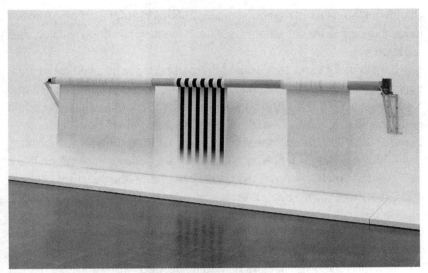

Figure 7.3 John Latham, *Time-Base Roller*, 1972 (image credit: photo Jean-Philippe Woodland © John Latham Foundation).

in which historical time, from its beginning to the end of the universe, was represented by the horizontal barrel of the roller. The turning of the roller was, through its turning, a reminder of present time passing, but as it turned it unfurled, vertically downwards, the stripes of the continuous presents of omnipresent time, bearing letters that appeared to form words or even phrases (Figure 7.3).

Because the roller turned, however, it was impossible to grasp all the words or letters at the same time, as they were obscured by the rolling or unrolling canvas – yet the knowledge remained, in the memory, that they were there. The flatness of the canvas, set against a wall, suggested another way of expressing time, but the idea of "Flat Time" – an ingenious expression for memory, because although it is the past we can only experience it in the present – only came to fruition when at last an opportunity came to give full expression to his cosmology as a coherent whole – an actual time-based-event: the Bellenden Renewal Scheme.

When the Bellenden project was announced in 1997, Latham remained aloof. First approached in 1998, he suggested a large-scale book sculpture, but

Southwark's director of regeneration, Fred Manson, in spite of being a knowledgeable supporter of Latham's work and meeting him several times, was not keen.

On the other hand, 210 Bellenden Road certainly qualified for renovation. Since moving in, Latham had made his studio a regular meeting place for artists and O+I. At first the artist Helen Foster Spragge, who also worked as his assistant, occupied the first-floor flat, while a gentle hippy, now remembered only as "Tom", lived in the stables. Then, in 1993, Latham's younger son, John-Paul, a geologist teaching at Queen Mary College, took refuge there following the breakdown in his marriage. John-Paul's little daughters, Harriet and Clara, came to stay every Wednesday night and every other weekend.

Harriet Latham, now a choreographer, speaks very fondly of her grandfather, and of the warm feelings that he generated – necessary in the spartan conditions of the house, unheated in winter: "There was consistency in his chaos." Using the green fingers he had developed while running a market garden in the 1950s, he grew strawberries and tomatoes on the rear roof, and a vine up the back of the house. His bedroom became a "den", where he loved watching snooker and Formula One racing on the television, left constantly on. He constructed a hammock for the girls, to discourage them from climbing into his bed in the mornings. It was, according to Harriet: "an adventure playground with lots of hazards". The children appreciated the kind attention and generous freedom that he gave them: "there weren't strict parameters, it was being free on a level with the parents". This private and domestic Latham was a very different character to the public controversialist who harried politicians and the Arts Council. In time, Helen Foster Spragge gave over her flat to John-Paul, who stayed on until 1999.

Latham was finally drawn into the Bellenden Renewal project by a former councillor for the Bellenden ward, John McTernan, who had tried to resolve a planning dispute over the right of way that ran along the back of 210 to give access to the other houses, but which was now blocked. McTernan, "a third generation Labour man", lived near Peckham Rye and became councillor for the Bellenden ward in 1986. When the Conservative government decided to wind up the Inner London Education Authority and pass responsibility down to the London boroughs, as chair of Southwark's Education Committee McTernan had to devise an education policy for the borough when it took over in 1990. An admirer of Latham and of the work of APG and O+I, he asked Barbara Steveni and O+I to look at ways to improve the borough's education system. In November 1989 they submitted their proposals for a much more creative way of engaging young people in the process of learning, and the Southwark Educational Research Project went on to place artists in 15 of the borough's schools. The project ran until 1995.

McTernan ceased to be a councillor in 1994, and in 1997 became an advisor on housing and development to the New Labour government, later working for Tony Blair as director of political operations, but he continued to live in Peckham and kept an eye on the area, and encouraged the development of Overground links to Peckham Rye Station. His connection with Latham prepared the way for a visit to 210 from Roger Young and Camilla Goddard. Together, they raised Latham's interest. Goddard recalled Latham as "an enthusiastic person, he had an open mind, wasn't interested in the politics. He was practical – chaotic – but easy to work with."

At the start of the scheme, everything seemed possible, and much was promised. The idea was that the shopfronts from 200 to 210 would be repaired, rendered, and painted, and that Latham would design a sculpture for the façade of 210. Somehow, the plans did not use the word 'iconic'. At first, £42,000 was promised for repairs to the house. The former shop on the ground floor would be converted into a display space as a "taster" of Latham's work, complete with the latest IT, and the possibility was raised of involvement from Southwark's museum services. As Latham wrote to Roger Young in July 2000:

The development entails a shift in the present appearance of the site from "anonymous zero-rated" (which I have been enjoying) to a "high profile public value-rated" site. Shockwave stuff, an awesome impact on the way I live, entailing as we discussed a lot of rearranging of internal areas and internal requirements. (I have some plans of the necessary shift but need to hear your side.)

Latham's immediate task was to design his sculpture. He chose to use two of his favourite materials, glass and books, but on a grand scale (Figure 7.4).

Working on a vertical axis, two outsize books, specially made by a bookbinder, would have their pages interleaved, with the boards of the upper book bent up and back like two wings, reaching up as high as the second floor, with

152 | "Incidental Person"

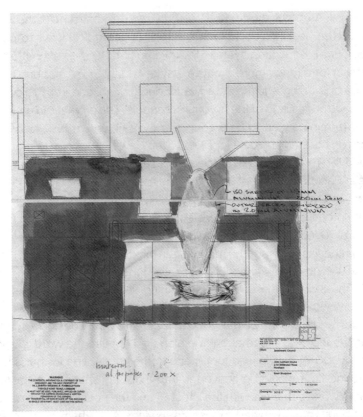

Figure 7.4 John Latham, draft design for *Face* or *How the Univoice is Still Unheard*, 2000 (image credit: © John Latham Foundation).

the lower section thrust through the glass of the shopfront. The blue binding of the lower book would bear the title "How the Univoice is Still Unheard". But while the materials spoke to Latham's regular themes of unity, there was also a figurative element to the design. In a link to the terrace's neighbour, the Faith Chapel at the corner with Danby Street, he presented the maquette to the Renewal Team as a "new (and unforeseen) scaled up modern version of the Pentecostal Image" (Figures 7.5 and 7.6).

The maquette, constructed in 2000 out of a sheet of glass, cardboard, and masking tape, was sufficiently convincing to be awarded a grant of £8,000 from the Henry Moore Foundation to secure its realisation. Latham

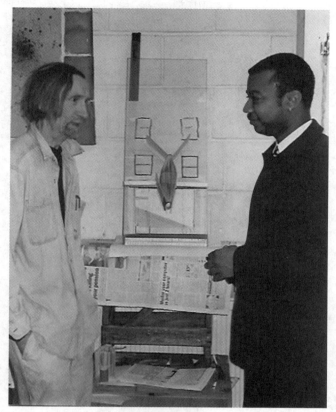

Figure 7.5 John Latham (left), sculpture maquette, and Roger Young, 2000 (image credit: photo Camilla Goddard © John Latham Foundation).

engaged a fabrication expert to design an armature to support the sculpture, and busied himself with clearing out the shop. But time – real time – began to be as divisive as money. As we saw in the previous chapter, with the passing of the financial year at the end of March 2000, the money supposedly available for repairs to 210 began to disappear into other budgets.

In December 2000, frustrated by the delays, Latham repeated a tactic he had used to challenge the Arts Council. In 1977, furious at the Arts Council's withdrawal of support, and apparent plagiarism in setting up its own artist placements, he had submitted an invoice "For Services Rendered", that is to say, for launching an art movement. He demanded £1 million for

Figure 7.6 John Latham, maquette for *Face* or *How the Univoice is Still Unheard*, 2000 (image credit: © John Latham Foundation).

APG, and £0.5 million for himself. His bill to Southwark was more modest, an entirely reasonable £4,000, but, like the Arts Council's invoice, it would not be paid. It was made clear to Latham that if the Southwark Council paid him for the sculpture, it would become the Council's property, so he would have to work for free. The Lisson Gallery was also vexed that Latham had not brought it in on the project. Latham and Stevini's view was: "the Lisson has made no sale of the work or promoted it abroad for a decade, so the original arrangement between L[atham] and Lisson is regarded as lapsed", but although the Lisson refused to help with a launch event for the Bellenden Renewal Scheme at the South London Gallery, relations with the Lisson (which stored much of his work) were not broken off.

A deadline for installation was set for March 2001, an important date for Latham as he was trying to raise funding for a project he was working on with Professor Chris Isham of the theoretical physics department of Imperial College. The grant did not materialise; the deadline was missed. A new completion date was set for February 2002 but it was not until July 2001 that the necessary planning permission was applied for. On 20 September, by one vote, Southwark refused planning permission for what was, in effect, its own idea. To make matters worse, the Renewal Team did not inform Latham until November. Once more, "planning" was the enemy of creativity. This particular "Event-Structure" seemed in danger of disappearing down a bureaucratic black hole.

Although Latham raged to Roger Young – "I am not interested in having my house half-transformed in difference [sic] to some planner's idea of what is appropriate – it would be a betrayal, a cop-out, a denial of reason for living" – the linear time made by these delays proved useful to Latham. It created more space for him to develop his ideas about what 210 could become, and to develop his ideas about time.

Latham's search for an all-embracing theory had led him to propose the "Event-Structure" as an "inclusive cosmology". He wrote in 1995: "Within it every conceivable action or idea is explicable relative to the rest … It is the most succinct theory of 'time' yet proposed, in that it subsumes all the variant phenomena reported on the subject while remaining simple and self-consistent." The idea developed in the following years, so that by May 1998 he was telling people about "a phenomenal discovery about the relation of art to materiality". The breakthrough was "the discovery of a dimensionality 'Flat Time'".

The thinking behind "Flat Time" goes back at least as far as the roller paintings he made in the 1960s, and the visual rendition of the two dimensions of time in his *Time-Base Roller* of 1972, where time moves on in one plane, but remains static in the other, as a form of memory (Figure 7.3). The thinness and two-sidedness of the unrolling canvas seems to have revealed the (one-dimensional) significance of "flat". His most explicit reference to this is contained in a handwritten footnote to his draft of "Flat Time 1–10 as Sculpture", written in November 2003, where he adds at the bottom of the paper: "'flat' refers to the double-sided membrane which unrolls from a cylinder". This membrane represents the static plane of time. In a letter to Yoko Ono, who had been giving him some financial help, in December 2000 he writes, more obscurely: "In Flat Time the rollerised canvas manifests a Nothing=Everything plane which (I maintain) is synonymous with the missing component called by space-bound physicists 'the vacuum'." This could be seen as the moment before the Big Bang that launched the universe, and the moment after the universe ends.

"Flat Time" turns out to be the basis for all "Event-Structures", embracing both passing time and the time-boundaries of observable events. It thus creates the illusion of space that allows us to treat continuous events as discrete and observable phenomena that can be described through language. Or, as Latham gnomically puts it in his notes on "Flat Time" in December 2002, the present universe "is a mindstructure and Flat Time is its architecture".

These ideas were partially the result of the three months between December 1999 and February 2000 that Latham had spent as "Artist-in-Research" at the Isaac Newton Institute for Mathematical Sciences at Cambridge. At the end of his assignment, arranged by the Institute of International Visual Arts, he issued a one-page statement from the Isaac Newton Institute, addressed "to whom it may concern": "Art and Culture – Cosmic Dimensions as Flat Time". This read, in part:

Flat Time shows up as art, and is contradicted by verbal logic. It is at odds with ways we have become accustomed to think. However, it purposes a stratagem for socializing this (T = time-based) map. When put into practice, it has been found to work. The result from art hatched spontaneously, and has grown like an organism. I have now to suggest that Flat Time contains in one envelope a map of all our cultural histories, and that for purposes of extending the future, it constitutes the most comprehensive 20th century legacy.

One scientist who appeared to find that "Flat Time" did indeed work was Christopher Isham, professor of theoretical physics at Imperial College London. In 2000 he and his colleague Konstantina Savidou gave a public lecture at Darwin College, Cambridge, subsequently published in 2002, on "Time and Modern Physics". It used Latham's *Time-Base Roller* as one of its illustrations (Figure 7.3). Isham was a leading expert on quantum theory, and was concerned with trying to reconcile the incompatible theories of relativity and quantum mechanics. Latham excitedly told Yoko Ono in December that year that Isham had thought the problem was insoluble, but that his *Time-Base Roller* illustrated what they had lately discovered: "two kinds of time". Latham and Isham linked up to submit an application to the Arts and Humanities Research Council for funding to create a computer model that would act as the mathematical equivalent to the *Time-Base Roller*.

The application was refused, but this intellectual activity and external encouragement had given Latham what scientists call a GUT – a Grand Universal Theory: "the new envelope concept of 'FLAT TIME'". The artistic realisation of this envelope would be 210 Bellenden Road. Not just the book-sculpture on the façade, but the whole house would become, in a phrase that goes back to the title of the Institute for the Study of Mental Images paper of 1959, "a psychophysical sculpture". Quoting his former colleague in APG, David Hill, Latham wrote that 210 would become a complete "Work in Itself". Unity would be achieved.

210 would be called Flat Time House – or, rather, since Latham could not resist multi-layering his references, "Flat Time Ho", where "Ho" was constructed from the numerals 1–10, a play on all that work on the "0 Structure".

These plans were possible because the Bellenden Renewal team was at last making progress, even though it meant artistic compromise. After the setback of refusal of planning permission in 2001, Roger Young had come up with a solution. If the sculpture were to be no more than six feet high, there would be no need for planning permission. It was agreed that the two books of the original vertical "Pentecostal Image" would be set horizontally within the glass of the shop window, while a flat, painted "ghost" of the original idea would be pinned to the façade above. By March 2002 the maquette of the second version was in the fabricator's workshop, and in April 2003 the book-sculpture was installed at 210, ready for an opening event on 9 May (Figures 7.7 and 7.8).

This was, however, just the beginning. In November 2003 Latham laid out his ideas for the "living sculpture" as a whole.

Figure 7.7 John Latham, *Face* or *How the Univoice is Still Unheard* (detail of the horizontal installation), Flat Time House, 2003 (image credit: photo Ken Adlard © John Latham Foundation).

The building at 210 Bellenden Road, London SE15 is an "abstract-real" figure sculpture where
> FACE is the street frontage, a relief sculpture, behind which
> MIND is the space behind the frontage where a series of forms as art (1954–1995) are presented in front of
> BRAIN the space behind Mind, a computer work-station behind which is
> BODY EVENT where practical present time activity occurs, including a spiral up to bedding and plumbing. Furthest back from Face is the
> HAND, where event-structured "things" are made and a current state of nature is cultivated.

It was Latham's intention that Flat Time House would become a public facility, with a staff of two or three, funded from Southwark's museum or educational departments, as had been originally half-promised in 1999.

Yet, after four years of delays, frustration of his ideas, and expense on his own behalf, in 2003, behind the repair and painting of the façade – in the Renewal Team's terminology a "facelift" – his home was in a worse condition than ever. The book-sculpture was protected by a glass screen, but Latham objected to the metal bar at its top, which obscured the composition, as did a new lamp-post outside, designed by Tom Phillips. The lamp-post was moved, but the metal bar remained. Otherwise, the whole house, which was attracting visitors and students at the risk of their safety, was untouched. In September Latham wrote to a Southwark Council officer:

Of greatest importance is the roof, which looks a century old and which leaks appallingly into parts of the house including my bedroom, where the ceiling has started to give way.

In short, while the condition to date may be a great asset to the Bellenden Road team, I personally have marked up losses in accommodation, accessory structural work, annual temporary roofing repairs and general lack of maintenance. I do hope you will require your contractors to attend to my interests in the projected work rather than call me just a resident and not to be consulted.

Latham was experiencing the problems that others were complaining of. His fears were realised when part of the ceiling of his bedroom collapsed in February 2005.

With the recognition of Flat Time House as a living sculpture, however, Latham's position began to improve. The acquisition of the APG's archive by the Tate in 2003 was a financial relief, and in September 2005 Tate Britain at last gave him the retrospective he richly deserved, "John Latham in Focus". That year he also showed at the Lisson, and in Venice. But he was not able to enjoy his success for long. He died on 1 January 2006, at the age of 84.

To preserve his legacy, his family set up a foundation in his name, and between 2006 and 2008 Southwark Council contributed £20,000 so that repairs were at last done on the house to make it accessible and safe. John Hill, a student at Camberwell, had started working in the house, using Latham's tools, and he set up a group of a dozen or so artists who would meet there regularly as the Mental Furniture Institute, an "anti-know" project on Latham lines that ran for four years. In May 2008 the Goldsmiths-trained curator Elisa Kay, who had worked on the Lisson Gallery's 2005 Latham show, *God is Great*, became Flat Time House's first curator, and John Hill joined her as education officer. The Flat Time House Institute came into being, with a succession of shows, discussions, and a residency programme.

In 2012 Kay was succeeded as curator by another Goldsmiths graduate, Claire Louise Staunton. Although the house was getting short-term project funding from the Arts Council and the Henry Moore Foundation, and Latham's personal archive was being conserved and digitised, the costs of maintaining Flat Time House were falling heavily on the Latham family foundation, which decided to move Flat Time House towards being an independent organisation. At the beginning of 2016 it looked as though the house would have to be sold, possibly to a developer, who would take advantage of the gentrification of the area.

Staunton resigned as curator, and in July the house closed, just as the Serpentine Gallery began to prepare a celebration of Latham in March 2017. However, Royal College of Art-trained Gareth Bell-Jones moved in as curator and was able temporally to reopen the house and archive. At the last minute, in April 2016, a Rome-based family of collectors, who had only discovered Latham's work in 2014, decided to buy the house. While the Dino and Ernesta Santarelli Foundation now owns the building, Flat Time House continues to operate as an archive, exhibition space, project hub, and artist residency facility. And as an "Event-Structure".

It shows what, in the end, the right kind of regeneration can achieve. While parts of the Bellenden Renewal Scheme have become shabby, or have disappeared altogether, 210 Bellenden Road remains a living, breathing sculpture. Such an "Event-Structure" is John Latham's masterpiece, and a fitting monument to one of the world's most remarkable incidental persons.

"One of the functions of art is to say 'Well yes I can see it, and it's fascinating, but what does it mean?'"
John Latham in conversation with Noa Latham, 1981

Sources

The bulk of the material cited in this chapter comes from the John Latham archive at Flat Time House, and I am very grateful to the curator, Gareth Bell-Jones, for all the help and access he has given me. Roger Young also supplied material, and Camilla Goddard gave me a very helpful interview. I would also like to thank the late Barbara Stevini, her sons Noa and John-Paul, and granddaughter Harriet for reviewing my chapter and allowing me to use their words. John McTernan helped with background. John Latham's *Report of a Surveyor* was published by Edition Hansjorg Mayer and Tate Gallery in 1984. Latham's *Event-Structure: Approach to a Basic Contradiction* was published by Syntax/Egg Press in 1981. Antony Hudek and Athanasios Velios edited *The Portable John Latham* for the Ligatus Research Centre,

Figure 7.8 John Latham, *Face* or *How the Univoice is Still Unheard*, Flat Time House, 2003. The "wings" of the original Pentecostal image reach above the second floor (image credit: photo Ken Adlard © John Latham Foundation).

Colophon, Camberwell College of Arts, in 2010. John A. Walker published his critical biography, *John Latham: The Incidental Person – His Art and Ideas*, with Middlesex University Press in 1995. There is a very helpful interview with Latham and Stevini, by Pauline van Mourik Broekman and Josephine Berry, "Countdown to Zero, Count up to Now (An Interview with the Artist Placement Group)", in *Mute* 1, no. 25 (Winter/Spring), 2003.

A version of this chapter was published in *Ants and Grasshoppers: reflections on the anxious object*, edited by Gareth Bell-Jones and David Thorp (Flat Time House, 2021), to accompany an exhibition of the same name.

Figure 8.1 Richard Wentworth, *Agora*, 2015, at Bold Tendencies. *Agora* (meaning a meeting place) snakes sinuously across the roof of the multi-storey car park, which Wentworth describes as "London's balcony" (image credit: photo Quintin Lake, courtesy Bold Tendencies).

8

Bold Tendencies: Culture and Creativity, 2000–2021

"What we are trying to have here is organic growth."
Jonathan Wilson, owner of the Bussey Building and Copeland Park, 2020

Early in 2006 a young Cambridge art history graduate, Hannah Barry, travelled to Peckham for the first time to see an exhibition at the recently opened Sassoon Gallery. It was in one of the railway arches at Dovedale Court, like Blenheim Court off Blenheim Grove, and next to Peckham Rye Station. The gallery had been launched by the architect Ben Sassoon as an adjunct to his Bar Story, a rough-and-ready café-bar popular with art students from Camberwell and Goldsmiths since its opening in 2003. Barry had been invited by the painter Shaun McDowell, a graduate of Chelsea Art School who had organised the show, and was sharing a place in Friary Road with a Camberwell graduate, Bobby Dowler. Balmforth and Dowler were survivors of !WOWWOW!, an artists' collective formed by another Camberwell graduate, James Matthew Stone, with the Central St Martin's-trained fashion designer Gareth Pugh, much featured in the magazine *Dazed and Confused*.

In 2004 Pugh, Stone, video artist Adham Faramawy (Slade and Royal Academy Schools), sculptor James Balmforth (Chelsea), and others squatted a former Co-Op store at 259 Rye Lane (replaced by housing in 2008), where the parties became more famous than the exhibitions and performances they put on. Peckham knew about squatters. Peckham Action Group used the device politically in 1979 when a house in Sumner Avenue threatened by the proposed town hall and four-lane highway was occupied, preventing its immediate demolition. In 1989 the former Department of Social Security offices in Collyer Place, off Peckham High Street, had been occupied by the Dolehouse Crew, a place for post-punk music and parties, from which emerged the short-lived Peckham band Ruff Ruff & Ready. They were evicted in 1990, but between 1998 and 2008 Southwark Council licensed a squat at 39b Consort Road, a former dosshouse which became the home of the Spike Surplus Scheme, which ran alternative community programmes and an urban craft business, recycling waste materials such as "Peckham Diamonds" (an idea worthy of Del-Boy), made from broken windscreen glass. Few squats had such cultural pretentions; empty pubs were popular. The Clayton Arms was squatted in 2011, the Gowlett Arms in 2018, but squatting became a less easy solution to finding somewhere to live after legislation was tightened in 2011.

In 2006 Dowler, McDowell, Balmforth, and others moved on to 78 Lyndhurst Way, a handsome four-storey Grade II-listed Georgian house, whose owner was waiting for planning permission to convert it into flats. This was not an ordinary squat. The house had been occupied by Poles and Ukrainians, but Dowler persuaded the owner that it would be far cheaper to allow him to live there as a caretaker than to fortify the house against squatters. A deal was struck, and a rent of £5 a month agreed. Dowler and his friends moved in, cleared out the stained and rotting mattresses and piles of rubbish, and painted the walls. As McDowell told *Dazed and Confused* in 2013:

Right from the off we didn't want to do what everyone did by throwing huge parties where the art was irrelevant. So, unlike those squat parties in Kensington that were full of rich kids, we improved the building. This set a serious precedent. Artists in the area started showing their work in alternative spaces. All of a sudden people were showing in squats that had white walls.

Hannah Barry was introduced to the Lyndhurst Way group, which included James Capper (Royal College of Art), Oliver Griffin (Falmouth), Christopher Green (Byam Shaw), and Oliver Eales and Simon Milner (both Bournemouth). She felt welcomed there, and offered to help arrange their shows, beginning with "Ten Rooms and a Sculpture Garden" in November 2006. The following summer the group did something more ambitious, when they were allowed to mount an exhibition on the roof of council offices in Sumner Road, North Peckham, which had served as the playground of a school. The show was called "Bold Tendencies". A fresh chapter was opening in Peckham's cultural history.

Figure 8.2 "Bold Tendencies 1", Sumner Road, 2007, with work by Shaun McDowell, James Capper & Nick Jeffrey, and Michael Allen (image credit: courtesy Bold Tendencies).

At the beginning of the 21st century, after a long period of decline shared by other parts of London ending only in the 1990s, the population of Southwark began to increase at a much faster rate than the rest of the country, from 256,700 in 2001 to 317,256 in 2018. (This is still considerably lower than 100 years earlier, when it peaked in 1911 at 579,338.) This population is younger than elsewhere, and more mobile, with a 10% annual turnover. It is ethnically highly diverse. In 2001 it was 63% White, 6% Asian, 16% African, and 8% Caribbean. By 2018 it was 53% White, 9% Asian, still 16% African, and 6% Caribbean. In 2001 the Camberwell and Peckham constituency had the highest proportion of Black or Minority Ethnic voters in the country, at 39.2%. Many of these were concentrated in the four wards around Peckham Rye Station. The Peckham ward itself was 36.7% African, 15.45% Caribbean, and 23.73% White. What is noticeable is the concentration of Africans, mainly from Nigeria. "Southwark is Britain's African capital", stated a study of African churches in the borough in 2013.

Although a survey in 2016, which looked at class rather than ethnicity, showed that Peckham ward's population was 32% ABC1 in 2001 and 40% in 2016 (the London average was 62%), the ward also contributed to the statistic that 25% of Southwark's population was suffering income deprivation. Out of the 21 wards in the borough, following the renaming and redrawing of ward boundaries in 2002, Peckham was the fourth-most deprived, Livesey the second, Nunhead the fifth, Rye Lane the sixth, and Peckham Rye, to the south, the sixteenth. The ethnicities of the population may have changed, yet the overall pattern is not very different from that described by Charles Booth at the end of the 19th century.

At the same time, Peckham has not escaped the phenomenal rise in the price of private property. In Peckham ward the average cost of a terraced house in 1995 was £52,000; in 2019 it was £535,000; a flat in 1995 cost on average £28,000; in 2019 it cost £351,000. In more affluent Peckham Rye the average cost of a terraced house in 2019 was £775,000 and a flat £405,000. These figures are partly mitigated by the fact that the borough still contains a substantial amount of rented property, just over half of all homes. In spite of the policies described in Chapter 4, Southwark has the largest proportion of social housing in England, at 43.7%; 31.2% is directly owned by the council, making it the largest social landlord in London.

The purpose of this blizzard of figures is to create a context for the arguments about gentrification that can be heard daily in Peckham. Peckham is not paradise. Crime rates may have fallen to around the average for the borough – though knife crime increased in and after 2017 – but there is still plenty of tension. In August 2011 Peckham saw its share of the rioting that broke out across London and other towns following the shooting by police in Tottenham of mixed-race Mark Duggan. About 500 White and Black rioters caused mayhem in Peckham High Street and Rye Lane. Shops were set on fire and others looted. The Clayton Arms in Clayton Road was ransacked, leading to its later being squatted. In all, 50 local businesses reported damage.

But there is another side to Peckham. A brick had smashed the window of Poundland, in the old Jones and Higgins building, and was boarded up. The blank face became a spontaneous memorial when members of the Peckham Shed Youth Theatre, led by their director Joy Tyabji, decided to hand out post-it notes and marker pens so that passers-by could express their love for Peckham by sticking their comments to what became known as the Peace Wall. The notes were subsequently transformed into a mural that stands beneath the Peckham Arch across the road.

The greatest threat to Peckham was planning. Planning is a long and cumbersome process, involving many competing interests. In London it is governed by a hierarchy of documents, descending from the National Planning Policy Framework, to the London Plan, to overall Borough Plans, a Borough Core Strategy, and specific Area Action Plans, which come closest in detail to the streets where people live. Once agreed by the local council, these, having been consulted upon, are subject to government inspectors and public hearings, and make their way back up the chain to be signed off by the secretary of state for the environment (or whatever title the department has since been given).

The years this takes mean that the process has to begin all over again almost immediately because conditions have changed. The mayor of London (head of the Greater London Authority established in 2000) and borough authorities are by no means the only interested parties. Transport for London will have its own ideas, as will individual rail companies and Network Rail. Between 2000 and 2012 the London Development Agency operated under the Greater London Authority. English Heritage can influence decisions for and against change. Private landowners and developers, such as the recent owners of Peckham's Aylesham Centre, Tiger Developments part of BlackRock venture capital (the site has been bought by Berkeley Homes), or of Copeland Park, have their own different agenda. Private citizens or groups representing their interests can have their say, though they are not automatically listened to, in spite of having a much better understanding of what is going on in their neighbourhood – and investment in it – than most transient professional planners.

After Labour regained full political control of Southwark in 2010, it pressed on with the development of a Peckham Area Action Plan that had been in preparation since 2007. A *Future Peckham* vision paper was released by the council in 2008, which took in Nunhead and identified five "development opportunities" across most of SE15. The council was also trying to cope with the fallout from the errors of the Five Estates project with its £3-million Peckham Programme, led by Russell Profitt, to address the lack of social amenities in the new-build and help encourage a sense of community. Profitt took a positive view of the potential in cultural activities, but earned the envy of other departments. In 2008 (the year of the financial crash) the Peckham Programme unit was disbanded, and Profitt took early retirement.

Abolition of the Peckham Programme left the council without a co-ordinated overview of Peckham's town centre. Although an earlier generation of councillors had been thwarted in their attempt to make the centre of Peckham a grand civic space, the council was well aware that this had the largest area of shopping floorspace in the borough, although following the exodus of the big chain stores – joined by Sainsbury's in 1992 – Rye Lane was taken over for multiple occupation by smaller traders, who answered the particular needs of a growing multi-ethnic population.

The "Golden Mile" was but a memory – Rye Lane was certainly not one of Britain's increasingly identical high streets – but financial imperatives meant that Southwark continued to be focused on making Peckham "attractive

Figure 8.3 Khan's Bargains in the partially restored 1930s Holdron's Building, 2021 (image credit: courtesy Benedict O'Looney Architects).

to shoppers", with larger chain shops and improved transport links. A long-term ambition has been to secure an extension of the Bakerloo Line from the Elephant and Castle to Lewisham along the line of the Old Kent Road but this is unlikely to happen for some years. The idea was to make Rye Lane and Peckham High Street a town centre as planners and developers imagined one, rather than the spontaneous vortex that was already there, and which was sometimes actively threatened by the planners' dreams. One provoked local police chief had wanted to see it all razed to the ground.

The first significant threat to Peckham after 2000 came from Transport for London. In 2005, in alliance with the council, it proposed building a Cross River Tramway running from north London that would terminate with a seven-acre depot on the site of the Copeland Industrial Park, a bus garage and other buildings, east of Rye Lane and south of the rail line. In effect these seven acres would be a vast marshalling yard for trams, with a supermarket on the roof. This would mean the demolition not only of the Industrial Park, but also the former Bussey factory (Figures 8.4 and 8.5), all of which was to be compulsorily purchased in preparation for demolition. Yet both had developed the potential for a lively mixed existence.

The Copeland Industrial Park, as it was officially known before 2012, was hardly a heritage attraction: a nondescript collection of warehouses, sheds, and workshops in the shadow of the raw Bussey factory, some of them left over from the demise of Holdron's store. A tall square chimney bearing the name "HOLDRONS" appears in the opening frames of Antonioni's film *Blow-Up*, shot in 1966; the chimney is still there, but was later shortened, and with it the letters to "RONS".

Back in 1993, when, following the 1990 recession, much of this site was semi-derelict, an affable surveyor in his early forties, Jonathan Wilson, was asked to make a valuation of the Industrial Park. The property was going cheap and, with an eye to acquiring a future personal retirement asset, the following year Wilson bought it in partnership with a potential developer. It took some time for Wilson to discover that his partner's potential and interests lay elsewhere but before then, in 2000, they added the Bussey factory – then known as the Notevision Building, the name of its owners, later becoming CIP House – to the site.

170 | Bold Tendencies: Culture and Creativity, 2000–2021

Figure 8.4 Copeland Park summer 2018. The "RONS" chimney is on the right (image credit: photo Peach Photo, courtesy Jonathan Wilson).

Figure 8.5 The Bussey Building before conversion (image credit: courtesy Benedict O'Looney Architects).

The Bussey factory was already in partial use by artists and others. An organisation called South and North Arts was letting out artist studios. There was a sweatshop clothing factory on the middle floor, elsewhere a printing-works and a couple of West African churches – at one time Wilson would be landlord to 13 churches and a mosque. In 2001 Wilson and his then business partner acquired Holdron's art deco building on Rye Lane (Figure 8.3), adding other parcels of land and buildings as he went along. He was content for the time being to let things stay as they were, although development in some form was always in mind. Then in 2005 came the tram.

The proposals for the tram depot were discovered by Eileen Conn, who alerted members of the Peckham Society, in the hope that it would lead a campaign, but it fell to Conn, working with Jonathan Wilson, to contest the scheme by raising community awareness and arguing that the site had a cultural potential that the planners had not considered. The objection was not to the tram itself, but to the location of the depot, which would have torn a hole in the town centre, driving out artists and small businesses, and reducing rather than increasing employment, as was claimed. At a large public meeting in the Bussey Building in January 2006 resistance to the tram depot and other proposals began to coalesce around an informal group, shaped by Eileen Conn and Jonathan Wilson. The group called itself Peckham Vision, on the grounds that Southwark Council utterly lacked one. It would not be until 2013 that it became formally constituted as a campaigning community organisation. It took three years of letter-writing, public meetings, and protests from 2006 to convince the planners that the Bussey factory and the Industrial Park had more potential left as they were.

Vital to the campaign was an energetic, fast-talking, and passionate Yorkshire-born Jamaican, Mickey Smith, whose combination of a knowledge of advertising and music promotion, and a love of DJ-ing brought new energy to saving the site. Born in Huddersfield and trained as an art director, Smith had spent seven years in Hong Kong, where he exchanged art direction for music promotion. On his return to the UK he ran events in Brixton, but moved on to Peckham, attracted by what he has called the "rawness" of the place: "the people here were real". He wanted to do more than play music and set up gigs, and in 2003 with three friends established the Chronic Love Foundation, an informal social enterprise – what he calls a "commercial humanitarian company" – dedicated to helping people to help themselves to deal with global change through arts projects, from hip hop to opera. He has managed this without outside funding, although the Arts Council came to his aid in 2020 through the Cultural Recovery Fund, a recognition of what he has been able to achieve on his own.

In December 2006 a chance meeting with Eileen Conn at Peckham Library, where she was leafletting outside an exhibition by Transport for London promoting the tram, led to an introduction to Jonathan Wilson. Working on temporary licences, Smith set up the CLF Arts Café on the first floor of the Bussey Building as a venue for performances, and joined Peckham Vision. Over time CLF would develop a relationship with the Royal Court Theatre, which created a performance space on the third floor. (The original idea had been for the Royal Court to use the semi-restored Peckham Rye Station waiting room, but there were access problems.) In the basement Wilson allowed Smith to set up Rye Wax, a vinyl record store that also serves as an incubator for food enterprises and gave its name to a club, where, as "Jazzheadchronic", Smith's personally DJed South London Soul Train nights that attracted up to 2,000 people. All these activities drew attention to Peckham Vision's campaign to save what was still officially called the CIP Building, but which campaigners referred to as the Bussey Building, so as to exploit its historic connections.

Eileen Conn, Jonathan Wilson, Mickey Smith, and the combined forces of Peckham Vision proved persuasive. In 2009 Transport for London retreated, accepting that the town-centre site for the tram depot was the most unsuitable of its options. Shortly after, the entire tram scheme was dropped in the face of Conservative opposition north of the river. London's new mayor, Boris Johnson, cut the proposal from his budget. In the immediate future, the Bussey Building, Copeland Park, and its surroundings were saved. In 2011 Mickey Smith and the CLF got a long-term entertainment licence. After Peckham Vision had done so much work to save the Bussey Building, and having mounted a series of campaigning exhibitions and events there, in 2015 Jonathan Wilson gave the now formally constituted organisation permanent studio space, rent-free.

In 2017 a minor fire on the fourth floor of the Bussey Building was quickly extinguished by sprinklers, but the floors below were flooded because the fire brigade failed to turn off the main sprinkler valve. Delays over the next three years worsened the damage, and in 2021 restoration work was still ongoing – as was an insurance claim for over £1.5 million. Needing premises, in 2019 Mickey Smith took over space temporally available at Peckham Rye Station to extend his activities as the CLF Art Lounge.

Southwark Council spared the Bussey Building and Copeland Park, though it continued to lobby for a tram to Peckham, and reserved land for it near the head of the former canal, the site known as Flaxyard from that earlier abandoned scheme. But the most important transport development, as significant as the opening of Peckham Rye Station in 1865, was the completion in December 2012 of the Overground rail network – its orange livery earned it the name the "Ginger Line" – a reorganisation of local commuter lines to link Clapham Junction with Dalston, and then up to Highbury and Islington. Now better connected east and west as well as north and south, the station began to have over 2.5 million users a year, far more than the 19th-century building was designed for. This had important implications for the gentrification process as Peckham regained its attraction for central-London office workers, heirs to the clerks of 1900. The arrival of the railway in 1865 gave Peckham its lower-middle-class and working-class profile; the Overground meant that would begin to change again.

It also had implications for Peckham Rye Station itself, whose core was the handsome beaux arts building designed by Charles Henry Driver (Figure 2.5). Features of its remarkable interior and its attractive façade had been rendered almost invisible when the forecourt between the two arms of the rail line was closed off by vaguely art deco buildings in the 1930s and the platforms were realigned. In 2004, with Russell Profitt's co-operation, Eileen Conn set up the Rye Lane and Station Action Group, to seek improvements to the station and its environs. In response to this local pressure, in 2008 English Heritage registered the station as a Grade II-listed building. Local discussions began about restoring the frontage of the building to its original condition by removing buildings so that the forecourt could be cleared and the station regain an open front to Rye Lane. Negotiations with interested parties began.

In a further success for local pressure, in 2011 the council agreed, after a campaign running since the 1990s, to declare the centre of Peckham a conservation area. The Peckham Society had begun the campaign, in the face of council reluctance. Peckham Vision took up the cause, and promoted the idea of an application to the Heritage Lottery Fund under its Townscape Heritage Initiative for money to restore historic buildings in the area. A very thorough assessment by the research department of English Heritage in 2009 had recorded buildings going back to the 17th century.

Figure 8.6 Peckham Rye Station waiting room during restoration, 2020 (image credit: photo Edmund Sumner, courtesy Benedict O'Looney Architects).

It was necessary to have a Conservation Area in existence for an application to the HLF to succeed; in 2011 Peckham Vision supplied 25 volunteers to conduct the necessary building surveys for the council's application, and in 2014 the Heritage Lottery Fund agreed to make a contribution of £1.7 million from its Townscape Heritage Initiative for a £2.3-million programme of improvements in the conservation area, together with a community engagement programme through a Peckham Heritage Regeneration Partnership. Work on individual buildings started in 2016 and was expected to end in 2022.

As far as Peckham Rye Station was concerned, the hidden gem of the station's old waiting room and later billiard hall (Figure 8.6) was already in the process of restoration through the Rye Lane and Station Action Group (an association between the Peckham Society and Peckham Vision, and initially supported by the council's Peckham Programme), when in November 2011, as part of a scheme to improve the lives of people in Peckham following the August riots, the Greater London Authority and Southwark agreed to put £11 million towards the recreation of the square in front of the station (Figure 2.6).

Peckham Rye Station is very much a live building, and though it has seen scenes of Dickensian squalor in the warrens of the forecourt, its curtilage contains valuable real estate, some of it held on long leases. The council set up discussions between Network Rail, Southern Rail, the Greater London Authority, and council planners as to how the project would proceed. In August 2011 the GLA and Southwark agreed matched funding of £10 million for the square, and discussions began with Peckham Vision, with its interest in the old waiting room. Secretly, however, the council favoured the complete demolition and clearance of all the commercial buildings around the site, prior to redevelopment, as Eileen Conn discovered in October 2013. In January 2014, following months of denial, it was revealed that Southwark, the GLA, and Network Rail were indeed planning an immediate demolition of surrounding unlisted buildings which, like the Bussey Building, had become part of Peckham's spontaneous new world of galleries, cafés, and restaurants. In January 2014 the council and Network Rail mounted a public exhibition of a model confirming the clearances, and showing the construction of five- to seven-storey buildings around the front and sides of the station.

The proposal was met by a comprehensive public rejection. Leading the fight, Peckham Vision proposed rethinking the plans, adopting the process of "co-design". Possibly with the imminence of council elections in mind, the council agreed, and appointed consultants to manage discussions throughout 2014, but with an unclear brief that covered only the frontage of the station and the building on the corner of Rye Lane and Blenheim Grove. Public participation was limited to aspects of the design of the front of the station, but excluded from challenging the design brief as a whole. The "co" in co-design seems to have been largely ignored; in November 2014 the consultation produced an "Atlas of Aspirations", but for Eileen Conn the process was "a total shambles from beginning to end". Relations between Network Rail and the council broke down and Network Rail withdrew. New architects were appointed in 2015, and a revised design received planning permission in 2016, with complex negotiations with leaseholders to follow. A programme of demolitions and improvements was not expected to be completed until 2023. Network Rail has re-entered the debate with proposals to rebuild access to the station via the railway arches at its rear, which would have serious implications for the current tenants.

As with the Copeland Industrial Park, Southwark Council has shown a remarkable knack for blighting those parts of Peckham that were contributing most to its distinctive character. The parallel lines of railway arches west of the station, framing Blenheim Court and Dovedale Court – formerly a police car pound – were home to Bar Story, Peckham Springs, the Brick Brewery, artists' and ceramists' studios, a small foundry, motor workshops, and an important metal construction firm, Tara Fabrications. In 2021 some occupants of Dovedale Court were facing the prospect of removal if Network Rail went ahead with its plans to create new access to the station and the platforms above at the rear of the restored station building. As we shall see, the junction of Blenheim Grove and Rye Lane had become famous for its African hairdressers. It was messy, but productive.

The teeming world of railway arches all over London was already in turmoil after Network Rail complied with the government's instruction in 2019 to sell off over 5,000 arches from its property portfolio. There was particular controversy in Brixton, where gentrification was further advanced. The Arch Company paid Network Rail £1.5 billion, a sale judged by Parliament's public accounts committee to be poor value for money. Arch rents rose generally by as much as 80%, and lease conditions changed. When Jane Muir rented an arch in Blenheim Court in 1997 the rent was £2,500 a year. It is now £11,000 a year. Other tenants have seen rents doubling and there is a general sense of insecurity about the Arch Company's plans.

The now familiar insensitivity to local interests was revealed when a draft of Southwark's Peckham and Nunhead Action Plan was made public in 2012. There were good things in it – 2,000 new houses, improved offices as well as shops, attention to green space, more cultural facilities – but the proposals affected several key sites in Peckham's urban renaissance: the railway arches, the Bussey Building and Copeland Industrial Park, the now semi-abandoned Sainsbury's multi-storey car park (Figure 5.3), and the area around the new Peckham Library (Figure 5.4). Central Peckham has a relatively low skyline, the tallest structures being the former Sainsbury's car park and the Bussey Building, both of which give public access to a remarkable panoramic view north towards the City and Canary Wharf, with a diminutive St Paul's Cathedral at the centre of a cluster of looming steel-and-glass giants (Figure 8.1). The council proposed to back the comprehensive redevelopment of the Aylesham shopping centre, north of Peckham Rye Station, complete with an at least 20-storey tower.

Civic vanity appears to have considered this an appropriate phallic marker for Peckham town centre, but it would wreck the view locally, overshadow the hard-fought-for conservation area, and threaten protected sightlines of St Paul's Cathedral. Not just the point block, but more seven- to eleven-storey blocks would completely obscure the view. The developers, who had the gall to produce sketches showing what looked like a sculpture park on the top of their buildings, argued that the existence of a 1967 20-storey block of flats, Witcombe Point, south of Queens Road, was an established precedent, but there was no gainsaying the effect a new tower and its companions would have on the magnificent views of London, from west to east, from the Bussey Building and the multi-storey car park.

Assuming, that is, that there would be a view, for it was proposed to demolish the former Sainsbury's building and its dominating car park. Sainsbury's had abandoned the site as soon as its first ten-year legal commitment ended in 1992, but in 1994 the supermarket space at the foot of the building re-opened, enterprisingly converted into an independent multi-screen cinema, the Peckhamplex, offering the cheapest tickets in London.

Not only would the cinema be a loss in itself, but it had an 80-year lease on the cinema space and some car spaces, causing a potential legal tangle that meant demolition could not be immediate. Although she had campaigned in 1981 against the construction of the multi-storey car park, on the grounds that it would demolish a whole street of solid Victorian houses, Eileen Conn now came to its defence, arguing for re-use. In May 2017 the council's cabinet member for regeneration got 5,300 emails, the result of five years of community action organised by Peckham Vision.

Consultations and objections to the Peckham and Nunhead Area Action Plan went on from 2009, with public hearings by a government inspector in July 2013. His modifications were significant. Whereas the council had been thinking in terms of offices and retail, the "creative industries", which embraced everything from artists' studios, to craft and design workshops, media and tech start-ups, architecture, and the cultural consumption associated with bars and restaurants, were changing the face of Peckham. The inspector's comments added emphasis on the creative industries, spared the railway arches, supported the creative use of the Bussey Building and its environs, and put a stay of execution on the Sainsbury's car park, inviting the council to find a better use for it – which it had already found for itself. That did not mean the planners had put down their pencils and slide-rules. Having formally agreed the Peckham and Nunhead Area Action Plan in November 2014, consultations immediately began on a fresh over-arching New Southwark Plan, which once more threatened the car park with demolition. A draft was published in 2017 and, after significant modifications by the council, would be subject to public enquiry in 2021. There were still battles to come.

As seen in Chapter 4, council action produced local reaction, beginning with the formation of the Peckham Society in 1975. The Peckham Society depended on volunteers chiefly interested in Peckham's past, and its fortunes waxed and waned. First the Peckham Action Group, then the Peckham Rye and Station Action Group, which morphed into Peckham Vision, led the resistance to the council's plans. As we saw, Peckham Vision and partner groups, with the support of the council's Peckham Programme and Network Rail, had begun the restoration of Peckham Rye Station's historic top-floor waiting room, with a view to making it a community space

(Figure 8.6). Its existence had been discovered in 2006 by Benedict O'Looney, who has become an important figure in the battle to rediscover Peckham's building heritage. English-born, he had spent his childhood in America where, while exploring punk rock, he began architectural studies at Yale, taking on summer jobs in London with Will Alsop. In 1992 he decided to move back to England, and qualified as an architect while working for Nicholas Grimshaw. Like other young creatives, in 1997 he settled in Peckham because it was still cheap: "There were hardly any pubs or restaurants you would want to go to." Transport was poor, but that did not trouble a keen cyclist. Always passionate about the historic architecture that he loves to draw, he joined the Peckham Society, where he met the architectural historian and English Heritage inspector Steven Robb. They and the conservation architect Bill Morris drove the Peckham Society's campaign to establish a conservation area in the town centre: "So much was coming down. We didn't think we could get individual buildings listed, but a conservation area was a start. The glue that held it all together was friendship." As we saw, Southwark agreed to the conservation area in 2011.

O'Looney did not work with Alsop on the Peckham Library, although he contributed to other Alsop projects such as *Le Grand Bleu*. He began to teach part-time at the Architectural Association, and set up his own practice in 2004: "We don't look for big profits. Rescuing dilapidated buildings is fun, the work is research-led, and we work mainly for immigrants." The rediscovery of Peckham Rye Station has been an ongoing project since the first stage of the restoration of the waiting room was completed in 2010. Influenced by the principles of the Italian restoration architect Carlo Scarpa, he has devised a contemporary solution to making the station's cast-iron staircase usable and the waiting room accessible without people having to go through the working station.

This is only one of his schemes: "Everyone can see the local townscape. Making it better makes everybody feel better." It was a personal triumph for O'Looney when, after a year of negotiations, in 2015 he got the clock on the tower of Jones and Higgins to tell the right time again.

Meanwhile, the battle continued over Southwark's Peckham and Nunhead Area Action Plan, as it wound its way towards adoption in 2014. In 2002 the

Figure 8.7 Benedict O'Looney's restoration of Peckham Rye Station staircase, 2020 (image credit: photo Edmund Sumner, courtesy Benedict O'Looney Architects).

ruling Liberal Democrats had introduced Community Councils, with planning functions. Their "Cleaner, Greener, Safer" scheme had helped with the station renovations, alongside the Railway Heritage Trust. Once back in office, in 2012 Labour removed the Community Councils' planning powers. Seeing the need to co-ordinate responses at public hearings on the 2010 Core Strategy and then the Area Action Plan, Peckham Vision contributed to the Southwark Planning Network, also supporting a Peckham Planning Network between 2013 and 2016. Between 2009 and 2012 Eileen Conn and others arranged meetings of a Town Centre Forum to co-ordinate thinking on planning matters, by which time it had become clear that Peckham Vision needed to formalise its structures as a campaigning community organisation, which it became in 2013. Peckham Vision has a mailing list of over 3,000 for its Peckham Vision Newsletter, a list that has steadily grown since Eileen Conn set up the Bellenden Residents Group in 2002, through the Peckham Residents Network, to the influential organisation it is today, with 3,600 followers on Facebook and nearly 10,000 on Twitter. But having successfully defended the Bussey Building, and having won a stay of execution on the multi-storey car park, when the New Southwark Plan emerged in succession to the Area Action Plan, Peckham Vision was still confronted by the council's plans to demolish the multi-storey car park, which it owns (Figures 5.3 and 8.8).

Figure 8.8 Concrete potential: Multi-Storey Car Park, 2021.

There had been earlier attempts to make something of this remarkable structure, which since Sainsbury's departure in 1992 had become a dank and dangerous place, the haunt of dossers and drug dealers. During his time as director of regeneration Fred Manson had been on the board of the arts agency Artangel, which specialises in commissioning site-specific art projects. Manson invited new music guru Brian Eno and Artangel's director Michael Morris to a picnic on the car park roof. (Coincidentally, Eno was a former student of Tom Phillips.) Eno offered to run a music programme there, but the council turned the suggestion down. Hannah Barry had more success following the "Bold Tendencies 1" exhibition on the roof of the council offices in Sumner Road in 2007 (Figure 8.2). Introduced to Jonathan Wilson by Eileen Conn, she had launched her own gallery in the Bussey Building in January 2008 (moving at the end of the year to a larger space in the Copeland Park complex), where she represented the Lyndhurst Way group. Barry was looking for a suitable site for another sculpture show. A helpful council officer, David Strevens, a member of Russell Profitt's Peckham Programme team, suggested the roof of Sainsbury's car park, and while continuing to run her gallery, in collaboration with Sven Münder *Bold Tendencies* developed into a not-for-profit annual summer event, run by a Community Interest Company, with a budget rising to half-a-million pounds a year, and paying Southwark rent.

Attendance in the first year, 2008, was sparse, and Barry realised that more than sculpture would be needed to attract people up the daunting stairwells. The next year Frank's Café appeared. It is run by Frank Boxer, grandson of the food writer Arabella Boxer and landlord of the Anchor and Hope in Waterloo, and was designed by Lettice Drake and Paloma Gormley, whose firm Practice Architecture had taken over Paloma's father Antony Gormley's studio in Bellenden Road. An ideal drinking and meeting spot for young Londoners, the lightweight structure, which comes down in the winter, was built for £5,000 in 25 days, by volunteers, among them future members of the architectural collective Assemble.

Barry had first been attracted by the building's cavernous interiors (Figure 8.8), and in 2010 Practice Architecture designed a straw auditorium on its upper floor as the *Bold Tendencies* programme expanded into talks, discussions, and music. The Multi-Story Orchestra was formed

Figure 8.9 Frank's Café at *Bold Tendencies*, designed by Practice Architecture, 2009 (image credit: photo Andy Matthews, courtesy Bold Tendencies and Frank's Café).

by composer Kate Whitley and conductor Christopher Stark in 2011. In 2016 the orchestra took part in the BBC Promenade Concerts, the music of Stravinsky and Steve Reich rising above the rhythm of passing trains (Figure 8.10). Their 2017 Prom, benefitting from an acoustic wall installed by Cooke Fawcett Architects, added the Multi-Story Youth Choir, with music by Whitley. (Orchestra member Hannah Catherine Jones spun off the Peckham Chamber Orchestra in 2013.) In 2019 a lower floor began to be used for dance performances. In her *Observer* review of two socially distanced concerts in August 2020 Fiona Maddocks commented: "the act of listening becomes more intense. Covered yet open to the elements, this concrete cathedral may be more important to our cultural future than anyone could have imagined."

Figure 8.10 *The Rite of Spring*, the Multi-Story Orchestra at Bold Tendencies, 2011 (image credit: courtesy Bold Tendencies and the Multi-Story Orchestra).

The Hannah Barry Gallery, run as a separate business, was sufficiently established by 2013 to move from Copeland Park to a large industrial unit in Holly Grove, part of the complex of buildings that had accumulated around Peckham Rye Station, and which had lain empty for a number of years following an attempt to turn it into a meat processing factory, defeated by Peckham Vision and residents of Holly Grove. (The building is now under threat from station redevelopment proposals.) Barry had already taken her gallery to the Venice Biennale with the Peckham Pavilion in 2009 and the Peckham Palazzo in 2012, and continued to add features to the car park. In 2016 the artist Simon Whybray was commissioned to devise a pink decorative scheme for the staircase rising beside the Peckhamplex, which he called *hi boo i love you*. (Comedienne Jenny Eclair remarked after a visit: "the staircase doesn't smell of wee and ganja anymore.") The following year Barry commissioned "The Peckham Observatory" from Cooke Fawcett, a wood-and-steel platform at the east end of the roof with admin space underneath. The observatory gives a good view of the snaking forms of *Agora*, painted by Richard Wentworth on the tarmac of the roof in 2015 (Figure 8.1).

Barry, who has developed a policy of annual art commissions, sees *Bold Tendencies* as a public space with a civic function.

The project represents, without sounding too communist, the will of many different people. Things don't survive for ten years unless a certain number of people will them to do so. It is not about the whim of the Council or fund-raising – it's about the robustness and resilience of the organization.

Bold Tendencies began to run educational projects with Peckham's schools and to work with the council's youth services, and launched an arts training programme for up to 20 people a year. This showed remarkable confidence in the light of the threatened demolition of the building. It had been spared in 2014, but the council still had long-term plans.

Directly across the railway tracks, the Bussey Building and Copeland Park (Figures 8.4 and 8.5) had been secure since 2009, although the new flats built between them and Rye Lane were to cause problems when the occupants complained about noise. What might happen next depended on Jonathan Wilson, his wife Lorelei, and their three sons. In the early days of the battle to stop the tram depot, Wilson was willing to give short leases, and took a genially relaxed approach to his tenants – Hannah Barry recalls "a certain lawlessness and lack of oversight that made things possible". In 2013 Wilson finally gained full control of the Bussey Building and Copeland Park. Although the properties have appreciated significantly in value, his view on development is:

If it happens, let it happen, but it is more important to create the vibe than spending lots of money. What we are trying to have here is organic growth. If you have a culture already, say in an old building, you maintain and enhance it, and use what's there. We can either knock it down, and build flats – as people do –, or we create something. But I didn't know that it was going to work until 2012.

In 2013 he opened, with Roof Top Film Club, a bar and an open-air cinema on the Bussey roof (Figure 8.11), refurbished Hannah Barry's former space as the Copeland Gallery, and acquired two derelict houses on the edge of the park, where Frank Boxer had run a bar and restaurant as the Peckham Hotel. In 2014 local artists Jo Dennis and Dido Hallett, who had been putting on events in the semi-derelict chapel of the Licensed Victuallers Institution in Asylum Road, took the buildings over as Safehouse 1 and Safehouse 2.

Figure 8.11 Bussey Building roof cinema (image credit: courtesy Jonathan Wilson).

Wilson's tenants come and go, but usually there are around 120, with spaces ranging from 160 to 13,000 square feet. Some 700 people, employed and self-employed, use them. About half are put to creative and cultural use; African churches rub shoulders with a saki distillery, four restaurants, a gym, and one psychiatrist, but there is no residential use.

Once the council acknowledged the new importance of the creative industries in its Area Action Plan, its attitude towards these two spontaneous and organic developments began to change. Hannah Barry has said: "Overall, Southwark has been very supportive, particularly in the last five years." Jonathan Wilson likes to say: "we gradually educated the Council". Indeed in 2020 Copeland Park won the Southwark Culture and Tourism Award. But there were still controversies. The council wanted to make more cultural provision at Eagle Wharf at the canal head, where a former timber warehouse, also known as Area 10, had been squatted by artists (Hannah Barry held an early Lyndhurst Way show there). As always, they wanted to profit from development. Late in 2016 the council voted to demolish the signature Peckham Arch in order to build flats in partnership with a developer.

This scheme also threatened a community art facility, Peckham Platform, which nestled beside the arch. It had begun life in 2010 as the Peckham Space, run by Camberwell Arts School as an outreach project after it had vacated a studio annex in Sumner Road (subsequently burnt down in 2009). In 2014 it became the independent Peckham Platform, and in 2017 moved to the Bussey Building to prepare for the erection of a much larger facility on Peckham Library Square, scheduled to open in 2021. The council abandoned immediate plans to demolish the arch, but Area 10 was cleared, and in 2018 Mountview Academy of Theatre Arts opened with a commitment to developing local talent in a rather grim-looking new building behind Peckham Library (Figure 5.5). The students, however, have added to the cosmopolitan mix of the town centre.

Southwark's attitude to its cultural assets was changing. In 2015 it still hoped to demolish the car park in five years' time, but was looking for a "meanwhile" use for the site. In April 2015 Peckham Vision persuaded Southwark's head of regeneration, Neil Kirby, to a "walkabout" of the building.

Figure 8.12   Peckham pioneers: Eileen Conn (left) and Jonathan Wilson (right) point out the multi-storey car park's potential to Neil Kirby, April 2015 (image credit: Corinne Turner).

The council decided to give *Bold Tendencies* a lease until 2021 on the seventh to tenth floors, and invited bids to take over the intervening levels between *Bold Tendencies* and the Peckhamplex – again, with only five years of life in view. There was no attempt to involve local interests such as Peckham Vision in shaping the brief for the use of the space before bids went in. Both Jonathan Wilson and Hannah Barry made pitches, Barry in partnership with Rohan Silva's co-working office business Second Home. They proposed creating 600 artists' studios, which would have made it the largest studio complex in London, potentially transforming Peckham. But in November 2015 the preferred bidder was Make Shift Limited, which had successfully converted a former car park in Brixton into Pop Brixton, a centre for over 50 small local businesses and social and creative enterprises. The proposed lifetime for the project was still five years until the intended demolition, which made the conversion an expensive proposition for Make Shift and any tenants. In October 2017, however, with a week to go before its finalisation, Southwark dropped the building's demolition from its New Southwark Plan. (Previous unsuccessful bidders were not invited to revisit their proposals in the light of this complete change of plan and timescale.) It also gave planning protection to the cluster of studios and workshops in Chadwick Road known as Print Village. *Bold Tendencies*' lease was further extended for 25 years.

Peckham Levels opened in December 2017, after a difficult period turning three-and-a-half levels of a car park formerly open to the elements into something watertight and livable. Its 90,000 square feet became home to over 100 small creative and social enterprises. Tenants – known as "members" – included a violinmaker, a conceptual artist, a composer, co-workers, and the obligatory street food traders, yoga studio, two bars, and a café. Local enterprises were given preference, with special rates and space prioritised for them, but the conditions and costs of converting the space necessitated high rents. Peckham Levels became popular with locals who enjoyed the bars and restaurants, or took on studios, but it had hardly got on its feet when the Covid lockdown closed the whole building until better times. The view from the roof remained threatened as the council still had plans for a 20-storey building on the nearby Aylesbury site.

A key tactic in Peckham Vision's campaign to save the car park was to argue that the council should list the car park and Peckhamplex as Community Assets, which it did in September 2017, shortly before formally

Figure 8.13 Creative industry: crochet and knitting studio, Peckham Levels, 2018 (image credit: courtesy Peckham Levels, London SE15).

withdrawing plans for the car park's demolition. The 2011 Localism Act had given local groups a new weapon against unwanted demolitions and developments. Once registered as an Asset of Community Value, land or buildings have additional planning protection, and the local community is able to make a first bid if they come up for sale. In 2013 the Ivy Pub in Nunhead became England's first community-owned pub, followed by the 100-year-old Liberal Club, nominated by Peckham Vision, the traditional working-men's club in Elm Grove.

Southwark's conversion to the creative industries became firmer in 2018, when, supported by a £50,000 grant from the Greater London Authority to explore the possibilities of becoming one of the mayor's projected Creative Enterprise Zones, it declared the formation of the Camberwell to Peckham Creative Corridor along the A202 link. A "refreshed" New Southwark Plan for 2018–2022, released in 2020, identified a "Creative and Cultural District in Camberwell and Peckham", as part of "economic revival". Camberwell and central Peckham are mapped as "opportunity areas" in the council's *Creative Southwark: Cultural Strategy 2017 to 2022*, a document focused on the "creative economy", but significantly short of detail.

Hearings on the New Southwark Plan ran on long into 2021. Tiger Developments continued to press its vision for a high-density commercial and residential redevelopment of the Aylesham site at the top of Rye Lane, including the now notorious 20-storey tower block. During the hearings in 2021 before a government inspector it was revealed that if it went ahead the whole redevelopment was not expected to be completed until 2035. The change of ownership in 2021 implied that Berkeley Homes would submit a fresh planning application, further delaying development. A successful planning application would depend on what the final New Southwark Plan turned out to be. Although the Bussey Building appeared to have a future, Southwark Council wanted to see more mixed development on Copeland Park, including housing, which would significantly affect the character of the site. When asked, while consultations were going on, about the inclusion of Copeland Park by Southwark Council in its plans, Jonathan Wilson replied: "We're in the planning zone, but the Council don't know what the plan is."

Sources

This chapter relies extensively on interviews with four of the people most responsible for helping to make Peckham the place its today: Eileen Conn, Jonathan Wilson, Mickey Smith, and Hannah Barry; Benedict O'Looney has also been very helpful with interviews and photographs. Much incidental information comes from *The Peckham Peculiar*, a local community newspaper and blog launched in 2014 that not only keeps a sharp eye on planning matters, but presents a positive picture of a multicultural society. Similarly the Peckham Vision blog. Shaun McDowell is quoted from *Dazed and Confused*, August 2013.

Population statistics and demographics come from the 2001 and 2011 national censuses and Southwark ward profiles. The Peckham and Nunhead Area Action Plan was published by Southwark as *Revitalize: The PNAAP*. The planning inspector's amendments are in "Peckham and Nunhead Area Action Plan: Table of Potential Main Modifications Required by the Inspector, Subject to Consultation", released by the council in October 2013.

Fiona Maddocks was writing in *The Observer*, 23 August 2020. Jenny Eclair made her comment in *The Independent*, 5 February 2018. Hannah Barry is quoted from *The Peckham Peculiar*, June 2016. Many of the individuals mentioned in this chapter have been profiled in *The Peckham Peculiar*.

The bid to become a GLA-supported Creative Enterprise Zone – an idea discussed further in Chapter 10 – did not succeed, but the idea lives on. Jonathan Wilson's closing remark was made in April 2021.

Figure 9.1 *Aladura Spiritualist African Church members buying Ice Cream*, from Sophie Green's *Congregation* (Loose Joints, 2019) (image credit: courtesy Sophie Green and Loose Joints Publishers).

9

On Road: Culture and Resistance, 1948–2021

> "When hipsters take selfies
> On the corners where our
> Friends died, the rent goes up."
> Caleb Femi, "On Magic/Violence", *Poor*

The conjunction of West African churches with studios and galleries in Copeland Park, of African import/export companies side by side with bars and distilleries, shows how rich and mixed Peckham's culture has become. Russell Newell, who has observed the changes since the 1970s, attributes a great deal of this to West African entrepreneurialism: "they are natural traders, they have transformed the place, buying up property, setting up churches". The 2014 report *Being Built Together* established a database of 252 of what are known as Black Majority Churches in Southwark, although it guessed there could be as many as 300. (The first such church was established in Southwark in 1906, testament to the immigration that preceded the *Windrush* generation.) This means that Southwark has the highest density of African churches outside Africa, of which the greatest number are in the Peckham postcode, numbering at least 118. That translates into as many as 20,000 Sunday worshippers in Southwark, which gives a different picture to the negative image of gangs and crime. Sundays in Peckham celebrate the customs and costumes of different local communities. Such churches are, in the words of the 2014 report, "a gift to London".

They are missionary, self-starting, highly individualistic, pastor-led organisations – competitive, and culturally very diverse among themselves. They can also reach people that other agencies have difficulty connecting with. The explanation for their strong presence in Peckham appears to be the same as that for the presence of artists: the availability of ambiguous space.

This has led to similar problems – planning issues were a motive for producing the *Being Built Together* report. Congregations have difficulties with the unauthorised use of industrial buildings or, as has happened at Copeland Park, neighbours complaining about parking and noise. The council itself can be a problem. In 2007 Community Outreach Ministries leased "The Old Mill" on Blackpool Road, a large former "British wine" and vinegar manufactory built in the 1870s, left empty in the 1980s and passed into council hands. The building was spared when the plan for a tram depot was abandoned, but then threatened with demolition in the New Southwark Plan.

Muslim communities also flourish. The pattern by which groups gather to create a mosque, first in private homes, then in whatever properties are available, while raising the funds to build their own place of worship, has had its impact on the Peckham skyline. In the 1990s work began on a mosque for up to 1,000 people on the site of a former school in Choumert Grove. The building ran into planning difficulties, and for a time remained unfinished, looking rather like a small power station. Having got to know local traders who supported the mosque, architect Benedict O'Looney was consulted about what was then, in his words, "the ugliest building that it could possibly be. This was a chance to give it some architecture." In partnership with architect Bill Morris he gave it a curved roof that conformed to the necessary local sightlines, and topped out the two minarets with cupolas that reflect Edwin Lutyens's work in Delhi. Completed in 2013, its success has meant further commissions to design mosques.

Unlike the former air-raid shelters that are part of the foundation myth of the Caribbean community in Brixton, having accommodated some of the *Windrush* arrivals in 1948, there does not appear to be a particular reason for Peckham to be so strongly linked to West Africa, apart from the natural clustering of nationalities. The Caribbean migration was encouraged in order to fill low-level jobs. Those who prospered in Peckham began to move away. The later African migration coincided with decolonisation; people came as students, with, or looking for, professional qualifications. Asian traders also saw the opportunities, producing a "layering" of distinct communities. Many of the shop owners were or are Asian, for instance, Akbar Khan, who arrived from Afghanistan in 1999. Having begun with a market stall he established "Khan's Bargain's" in the former Holdron's art deco store (Figures 8.3 and 9.3).

Figure 9.2 Peckham Mosque, Choumert Grove, 2018 (image credit: photo Quentin Lake, courtesy Benedict O'Looney Architects).

In this business model, leaseholders were prepared to sublet spaces that allowed traders with little capital – and who would have difficulty raising it from British banks – to start up. Multiple occupancy keeps Rye Lane alive, though Southwark planners hate it. The secret is food: saltfish, goat, palm nut oil, and yam; malagueta pepper, shea butter, and plantain; baobab fruit, garri, okra, and cassava; sorghum and sumbala – a poem of West African commodities hard to find elsewhere. The odours around Peckham Rye Station have become as ripe as the mixture of cultures on the street. While Asian traders are generally male, the West African enterprises tend to be female-led. Bim's African Food Store in Rye Lane is an example of a now second-generation, female-run food store.

Figure 9.3 Akbar Khan beneath his rediscovered art deco ceiling, 2018 (image credit: photo Edmund Sumner, courtesy Benedict O'Looney Architects).

Clothes shops, hairdressers, and nail bars have followed. Since 2009, founded by Cephas Williams, "Drummer Boy" on Peckham High Street has developed from a clothing brand into a "motivational space" with its own photographic studio, aimed at encouraging entrepreneurship. "Korlekie" is the brand name for Peckham knitwear designer Beatrice Newman. Sadly, some of the successful hairdressers who began by renting a single chair in the spaces in Blenheim Grove have had to move out because of the station redevelopment. Their co-managed new homes, designed by the council as a relocation project with the intention of providing training and better management under female control, is in an unattractive shed-cum-galleria, absurdly called Peckham Palms, away from their former footfall, in Bournemouth Grove. Progress has a price.

In 2017 Nigerian-born Clement Ogbonnaya took over the derelict Clayton Arms and re-opened it as the Prince of Peckham, an allusion to Lee Stanley, the ebullient free-dealing "Peckham Prince" in *Desmond's*. The same year the photographer Eugene Codjoe opened his ECAD gallery and studio in Consort Road, later moving to Bellenden Road (Figure 6.4). In 2010 Nicholas Okwulu, London-born, but who had spent time in Nigeria after trouble with the police as a young man, set up the social enterprise Pempeople (People Empowering People) and has been energetically promoting local enterprise. Kenny Imafidon has used his experience of being wrongly charged in 2011 with gang crimes, including murder, to become a campaigning social researcher with his own firm, ClearView Research. Kelechi Okafur has fought male prejudice to establish herself as an entrepreneur, running her Kelechnekoff fitness and pole-dancing studio in the Sojourner Truth Association. Okafur proudly points to the difference in body-image between the cliché skinny White pole dancer and her confident clients. The blogger Chidera Eggerue, also known as Slumflower, leapt to popularity in 2017 with her hashtag SaggyBoobsMatter and has become a successful lifestyle writer with *What A Time To Be Alone* (2018) and *How To Get Over A Boy* (2020).

Well known as a commercial and fashion photographer, Liz Johnson Artur has been documenting the lives of the Black diaspora since 1985. Born in Bulgaria of a Russian mother and Ghanaian father, she studied at the Royal College of Art, and lived in Peckham for some years before having to leave her high-rise apartment and studio when it was declared unsafe following the Grenfell Tower fire in 2017. In her parallel artistic practice, since 1991 she has been continuously adding to her *Black Balloon Archive*, first exhibited in 2016, and shown in part at the South London Art Gallery in 2019. These images, some posed, some taken on the street, are intended to respect individuality and challenge stereotypical views. Her photographs can be found online – for instance, of a stop-and-search in Peckham – but she prefers them to be seen in the overall context of her archive.

The changes to Peckham's prosperity have been observed, almost sociologically, by Natalie Wongs (also known as Natalie Wo), born of Jamaican and Panamanian parents in Birmingham, who first came to Peckham in 2000 as a student at the London College of Communication at the Elephant and Castle. A marketing specialist, stylist, and "fashion facilitator", she has watched the changes from her homes in Danby Street and Choumert Road, commenting in her blog natalieblagsfashion. In 2016 she launched a new project, gIRLS aBOUT pECKHAM, which encourages mutual female solidarity, and records the changes in local fashions. Peckham girls, she says, are now more "stush" – Jamaican for both stylish and snobbish: "Others were seeing the changes round here in the way the buildings were coming down. I saw them in the way the girls were dressing."

While Black masculinity has long attracted official White concern, as we shall see, Black female power and solidarity has had less attention, but, as in relation to entrepreneurship, it has significant social power. Set in Hackney, Sarah Gavron's much-admired film *Rocks*, premiered in 2019, paints a touching picture of female friendship among a group of adolescents, led by Bukky Backray as a schoolgirl faced with adult responsibilities.

It was only a matter of time before Peckham's West African community was celebrated in television comedy. In 2010 Andrew Osayami, a former investment banker, set up MTA productions with the writer and director Debra Odutuyo to make *Meet The Adebanjos*. It took self-funding and enterprise to make seven episodes without a buyer, having been turned down by all the leading British broadcasters. Undaunted, Osayemi was determined to prove that "it is possible to get a Black show on TV". The answer was to sell it directly to African television stations, where three seasons and 50 episodes since 2012 have proved a great success and the programme has become available on Netflix. The producers worked with some of the writers from *Desmond's* on the studio-based show, with a Peckham setting as a common thread. The self-mockery in the comedy suggests that the Nigerian Adebanjo family have a confidence that Desmond Ambrose's lacked.

The Adebanjos' family conflicts recall those of *Desmond's*, with parents having more traditional ideas about their children's future than their offspring. Though hardly an entrepreneur, Bajo Adebanjo (Wale Ojo), who works variously and, it appears, simultaneously as mini-cab driver, security guard, and housing officer, sees himself as "a traditional Nigerian man". His concept of masculinity and his attempts to impose discipline are gently satirised by his family: his higher-class wife Gladys (Yetunde Odewale) and his much more English-mannered daughter Sade and son Tobi. Tobi's best friend is White, mocked for his imitation of African cool. Two of the characters would have been comfortable in Chaucer's *Canterbury Tales*: Auntie (Moji Bamtefa), Gladys's older half-sister, and Pastor Michael (Andrew Apraku). Auntie is a large lady slowly adapting to Peckham ways, and looking for a mate: "the best way to get a good man is in church". Pastor Michael's Pentecostalism does not prevent displays of greed or an eagerness for "tithes". Prayer meetings, Halloween exorcisms, and the spiritual healing of a washing machine delight a studio audience that rises to every Nigerian reference. Religion, money (or lack of it), and status are constant themes, but in an African context, and though not without hints at racist discrimination – feckless Auntie correctly says she cannot get a job because she does not have an English name – such White characters as do appear are relatively benign. Debra Odutuyo's follow-up, *The Tboy Show* (2014, 2016), has the same sense of agency, when a well-off Nigerian student comes to stay with his working-class Auntie in Peckham, but pretends to be living the high life.

Being a sitcom, *Meet the Adebanjos* inevitably presents a less conflicted view of Peckham than the reality. We hear nothing of the "mandem", a word that has emerged from the mixture of Caribbean, West African, American, and Black British dialects to describe young working-class men, mainly but not exclusively Black, who live – in another phrase from this patois – "on road". The "road" is a physical space shaped by the walkways, stairwells, and tight

Figure 9.4 Members of Peckham's Zone 2. Left to right: Skully, Karma, Narsty and two friends (image credit: Tim and Barry).

geography of the estates, where they are constrained to spend their time in and around "the block". It is also an imaginative space, a site of resistance defined by its own culture in terms of how social relations are managed, and by the language and music used to describe them.

Though often dependent on maternal support, it is an exclusively male culture, and shapes a particular form of masculinity where "respect" must be maintained, if necessary with violence. In her important study *'On Road' Culture in Context*, Ebony Reid describes the lives of a group of young men living in the pseudonymous "Northville" – an estate in Brent, North London – that has passed through the same process experienced by North Peckham: failed social housing provision in the 1960s and 1970s, followed by "regeneration" in the 1990s.

Reid argues that a particular territorial group, sometimes a mixture of ethnicities, is not to be treated as an organised, hierarchical "gang" in the demonising language of some sociologists and the popular press. Rather, they are a group of friends who form "a cohort of marginalized men immersed in criminality and violence". She draws attention to the poetically ambivalent term "trapping", which means both the drugs trade – "the trap" – and being trapped by the consequent lifestyle and sense of identity, such as exchanging your real name for an "on road" one. The trap includes confinement to one's territory or postcode, for rival groups patrol the invisible frontiers that make it dangerous to stray. Reid's argument is brutally dramatised in the 2019 film *Blue Story*, where the postcode rivalries of Deptford and Peckham trap young men from the two communities in a Jacobean cycle of killing and revenge. Under his *nom de plume* of Rapman, Andrew Onwubulo writes, directs, and supplies a rap commentary to a story that draws on his own experience of crossing the line between territories, and the consequences that can follow.

Although Reid shows that while illegality is necessary to establish and maintain a respected identity, and to sustain a career in the drugs trade, the irony is that, far from being a liberating alternative to the regular kinds of employment from which the mandem are excluded, dealing encourages "conservative/capitalist aspirations". The lifestyle turns out to be a curious parody of the bourgeois world, driven by a neoliberal business ethic and the desire for conspicuous consumption that just happens to be supported by dealing in drugs, and protected by violence. In the case of Peckham, the turf wars that characterise the drugs trade may have been exacerbated in the 1990s by the arrival of young, White professionals, including artists, with a taste for cannabis and cocaine. The previous local market, chiefly for cannabis, expanded and became more profitable, with consequent struggles over control. It is a further irony that the apparent distance between Black and White social lives in Peckham conceals a mutual dependence when it comes to the supply and purchase of drugs.

From her participant observations, Reid concludes that, having passed through the "liminal" passage from youth to adulthood, some in the mandem appreciate that they have become trapped, and want to escape, but the only alternative is a rubbish job. The other possible exits are prison or death, although religion, in the form of Islam, can offer transformation. She does not, however, mention two escape routes that traditionally have been open to working-class youths: music and sport. Football hero Rio Ferdinand grew up in the 1980s on Peckham's Friary Estate (using ballet classes to improve his physical skills), but sport may now be less of an option to the mandem because of the lack of facilities resulting from cuts in social spending – be it dance classes or sport. But music still offers possibilities, even when, as in the case of grime, and latterly drill, the music is associated with the violence and criminality from which it also offers escape.

In effect a continuation of the Jamaican dub music pioneered by reggae DJ U-Roy in the 1970s, where the "toaster" or MC semi-improvises over music tracks, often as part of "battles" with rival MCs, grime emerged in Britain as a distinct form in the early 2000s. In his study *Teklife, Ghettoville, Eski*, Dhanveer Singh Brar describes grime as both "a musical signature and a means of social organization, finding a highly effective technology in pirate radio". Pirate radio has been an irritant to governments since the 1960s; they have tried suppression, and then forms of accommodation. In 1988 licenses for "community radio" and an expansion of commercial radio were conceded. As we saw, Kiss FM had begun as a pirate station, and it took two years to obtain legitimacy in 1990. But in the process it lost its oppositional authenticity; the demand for the music that pirate stations put out remained, but unlicensed broadcasting was now a serious criminal offence.

The pirate stations that continued to operate in London found themselves in a similar situation to the Jamaican sound systems from which reggae was born, even if the technology was different. The music was a collective creation, reflecting working-class experience, self-directed, resistant to corporatisation, and framed by its illegal transmission. The various stations were at the same time in violent competition with each other and the authorities as they constantly shifted their illegal aerials from council-block rooftop to rooftop, to avoid the attentions of officialdom and their own rivals. Brar remarks: "antagonism is the primary mode of Grime". Having begun as a form of aural graffiti, it was only as the internet emerged as an alternative means of communication that grime artists could establish themselves legitimately, and a second wave has achieved industrial recognition and commercial success. The Peckham rapper Giggs has overcome imprisonment for gun crime and attempts by the police to thwart his career to become an award-winning artist.

Yet grime has continued to be held responsible for the negative aspects of the road culture that it reflects. The war on the pirate radio stations was matched by the police's introduction in 2004 of Form 696, a risk assessment that had to be filled in by promoters of live music events. At first applying to all events, its attention was narrowed down to grime, enquiring not only about what kind of music was to be played, but the ethnicity of the potential audience and the police records of performers. The wrong answers meant the event could not go ahead; people who went to licensed events would be the subject of stop-and-search. In effect, a mode of music was being made illegal. The system was dropped in 2017, but it firmly established a closed circuit of criminality between grime and its outlets, and with drill it continues to be treated with official suspicion and censorship.

Brar describes how grime emerged from a very specific urban territory in East London, but it quickly caught on in similar areas, such as Peckham. Its even more nihilistic successor, drill, was transplanted from the urban battlespace of South Chicago in 2012 to Brixton. The traditions of challenge and insult between drill groups – "diss tracks" – found a welcome on the internet, but with murderous consequences. Threats made in videos became a reality in 2018 when a member of Camberwell's Moscow 17 died, apparently at the hands of an associate of Peckham's Zone 2, and there have been other drill-linked deaths. In an effort to stifle the messenger, Criminal Behaviour Orders have been used against drill musicians to prevent them making records and videos that are believed to promote violence.

The music that has emerged in South London has an articulate defender in the poet and filmmaker Caleb Femi. Femi's personal story gives him authority to speak. Born in Nigeria, at the age of seven he joined his pastor father in Peckham, where the family of seven lived in a one-bedroom flat in the same North Peckham Estate block as Damilola Taylor's, whom he knew. In spite of being an educational high-flyer, Femi experienced exclusion from school, drugs, has been stabbed and shot, and has lost four friends, one shot at another's funeral. "Thank God for poetry", he has said, "because I wrote it all down". These experiences have led to what he calls "a heavy hand of PTSD". In hospital after being shot in the leg, Femi discovered literature, escaped the mandem, went to sixth-form college away from Peckham, and then to London University. He became a secondary-school teacher until disillusioned by the Gove "reforms" to the curriculum, and then became Young People's Laureate for London between 2016 and 2018. After a period away from Peckham, when he returned in 2017 he noticed, like Natalie Wongs, the changes: "even getting on the bus has changed".

Femi acknowledges the "violent, misogynistic, crime-endorsing content" of grime, which is certainly abusive to women, but he points to the common experience of the artists and their listeners: "Life in an inner-city, low-income council estate is not an easy thing. Sometimes it is good, sometimes it is bad, but most of the time it is just pure unimaginable madness." The irony is that now the music and fashion styles associated with grime have seeped into mainstream culture: "the culture itself is seen as cool, but the people of the culture are seen as a scourge to their community". The fashions of this stigmatised movement have been appropriated, "fetishized by a particular group of society: White middle-class youths ... wearing this working-class aesthetic like it's a day out at the safari." He reads grime as a means of processing, not a post-traumatic stress disorder, but a permanent stress disorder.

I want us also to recognize the culture not as a brutish or comedic troupe, and its people as violent and undereducated criminals, instead I want us to recognize that without road culture, we wouldn't have Grime, and the landscape of UK rap would look very different from what it is today.

In his own practice, Femi has integrated the modernity of photography, video, and rap with the traditional confessional themes of verse. His video-poems depict his friends and South London streets, with music and speech rhythms echoing that of grime, which he began by writing. But his first collection, *Poor*, published in November 2020, is mainly in free verse, without the relentless rhymes of grime. (His opening epigraph is from T.S. Eliot; there is a silent quotation from W.B. Yeats.) Illustrated by his own photographs of people and places and deploying the vocabulary of the mandem, his themes are the enclosed life of the estate, the oppression of the "boydem" (the police), the 2011 riots, the violent deaths of friends (and his own near death when a gun jammed), the trauma of violence, and his own survivor's guilt. Although he expresses his love for this neighbourhood of concrete, a poem towards the end of the book, "On the Other Side of the Street", suggests that he may indeed have left the mandem behind: "I crossed over and now the hood won't take me back."

There is a similar ambiguity about territorial entrapment in Bola Agbaje's Olivier Award-winning play *Gone Too Far!*, produced at the Royal Court in 2007 and released as a film in 2013. Agbaje was born on the North Peckham Estate, but she also spent some time as a child in Nigeria. After Greenwich University, in 2003 she joined the part-time Identity School of Acting set up at the Arcola Theatre in Dalston by the RADA-trained actor Femi Oguns, now an agent. In 2006 she got onto the Royal Court's Young Writers Programme, taking part in the "Critical Mass" scheme for Black writers, hosted by Mickey Smith in the CLF Café theatre at the Bussey Building. *Gone Too Far!* was the result.

Though very funny, the play is a serious take on Agbaje's favoured themes of "identity, belonging and a sense of home". Protagonist Yemi is Peckham-reared and Peckham-smart, and finds he has to teach the ropes to his elder brother Iku, who has arrived in Peckham after being brought up in Nigeria. They have to deal with the threat represented by Jamaican Razer and his sidekick Ghost, whose insistence on "respect" betrays the mandem's need to assert a road identity won by violence, a toughness that these young males may not actually possess. Ethnic identity within Blackness is debated as the characters argue over the right of Africans to appropriate the Caribbean culture of rap, or the degree of Britishness that a mixed heritage allows. The loss of a secure identity is reflected in Yemi's inability to speak the Yoruba language that his mother and his elder brother still share. By the time the play became a film directed by Destiny Ekaragha in 2013 – making it the first British movie to be both written and directed by Black women – the script has firmly become a comedy, ending in reconciliation, rather than with the death of Iku, as in the play's first draft.

Bola Agbaje's follow-up, *Off The Endz*, premiered at the Royal Court in 2010, offers a less reassuring view of the Black experience in Britain. This too is semi-autobiographical, in that Agbaje's brother has done time in prison. The "endz" of the play's title is patois for "neighbourhood" – defending one's neighbourhood is known as "repping the endz" – but the title also suggests the extremities that the three lead characters experience as they seek alternative forms of escape: crime or bourgeois affluence. David is an arrogant young man, fresh out of gaol, who moves in on a former girlfriend, Sharon, now a nurse, whose partner Kojo, former schoolfriend of David, is trying to hold down a good office job in a White business; "Life is ten times harder for us", he says. David, played in the first production by Peckham-born Ashley Walters (Figure 9.5) (whose successful acting career from the age of 14 was interrupted by a prison term in 2001) finds a fatal solution in returning to drug-dealing; Sharon and Kojo are trapped by aspirations to an affluence that they cannot achieve. David deploys the rhetoric of masculine solidarity to involve Kojo in his crimes, and though Kojo and Sharon survive, the trio do not end well. Ashley Walters starred in two Hackney-set dramas about struggles to control the drugs trade, the film *Bullet Boy* in 2004 and the television series *Top Boy*, launched by Channel 4 in 2011 and taken up by Netflix in 2019.

Just as *Blue Story* portrays fatal rivalries between Deptford and Peckham, the White-British comedian and filmmaker Joe Cornish's 2011 science-fiction film *Attack The Block*, where furry alien monsters descend on the Heygate Estate, reinforced Peckham's image as a place of dystopian structures, feral children, dope dealers, and ruthless street gangs. It did, however, give a starring part to John Boyega, who began acting at the age of nine at the performing arts academy Theatre Peckham in Havil Street, and later spent time at Femi Oguns's Identity School.

Boyega has said that one of his inspirations to become an actor was a series of portraits of celebrated Black actors (among them Ashley Walters) by the photographer Franklyn Rodgers. Following their exhibition at the National Portrait Gallery in 2008 these were installed as *Peckham Portraits* on a hoarding along Peckham Hill Street by Rodgers and the actor Fraser

James under the aegis of their organisation Underexposed Arts, which sets out to offer role models to Black or minority artists. The portraits survived the 2011 riots, and there was local protest when they were taken down along with the hoarding. After transfer to the Peckhamplex cinema, in 2019 they also appeared on their original site, this time on the walls of the newly built Mountview Drama School, where they serve their original purpose. As Franklyn Rodgers has said: "If you can see yourself *on* the building, you can see yourself *in* the building."

John Boyega has gone on to play in three *Star Wars* movies, though he has since made it clear that this was not an easy experience for a Black

Figure 9.5 Role models: *Peckham Portraits* by Franklyn Roberts, redisplayed outside Mountview Academy of Theatre Arts, 2021.

actor. His feelings overflowed in an impromptu speech at a Black Lives Matter demonstration in June 2020. Steve McQueen cast him as one of the first Black officers in the Metropolitan Police in *Red, White and Blue*, part of McQueen's 2020 TV series *Small Axe*, about the *Windrush* generation. When the cologne company Joe Malone replaced him with a Chinese actor in the Chinese version of a commercial that he had produced and performed in – recalling Femi's video poems, it was filmed in Peckham with brief shots of Rye Lane, a market, a playground, and Peckham friends – his response to this uninvited cultural appropriation – rather, censorship – was "I don't have time for nonsense", and he broke with the company.

In *Attack the Block* Boyega plays the young gang leader, "Moses" (note the name), who saves his community. There was no such redemption, however, for real-life Sodiq Adeojo in Adeyemi Michael's 2013 documentary *Sodiq*. A graduate of the National Film and Television School, Michael uses parts of an earlier short film he had made, *Crossing The Line* (2008), about Adeojo's ambition to become a doctor. But *Sodiq* records how this promise ended when he was sentenced to 30 years in prison following the shooting and stabbing of another boy in a stairwell at Heron House on Peckham's Pelican Estate in 2010, at the height of Peckham's "civil war". Regretfully, but without making judgements, *Sodiq* shows how the mandem can act as a replacement family, and that the demolition of the most notorious estates has not solved local problems. But there is joy to be had from Michael's fantasy short for Channel 4's "Random Acts" series in 2018, *Entitled*, in which he re-imagines his mother's journey from Nigeria to Peckham. Dressed in the magnificence of traditional Yoruba costume, Abosede Afolashade rides a horse down Rye Lane, a proud assertion of culture and tradition.

In his video-poem "Coconut Oil", about the changes in Peckham, Caleb Femi asks: "Is gentrification just another word for chemotherapy?" Somehow, he suggests, the cleaned-up streetscape is losing its texture, and going bald. Gentrification is a running theme for Peckham's writers and filmmakers. It gives a thread to *Peckham the Soap Opera*, a project by the Royal Court's Theatre Local scheme that brought 16 Peckham residents together to perform ten five-minute episodes of an imaginary soap opera, first presented in the CLF Café theatre in the Bussey Building in 2013, with Bola Agbaje and Rachel De-lahay as lead writers alongside eight other Royal Court contributors. (The Royal Court and Theatre Local also encouraged Diana Nneka Atuona to write her first play, *Liberian Girl*, premiered at the Royal Court in 2015.) James Barber's 2019 internet series *Flatshare* is a brief soap opera written from the point of view of a Black gay man, mixing gentrification and LGBT issues. A video series by Selicia Richards-Turner and Kate Debra, *Peckham Heroes*, found local witnesses for and against the changes in their area.

In 2018 Shane Duncan tackled the issue head-on with a trio of documentaries, *This is Brixton*, *This is Peckham*, and *This is Croydon*. Brixton represents a spoiled past, Peckham a successful present, and Croydon a potential future: "When I was putting the film together I realized that Peckham is a completely different area to Brixton, completely different ... The way the community are more intertwined with each other; it is so close knit." Clement Ogbonnaya, landlord of the Prince of Peckham, comments in the film: "you will never find a more integrated multicultural community than Peckham". Social researcher Kenny Imafidon tells Duncan that while gentrification is causing tension in Peckham and there will be change, "I don't think that the gentrification that took place in places like Brixton is going to happen in Peckham. I don't think it is going to get that far."

That is not the view of Natalie Wongs.

The culture that I came from has been stripped away. Those who were here originally are not getting the same deal as the newcomers. It feels like a board game, like Monopoly. The houses change hands without "For Sale" signs going up. A lot of what I love about Peckham has all gone. The substance was that you felt celebrated. Now it's all hype. It was a rough stone that was sometimes shiny – you could see the beauty of it. Now it is just shiny. There's no culture in it.

In April 2015, gentrification protests in Brixton, during which a "Reclaim Brixton" demonstrator smashed the window of the estate agent Foxton's, were a gift to Shola Amoo, who has lived in both Brixton and Peckham. His feature film *A Moving Image* (2017) is a Brechtian fiction about making a documentary about gentrification. His protagonist, played by Tanya Fear, is an artist who has returned to the neighbourhood from East London and who is treating gentrification as the subject for an art piece. (Amoo has described his film in similar terms.) The changes to Brixton reflect the changes witnessed by *A Moving Image*'s producer Rienkje Attoh. Amoo's Godard-like direction suggests that it is the artists themselves who are the gentrifiers, and Fear's character meets little sympathy from other campaigners. An angry demonstrator on the Reclaim Brixton march speaks directly to camera.

I'm from Peckham... they're saying its gonna become trendy like Brixton has become. Peckham has got the largest Nigerian community in London. What you see is what you get. There's no Costa fucking Coffee. Or Foxton's. Please. Don't. Make. Peckham. Trendy. Like. Brixton.

We shall see. By 2021 Costa Coffee was installed beneath the Jones and Higgins tower, and Foxton's had set up in Rye Lane.

Sources

The epigraph is from Caleb Femi's *Poor*, published by Penguin in 2020. The report *Being Built Together: A Study of New Black Majority Churches in the London Borough of Southwark* was published by the University of Roehampton, Southwark for Jesus and Churches Together South London in 2013. Natalie Wongs is quoted from an interview she kindly gave me in 2020. *Rocks*, directed by Sarah Gavron, is streamed by Netflix. *Meet the Adebanjos* is likewise available on Netflix.

    Ebony Reid's doctoral thesis, *On Road Culture in Context: Masculinities, Religion and "Trapping" in Inner City London*, was published by Brunel University in 2017. *Blue Story*, written and directed by Rapman (Andrew Onwubulo), was produced by BBC Films and is distributed by Paramount. Dhanveer Singh Brar's *Teklife, Ghettoville, Eski: The Sonic Ecologies of Black Music in the Twenty-first Century* is published by the Goldsmiths Press (2020). Caleb Femi's comments are assembled from recordings of TEDx Talks on YouTube, an essay in the web journal *Trench*, a 2017 interview on Oya Media, and an interview with Claire Armistead for *The Guardian*, 31 October 2020. He was profiled by *The Peckham Peculiar* in June 2015. Several of his video works, including "We are the Children of the 'Narm", produced with the SXWKS collective, are available on YouTube or the BFI network.

    Bola Agbaje's *Gone Too Far* appears in *The Methuen Drama Book of Plays by Black British Writers* (2013); the screen version was produced by the British Film Institute. *Off the Endz* was published by Methuen in 2014. She was interviewed in a podcast for the Royal Court by Simon Stephen. *Attack*

The Block was produced by Studio Canal. Boyega is quoted on *Peckham Portraits* from the Mountview website, Franklyn Rodgers from the Flannels fashion website. The Joe Malone/Boyega row broke out in September 2020. John Boyega was interviewed by Jimi Farurewa in *GQ*, October 2020. Adeyemi Michael's *Sodiq* and Shane Duncan's *This is …* series can be found on YouTube. Shola Amoo's *A Moving Image* was produced by the British Film Institute.

Figure 10.1 Former shopfront and entrance to Kennedy's Sausages, Peckham Road, 2020.

10

Next: The Space of Possibilities, 2022–

"The hipster these days is a capitalist."
  Matt Hancock, Secretary of State for Digital, Culture, Media and Sport, September 2016

On 23 March 2020 a UK-wide government-imposed lockdown to tackle the coronavirus pandemic dragged a stifling facemask across Peckham. The historian Peter Hennessey spoke on the radio of "BC and AC" – before and after Covid-19. At the end of that year of social and economic distress, Britain left the European Community, accepting further damage. The economy had already shrunk by more than 10%. The National Institute of Economic Research has calculated there has been more than £700 billion in lost output. The scarring has been deep. Inflation threatens.

The arts, especially the performing arts, have been badly hit, with theatres, concert halls, arenas, discos, comedy clubs, and music venues closing, cinemas suffering, and a largely self-employed workforce left stranded, many unable to take advantage of temporary government support. Film and television production has been interrupted; an army of technicians, designers, and workers in the creative industries have been left unemployed. By the start of 2021 a third of the cultural workforce had lost their jobs. In spite of a post-lockdown spree, the British economy is not expected to recover fully until at best 2022, and there is a reckoning to pay in terms of tax rises, public expenditure cuts, and a squeeze on pay and social benefits, all leading to shrunken household incomes. A lost generation of young creatives have been unable to launch their careers, or have seen their start-ups stop down. The cultural economy will especially take time to revive; it has had to cope with lost venues, lost connections, lost skills, changed patterns of consumption, and, after an initial splurge of temporary savings, the public's shortage of disposable income. Culture will have to return in altered form.

Peckham has been hit in a number of ways. The Covid crisis has exposed the profound structural inequalities in health, wealth, and social trust in deprived areas of Britain, including Peckham. Unemployment, especially youth unemployment, bears down particularly on the non-White population, bringing the risk of social unrest. Already a deprived borough, Southwark Council is unlikely to be favoured by a national government ideologically unsympathetic to local authorities – particularly Labour-controlled ones. Low central government support and the loss of business rates present a challenge to Southwark's ambitions for regeneration and house-building. The expansion of online shopping forces a rethink of traditional approaches to high streets and shopping malls, as former "anchor" outlets disappear. Pubs, restaurants, and cafés have suffered badly. Private developments have been on hold, and more industrial and commercial property has been left vacant.

Yet, looked at differently, Peckham stands to gain from the economic shock of 2020 and 2021. The shift to home-working during the pandemic led to a retreat by both people and businesses from the centre of London, not unlike during and after World War II. This might not be permanent, but large-scale companies have begun thinking in terms of satellite offices further out of town that could reduce overcrowded and time-wasting commuting. Home-working seems likely to continue for those in occupations that managed the transition during lockdown. Individual families who could afford it started to move out of London, in search of more living room and greener space. Peckham is hardly the *rus in urbe* it was in the early 19th century, but it has 21st-century opportunities in terms of transport, commercial space, housing stock – and celebrity. Assuming you can buy into it.

This is written before the end of 2021, and so is speculation. The gentrification cycle described at the beginning of this book – the Peckham paradigm – has been stalled, just when it might be expected to reach its climactic phase. Owen Hatherley's anticipated transfer of Peckham from the working class to the banking class is unlikely. Nor is Peckham by any means yet a settled milieu. But the signs are that once the economy has recovered, gentrification – policy-driven or self-generated – will continue, and even accelerate. Here is a moment to take stock, and to look for a better way forward.

Some argue it is already too late. The bankers may not have settled in, but artists have begun to move out. One remarkable example is that of Peckham-born Rósza Farkas, who set up her Arcadia Missa Gallery in Lyndhurst Grove in 2011 as an art space. A success, in 2014 it became a commercial gallery, and a publisher, but in 2018 Farkas reversed the gentrification process by moving north across the river to Soho. Similarly, in 2009, while still a painting student at Camberwell, Will Jarvis co-founded the Sunday Painter in the abandoned function-room of a pub, while supporting himself as a chef at Bar Story. In 2013 he and colleagues took over the top storey of the art deco building at the junction of Blenheim Grove with Rye Lane, letting out part of the space as co-working studios. In 2017 the Sunday Painter moved to Vauxhall. The landlord, Ivo Hesmondhalgh, wanted the property back, but Jarvis said at the time: "The group of artists and wider scene we came up with has for the most part moved on, it's time we did the same." In 2020 the building began to be redeveloped as part of the Rye Lane Station scheme.

Other galleries have come and gone, such as Guy Roberts's Sun Gallery in Copeland Park (2009–2012). The changes have been observed by Russell Porter, landlord of the Montpelier Pub in Choumert Road, whose clientele are in the main new, rather than old, Peckham: "The original [artists] who had studios around here and were here for the community and the vibe, most of them have moved on." For a time he also ran a club, bar, and, by day, vegan café, Ghost Notes, in the Peckham Levels, but gave up the space in February 2019. Some have been holding out, while regretting that they were not able to buy in earlier. In Bellenden Road artist Clive Burton remarks: "High rents are always a struggle for the street." Rising rents for spaces like the railway arches are a similar worry. Artists who would like to move to Peckham decide they can no longer afford to.

From her arch in Blenheim Court ceramicist Jane Muir and her colleagues have seen the changes.

We reminisce about how it used to be. We seemed to integrate quite well with the local community, who have been very supportive, that was what was so nice about it. There was a change around 2010. Rye Lane and Bellenden Road are poles apart now, it's a bit like walking through the pages of a lifestyle magazine. It is more busy, there are more artists, but for me it is less interesting because there are fewer characters around. People see more homogeneous. I don't see as many oddballs as I used to.

What has happened to Hackney, Hoxton, Shoreditch, and Dalston has reached Peckham. There are those who question whether the "hipsters", with their old-fashioned bicycles and curated beards who have turned an ordinary street into "Bellenden Village", have really contributed much, beyond pushing up rents and pushing out people. The mobile, freelance life of laptops in cafés with free Wi-Fi does not encourage setting down roots in a community.

Questioning the booster-ish rhetoric about the liberating effects of the creative industries, the geographer Oli Mould asks whether the contemporary art "scene" (signalled in Peckham by the murals that embellish Bellenden Road) is really as progressive as its participants might think.

Galleries, public art and hyper-commodified street art play to a particular version of aesthetic consumption that is high-culture and overly White. It is art that is "aware" of inequality within urban space, but "performs" this as part of a consumption cycle. The knowledge of protest and critique toward such injustices is *given* to an audience to consume rather than as something to enact. Therefore creativity in this rhetorical world is just a pastiche of consumption, more often than not modelled on the consumption patterns of White, middle-class people.

Mould is writing of the fashion among developers and city planners for inventing "creative quarters", but Julian Henriques, director of *We The Ragamuffin* and now a professor at Goldsmiths, has noticed something specific about Peckham. He has spoken of a "vertical apartheid", emblematised by the millennial rooftop culture celebrated at Frank's Café and the open-air cinema and bar that tops the Bussey Building (Figures 8.9 and 8.11). It is observable that there is a distance between the pleasure-seekers enjoying the view of London's gleaming money-scrapers, the arts aficionados at a car-park concert, and the urgent, untidy, sometimes tricky life in the streets below — even if that too is part of Peckham's attraction. The CLF Café's Mickey Smith has regretfully observed that events he puts on tend to attract separate audiences, even when they could be expected to appeal to people of different communities. Film director Shola Amoo is blunt: "British gentrification is about class. But break it down and race re-enters the picture." In the case of Peckham, where much of the local population is both working-class and Black, gentrification divides.

It is not unusual that long-term residents of an urban space treat incomers with suspicion, and will seek to defend their territory. Caleb

Femi's poem, ironically titled "Community", voices an angry and aggressive member of the mandem challenging a visitor to his endz. Charmaine Brown of Greenwich University, a long-term resident of the former Bellenden ward, has linked gentrification in Peckham to what she calls "Black urban removal worldwide". She points to Bellenden Road, Chadwick Road, Ivanhoe Road, and Avondale Rise, where Black residents have moved on. Some sold their houses; others were compulsorily purchased and their owners moved to the North Peckham Estate. Brown describes gentrifiers as suffering from the "Columbus syndrome" of thinking they are the first arrivals in virgin territory. This produces a "separation of communities", where it is the gentrifiers who live separate lives and refuse to integrate. But she also distinguishes between recent incomers and long-term middle-class residents. It is fair to comment that these too may resent the changes since the 1990s – but if they own property or run businesses, they may also have benefited. One protection for Peckham is that it has a relatively long-established population that has gained from the greater prosperity of the area.

As we saw in the last chapter, gentrification divides opinion in the Black community. Natalie Wongs is hostile; Kenny Imafidon (speaking before the 2020 crisis) acknowledged that shops will change hands and some older businesses move out, but still felt that Peckham would not essentially alter. Fearing a Rye Lane packed with bars and restaurants, Mickey Smith says: "It is really at a turning-point now. It is going to be hard to stop the roll." Clement Ogbonnaya, landlord of the Prince of Peckham, regards the process as inevitable, but as a force that can be used to people's advantage: "I am pro-regeneration, I just think gentrification isn't done responsibly."

That is the issue.

Ogbonnaya speaks both of regeneration and gentrification. I have proposed that although they are both aspects of urban change, they exist at different ends of the policy spectrum. This is not necessarily how they are perceived on the street. In 2002 the business sponsorship agency Arts and Business commissioned an evaluation of the impact of its contribution to the Bellenden Renewal Scheme. The report noted that house prices had begun to rise, and that there were concerns about gentrification, pointing out: "There was general confusion as to who, what or how the regeneration and arts programme had been funded, other than 'The Government'." Bellenden Renewal is described there as a regeneration project, using the arts to change the economy. Larger-scale regeneration programmes, such as described in Chapter 5, can be attributed to "The Government" in the form of the state or local authorities, but it is harder to identify who is "doing" piece-meal gentrification, responsibly or not. Individuals have made a lifestyle choice, with property developers hard on their shoulders, but these individual decisions are driven by deeper structural changes in society and the economy.

That is the persuasive argument of the geographer Neil Smith, who in 1979 posited what has become known as the "rent gap" theory. What appears to be a culturally determined consumer choice is in fact the result of the search by owners of capital – individuals or businesses – for increased profit. Under conditions of urban expansion, such as during the later 20th century, the rent gap opens when there is a significant difference between what a property earns at that moment – say, in the run-down streets of 1970s Peckham – and what those properties could earn if they were done up, and sold or rented to incomers willing to pay more. It may even be in the interest of landlords to let properties decay before beginning rehabilitation or redevelopment, in order to widen the gap between what a property is currently worth – its ground rent – and what it could return.

As filtering [of population] and neighbourhood decline proceeds, the rent gap widens. Gentrification occurs when the gap is sufficiently wide that developers can purchase structures cheaply, can pay the builders' costs and profit for rehabilitation, can pay interest on mortgage and construction loans, and can then sell the end product for a sale price that leaves a satisfactory return to the developer. The entire ground rent, or a large proportion of it, is now capitalized; the neighbourhood is thereby "recycled" and begins a new cycle of use.

Smith's "recycling" brings to mind Luna Glücksberg's observation on the regeneration of North Peckham: "if recycling is about turning waste into something useful again, this process was more akin to throwing something away and buying, or bringing in, something new altogether, in terms of a new group of people". As a Marxist, Smith (who died in 2012) would have deplored the throwing away of people during the course of capital's restructuring of social space, but under capitalism it appeared to him to be unstoppable.

Gentrification is not a chance occurrence or an inexplicable reversal of some inevitable filtering process. On the contrary, it is to be expected. The de-valorisation of capital in 19th century inner-city neighbourhoods, together with continued urban growth during the first half of the 20th century have combined to produce conditions in which profitable re-investment is possible.

Smith's Marxist production-side explanation is disputed by fellow geographer David Ley, whose "humanist" approach to the drivers of gentrification emphasises the influence not of finance capital, but cultural capital. By this he means that the long post-war boom – he was writing before 2010 – has produced a situation where most people's basic wants have been satisfied, and the shift from production to consumption has placed ever greater value on symbolic goods and aesthetic satisfactions – in short-hand, lifestyle – that give social status in the form of cultural capital. This helps to explain why the cultural and creative industries have been reframed as a distinct economic activity and why they are believed to have such economic importance. A commodified culture understood as "style" is their principal product. As Ley's argument presents it, it is not the artists who are responsible for the emergence of "Bellenden Village", but those who like the idea of sharing urban space with them.

To blame artists for the gentrification that so often follows their residency in a district is a misplaced charge; it is the societal valorisation of the cultural competencies of the artist that brings followers richer in economic capital.

It is a relief to me to read that the artists who came to Peckham in search of somewhere cheap to live and work are not guilty for what has begun to happen. After all, they are themselves also victims of the process. In 2014 a report for the Mayor of London's Office identified 298 artists' workspaces in London that were being used by five or more tenants, meaning there were approximately 11,500 occupying these studios (750 of the studios were in Southwark). But short-life properties and insecure tenancies meant that at least 3,500 were expected to lose their workspaces in the next five years. Whether as innocent pawns in the invisible hand of capitalism, or players in the post-modern drama of the cultural spectacle, artists are in the power of these structural forces. They have no more agency than the discarded tenants of the Five Estates.

Neil Smith, however, thought that something could be done.

Gentrification has been the leading residential and recreational edge (but in no way the cause) of a large restructuring of space. At one level, restructuring is accomplished according to the needs of capital, accompanied by a restructuring of middle-class culture. But in a second scenario, the needs of capital might be systematically dismantled, and a more social, economic and cultural agenda addressing the needs of people might be substituted as a guiding vision of restructuring.

Short of a revolution, how could that scenario be achieved?

Unless the forthcoming Act of Parliament proposed in the Conservative government's 2020 white paper *Planning for the Future* weakens local powers even further, as the local planning authority, Southwark Council could have a significant influence, beginning with the space it already controls. Southwark still has one of the highest proportions of residents renting their home from a council. Approximately 25% of residential properties are managed by Southwark, or by tenant management organisations that operate in its name. This does not include properties run by housing associations. There are 24,000 residential properties in the four wards of Nunhead and Queen's Lane, Peckham, Peckham Rye, and Rye Lane, of which 6,700 are council- or tenant organisation-managed (almost 17%). Like all local authorities, Southwark influences or controls land use and redevelopment, including permission for change of use from industrial to commercial or residential purposes. These are subject to local plans, such as that for Peckham and Nunhead discussed in Chapter 8, but that is the nearest it gets under present law to "zoning", as in the United States, where land use is limited in specific areas, and can be used to protect defined areas against unwelcome change. (It may also freeze what could be organic change, or act against local interests, as in *Planning for the Future*.)

As we have seen, until recently Southwark Council's focus on offices and shops that will have high rateable value has been as threatening to Peckham's artists and cultural entrepreneurs as any developer, but recognition of the potential of the creative industries has led to projects such as the Peckham Levels – even if locals complain of the high rents being charged. The council could, if it wished to, put some meat on the bones of its proposals for a "Creative Southwark", sketched in its *Cultural Strategy 2017 to 2022*. Beyond the planning powers it already possesses, there are a number of ways in which it could shape not a gentrified, but a balanced community, where the social inclusion, educational improvements, and environmental benefits promised by regeneration – but so rarely delivered – might become a reality: "a more social, economic and cultural agenda addressing the needs of people", as Neil Smith has put it.

Councils have powers that shape the way social space is used. The granting or withholding of planning permission is an obvious example but, as in the case of Peckham town centre, they have the power to declare conservation areas intended to protect the character of a neighbourhood by preventing demolition or inappropriate alterations to buildings. That assumes that they will be willing to enforce the sort of protection recommended by Historic England, which is not always the case. Local authorities are not directly responsible for "listing" individual historic buildings or other features, a protection managed through Historic England, but they can encourage a listing, or apply to have a building listed themselves. Once a building is listed, a council, as the local planning authority, must be consulted before it can be demolished or altered. But conservation areas and listed buildings presuppose that the built environment has sufficient merit to warrant such protection, a decision that will reflect class-conditioned cultural tastes. Is it possible to imagine the Bussey Building being listed (Figure 8.5)? If it were, would this affect its organic development?

When it comes to community assets, which are not just pubs but green spaces and other leisure facilities, the legal protections are far less than a listing, but a voluntary group can nominate a building or site as a community asset. This becomes a factor in any planning application, and gives local groups an opportunity to acquire it, though this is not guaranteed. Councils can transfer properties to community ownership as such an asset.

These measures only relate to the built environment. They would not necessarily prevent gentrification, but they are a means to inhibit unwelcome developments. Rebuilding and environmental improvements are not necessarily a bad thing. The question is who approves, and who profits. There is one aspect of planning law where developers can be made to return something to a community, especially where the combined results of individual efforts have made neglected areas attractive: by putting a price on planning permission. Section 106 of the 1990 Town and Country Planning Act in effect imposes a premium on permission to redevelop. The most familiar use of Section 106 is for councils to require developers to include a proportion of so-called "affordable" housing within a development, though, sadly, affordable does not mean that people can afford it, and developers notoriously wriggle out of the original commitments they undertake. Nonetheless, developers can also be made to contribute to infrastructure costs, accept impositions on land use, or simply help to pay for community services such as education. Used determinedly, Section 106 (if it survives new legislation) and planning law could balance the interests of capital and community to the benefit of both.

Ultimately, this requires change at national level, but is Southwark, or, for that matter, any other local authority, ready to try to achieve such a balance? This is about people, not just buildings. It demands a change of mindset. Throughout this book we have seen how a local authority – note the word, *authority* – has thwarted rather than served its electors. There appears to be a collusion between council officers and elected councillors that excludes most ordinary citizens. The Bermondsey Mafia held on to power so tightly that it generated an opposition within its own ruling party. Since the 1970s, we have seen time and again how local groups were brought into being in order to oppose the plans of the council. Even the more enlightened councillors of the 21st century seem determined to impose unwelcome development in Peckham town centre, and wreck the cultural assets that they have – almost inadvertently – created.

In the light of her personal engagement in these battles, it is appropriate that Eileen Conn, helped by her experience as a former civil servant, should propose a philosophical explanation for the conflicts that so regularly occur between large institutions and the public they are supposed to serve. These conflicts occur within what Conn calls "the field of possibilities", which is that space between public organisations, both governmental and commercial, and civil society as a whole. Almost exclusively, formally constituted organisations exist as hierarchies, be they armies or arts charities. They operate in what Conn calls a "vertical hierarchical" mode; they employ staff, have offices, regular finances, and use the discipline of line-management to deliver their services vertically downwards to whomever is using them, as disempowered "clients" or supposedly independent "customers".

But civil society is not shaped like that, especially when it comes to the many forms of voluntary organisation that exist in the same civic space as these "vertical hierarchical" institutions. Think of the action groups of Peckham, who have doggedly resisted the vertical impositions of planners and developers to produce organic solutions to the use of social space. They are free associations, depend on personal links, are unpaid, and rely on insecure fundraising. Conn calls them "horizontal peer" systems.

Civil society is not like regulated organizations, where people are recruited to particular defined jobs. Instead, individuals, when they come together voluntarily through their shared interests, connect to give each other mutual "peer" support in some way. These personal connections are the source of nourishment for the *horizontal* relationships between *peers*. They have their roots in life and death experiences in the community, not in contractual hierarchical relationships, nor in the needs of public agencies to deliver their services.

It is no surprise that Conn illustrates her article with an image of grassroots: "These social networks, and the need to nurture them, are fundamental to resilient communities." In Peckham, they have proved the power of their resilience against the vertical forces of capital and state.

The organic image is more than a metaphor, however, for society is not a machine, but an eco-system. Within the field of possibilities, the different frameworks of vertical and horizontal organisations perform what Conn calls "the social eco-system dance". Neither frame is impermeable – church organisations, for instance, are a hybrid form – but the challenge is to execute the dance in step, rather than tripping one another up and treading on each other's toes. It would be difficult in a democracy to force horizontal modes into vertical frames, but so long as vertical organisations fail to acknowledge the horizontal modality they will continue to be frustrated in their attempts to impose schemes that civil society, or, to put it less grandly, the local community, opposes. Such as 20-storey tower blocks.

Artists, we have seen, have been both agents and victims of change, mediators between the vertical and the horizontal worlds. Their positive contribution merits protection. John Latham's contrast between the modalities of authoritative space and open time has resonance here. His struggle to achieve the work of art that is Flat Time House is a rare – and, even then, compromised by the planning authorities who prevented him from fully realising his original conception – achievement for the horizontal world.

Two initiatives from the Mayor of London's Office offer some hope that they will not be priced or developed out of existence. As described in Chapter 8, at the end of 2018 the Greater London Authority announced £11 million in funding for six Creative Enterprise Zones intended to support local creative enterprises and training, and generate new workspaces. Twenty-five boroughs, including Southwark, put in bids for funding, which shows the growing appreciation of the importance of the creative industries, then employing one in six workers in London. The nearest subsequently designated Creative Enterprise Zone to Peckham is at New Cross, centered on Goldsmiths. In 2019 the mayor followed up with £4 million to help set up the Creative Land Trust, together with £2 million from Arts Council England and further help from Bloomberg Philanthropies and the Outset Contemporary Art Fund. Its purpose is to try to stop the steady decline in the number of artists' studios by buying or leasing buildings, inserting studios into developments, and exploiting Section 106, in order to let them at reasonable rates.

These initiatives suggest that artists, and other creative workers, are not quite the marginalised figures they were. But they are still at the mercy of capital and the market. Even more so are Peckham's working class, its small shopkeepers and local businesses. What they all need is agency, some control over their lives and space, beyond spurious consultations over planning proposals. Deprived of agency, not listened to when they are consulted, pushed to the edges of decision-making, especially if they are in a minority group, and deprived of the means of participation, they will experience alienation, and enact it, passively or aggressively. Given agency and empowerment, they will take responsibility and contribute their creativity. The vertical world must acknowledge the horizontal not as passive recipients of administrative kindness or as the recalcitrant subjects of managerial discipline, but as the ultimate source of that world's own authority.

The local, the human scale, and the organic must govern the space of possibilities. Peckham had a community of artists before they were recognised as potential economic assets and contributors to the policy invention that is the "creative industries". The Bellenden Renewal Scheme enjoyed an unusual moment when policy objectives – neighbourhood renewal – and economic growth were in alignment. The post-2010 recession and austerity stopped that. For all of the frustrations of its delivery, the scheme did consult and involve its intended beneficiaries, who responded by investing their own money in improving their own properties. It set out to engage artists, themselves residents, who collaborated with the public and shared in the benefits. Unusual partnerships produced fresh ideas.

It is impossible to plan for creativity, but it is possible to create the circumstances in which it can take place. As Jonathan Wilson, owner of the Bussey Building and the spontaneous "cultural quarter" that has evolved around it, has said, "what we are trying to have here is organic growth". Southwark Council appears now to appreciate the benefits that local initiatives have brought, yet, since the formation of the Peckham Society in 1975, just about every cultural asset that Peckham has acquired – conservation areas, the railway arches, the Bussey Building, the multi-storey car park – has been wrested from official control. No planners could have designed present Peckham, any more than the village from which it grew, but they have a responsibility to protect its character and to judge between positive and negative growth. Genuine creativity requires imagination and risk; the creators must be trusted; the benefits must be shared.

Peckham is just as "authentic" as it was, with a rich texture of people and places. It is also a more productive place, in terms of land values and employment, but much more importantly in terms of a better way of life. In contrast to the erasures that North Peckham has experienced, not once but twice, "done responsibly", gentrification has the potential to be a more benign process, with less enforced displacement. Even the critics of gentrification concede that Peckham is a safer place, and a more pleasant place to live. It could be even better, if the deprivation on the estates is tackled, and the developers are not allowed to run amok. Above all, it is a more creative place, with an entrepreneurial energy that demonstrates itself in art, music, movies, food, fashion.

But before these cultural goods can be consumed, they must be produced. That requires skills that must be learned, and jobs that must be done. There is no shortage of people in Peckham to do them, and they should be given the chance. With changes to the use of redundant shops and offices, the demand for housing could be met without disturbing the social patterns of established citizens. A reduction in commuting would reduce environmental damage, stimulate local enterprise in the service industries, fill the streets during the day, boost the local economy, and generate more social mixing and a stronger sense of community.

Although it has tried to cover all of the saucer of land that is Peckham, much of this book has focused on the space of possibilities that is the town centre. In the post-Covid world there is an opportunity to rethink what this public space could be, and to approach it in a more collaborative way. As I have discovered, Peckham is not one but several communities, with different customs, cultures, faiths, languages. I have, like Mickey Smith, observed a reluctance to engage with each other. There is no obligation to do so, but all communities have a common interest in the public space of Rye Lane, Library Square, and Peckham High Street. They all use it, they dodge the same scooters, are annoyed by the same traffic, are frustrated by the road layout, and avoid the same hustlers. They also draw energy, sometimes profit, and always life from the apparent chaos. Underneath it is still the twisted T-shape of roads and meeting-places that it has been for 1,000 years. They are all citizens, with the same rights to education, social services, and health – even if the Covid pandemic has revealed a reluctance by some to trust authority.

One reason for that is they do not have equal agency in the decision-making about the space they occupy. The "vertical" may be able to impose its will on the "horizontal", but it cannot make Peckham a better place without honestly engaging with those who live there. There needs to be a collective discussion about the town centre's future, a forum – better, an *agora*, a metaphorical meeting-place for all interests and communities.

Cities do not stay still. Peckham could yet become more like the self-sustaining village it once was, without losing touch with modernity.

Almost opposite Camberwell Art School and behind the South London Gallery's new extension in the Victorian fire station stands the former Kennedy's sausage factory. The business began in a shop in Rye Lane in 1877, just as Peckham was beginning to settle into its modest suburban character. Other branches opened across South London, and in 1934 the firm established its head office at 86 Peckham Road, fronted by a new-built shop whose façade and signage survives (Figure 10.1). The firm also took over two adjoining Victorian houses and the retired 1867 fire station next to them. These and a house at the bottom of Talfourd Road, to the west, backed on to the new factory built behind them. The story of this block, numbers 78 to 102

Peckham Road, from Talfourd Road to Grummant Road, is a recollection of Peckham in miniature.

Today, the corner of Talfourd Road and Peckham Road is occupied by a modern fire station, but this was once the site of Talfourd House, home of the comic actor and playwright John Baldwin Buckstone (1802–1879), who had made his debut at the original Peckham Theatre in his teens, and who went on to run London's Haymarket Theatre as actor-manager from 1853 until 1876. He went bankrupt in 1878 and died the following year in Sydenham. In 1925 Talfourd House made way for a new fire station next to the original 1867 building, which no longer suited modern requirements. In 1989 this in turn was replaced by the present buildings.

Both ends of the terrace suffered bomb damage during World War II, as did the free library on the other side of Grummant Road, and the former AUEW headquarters, now part of a Best Western Hotel, fronted by Del Boy's van (Figure 3.1). At the western corner with Grummant Road is the former Victorian pub the Walmer Castle, which latterly became celebrated for its strip shows, before ending its days as a place called Pharaoh's, seeing a fatal shooting in 2002 before closing in 2004 after a fire. After a second fire in 2009 what survived was converted into flats. A pub sign declaring this to be "Walmer Castle Court" and the graffitied, boarded-up windows of the public bar at the front are melancholy reminders of what was once the watering-hole of Camberwell Art School (Figure 4.2).

Next to it stands the banal façade of Pelican House, built on the site of an 18th-century gentleman's property that took its name from the stone pelicans that guarded its entrance. In the 1820s it became one of the many private girls' schools established in still semi-rural Peckham. After the railways came, the school moved to Grove Park, and the buildings were taken over as workshops by the London Association for the Blind (now the Association for Blind People). In 1936 the Association built a modern steel-framed factory on the site, retaining the Pelican name, where the Association stayed until 1976. When Southwark Council began construction of social housing on bomb-blasted land behind it in 1956, it gave each of the four blocks the name of a bird, and called the whole the Pelican Estate. In 2010 Crane block saw a killing and two stabbings.

After the Association for Blind People sold its factory in 1976 Pelican House became council offices, and in 1989, presumably oblivious to *Only*

Fools and Horses, it was renamed Winnie Mandela House. The name did not survive the loss of reputation of the nominee, and in 1995 it once more became Pelican House. Sold off by the council, in 2008 the building was enlarged to become housing association flats. With a nod to the heritage industry, the 1930s façade was incorporated in the frontage and, in the spirit of the new Peckham, a gallery-bar opened on the street.

In 2007 Kennedy's Sausages closed its factory next door, and in 2010 developers of the Kennedy's site, including the now Grade II-listed former fire station, were given planning permission for a large redevelopment. The two houses between the shop and the fire station on Peckham Road were demolished. But, this being the start of another recession, the project stalled. As if to exemplify the Peckham paradigm, an artist saw an opportunity. In 2011 the site was acquired by the Kashmiri-British artist Raqib Shaw. Born in 1974 of successful Kashmiri parents, who traded in textiles and had a shop in London's South Audley Street, in 1992 Shaw spent a year at the private Blake College in London, with the intention of becoming a fashion designer, but quickly found that what he really wanted to do was paint. He continued to work at South Audley Street, but was a reluctant businessman and, "banished" by his family for becoming a painter, in 1998 he started a BA in fine art at Central St Martins (then still in the Charing Cross Road). To support himself, Shaw kept a successful pashmina stall in the Portobello Road. This was the heyday of film, video, conceptual, and installation art at St Martin's, and Shaw found that he and the few who continued to paint "were regarded as primitive savages". Nonetheless, he was awarded a first-class degree, his degree show sold out, and he stayed on to do a one-year MA.

Shaw's MA show attracted the interest of Glenn Scott Wright, co-director of the Victoria Miro Gallery, whose move from Cork Street, Mayfair, to Islington in 2000 was part of the eastward reconfiguration of the art world. Helped by a former Audley Street client, Charlotte Rhodes, Shaw spent a further year developing his art at a studio in Hackney, and became a Victoria Miro artist, moving into a studio lent to him rent-free by Peter Doig in Wharf Street, near the Miro Gallery. His 2004 show with Miro, *The Garden of Earthly Delights*, was subsequently shown in New York by the celebrated American dealer Jeffrey Deitch in 2005, and then the Museum of Contemporary Art in Miami. After leaving Victoria Miro he was without representation for a couple

Figure 10.2 Part of Kennedy's Sausages factory, pre-conversion (image credit: courtesy Raqib Shaw).

of years, before joining Jay Jopling – former Camberwell resident – and White Cube.

By this time Shaw was feeling the need for a bigger studio than in Wharf Road. He was shown many studio properties, but could find nothing that appealed until he discovered – at the bottom of the estate agent's pile – Kennedy's Sausages: "the council had given planning permission for a hideous block of flats", he told me, "but this felt like a project. The space had a weird energy that wanted me to do something that was not commercial." In 2010 he took the building on.

We were talking in the courtyard that lies between the back of the former fire station and the factory building. This secret space, which attracted him because it reminded him of the hidden courtyards of Rajasthan, has been transformed into a Himalayan rock garden, full of the sound of water tumbling into pools where flamboyant goldfish have multiplied during lockdown. A California redwood *Sequoiadendron giganteum* pine already towers over Japanese acer trees whose rich orange and purple leaves echo the voluptuous forms and colour schemes of his paintings. They are the complete opposite of John Latham's passionate austerity. Heather, aubretia, dwarf Himalayan pines, and maples complete the picture.

All that Shaw knew of Peckham before he came here was the mythical *Only Fools and Horses*. In spite of being discouraged from buying the property, Shaw has gradually transformed it into a sequence of studio spaces for creatives, used by artists and makers. The factory floors have been made into a private viewing gallery, a drawing studio, paint workshop, and a painting studio, where he employs a small team of assistants.

His personal space, complete with hanging gardens, is at the western end. He had considered living, as Peckham's original firemen's families had done, in the old fire station, but decided it would be better as an art gallery, hence the generous gift to the South London Gallery. Raqib Shaw had a principle in mind: "Every artist has a debt, a duty to consider and inspire young minds." Peckham, and Peckham's artists, are benefitting from both the space and the employment that this distinctive, and benign, form of gentrification has created.

This last visit brings us back to the bottom of Talfourd Road, among the "mean streets" where the artist Tom Phillips once thought he could discover

Figure 10.3 Creative quarters: from sausage factory to studio space (image credit: courtesy Raqib Shaw).

no magical feeling at all. Except that he has, and his annual circumambulation of 20 sites will, with good fortune, continue to do so, into infinity. As he says:

In a hundred years' time the whole area might become an airport, or Disneyland, or a post nuclear desert; in a thousand years' time it might become a rain forest, or be indistinguishable from the Sahara, or have reverted to the hilly hunting grounds where King Charles first saw the Camberwell Beauty, or some Phillips yet to come might be trying to find both marks and a foothold on a glacier in the dark noon as he/she/it/ attempts to manipulate the camera with a mutant's cloven hoof.

There *is* life in Peckham.

Sources

Peter Hennessey was speaking on "The World at One", BBC Radio 4, 16 March 2020. The best information on the state of employment in the cultural sector comes from the regular updates from the Centre for Cultural Value, Leeds University. Will Jarvis is quoted from *The Peckham Peculiar* 19, February/March 2017, Russell Porter from the *Financial Times* magazine, 11/12 November 2017. Clive Burton and Jane Muir were (separately) in conversation with me. Oli Mould's *Against Creativity* was published by Verso in 2018. I am aware this book is open to his critique. Julian Henriques made his comment in an interview. Shola Amoo was speaking to the *Financial Times*, 22 April 2017. Caleb Femi's poem "Community" appears in his *Poor* (Penguin, 2020). Charmaine Brown's paper "The Gentrification of Peckham and Black Removal Worldwide" was given as a webinar for Black History Walks on 19 November 2020. Kenny Imafidon and Clement Ogbonnaya were speaking in Shane Duncan's 2018 documentary *This is Peckham*; Mickey Smith in an interview.

Kathy O'Brien produced the Arts & Business evaluation in 2003. Neil Smith is quoted from *The New Urban Frontier: Gentrification and the Revanchist City* (Routledge, 1996). David Ley is quoted from his article "Artists, Aestheticisation and the Field of Gentrification", *Urban Studies* 40, no. 12, November 2003. The *Artists' Workspace Study* was published by the GLA in September 2014. There are inevitably more artists and studios in London than those captured by the terms of reference of this report.

The data on residential properties come from Southwark's 2019 ward profiles, but relate to 2011, which may be out of date, but not much.

Eileen Conn's "Community Engagement in the Social Eco-System Dance" appears in *Moving Forward With Complexity*, ed. A. Tait and K.A. Richardson (Emergent Publications, 2011).

I am very grateful to Raqib Shaw for talking to me, giving me access to his studios, and lending photographs. Tom Phillips is quoted from his comments on "20 Sites n Years" in his *Words and Texts* (Thames & Hudson, 1992).

Index

For ease of use, this index is divided into five sections: "People", "Places", "Culture and Creativity" (meaning ideas, artefacts and arts organisations), "Organisations and Institutions", and "Concepts and Themes".

People

Abbensetts, Michael, writer, 60
Adamson, Steve, artist, Figure 4.5
Adeojo, Sodiq, 207
Admiral Ken, DJ, 55
Afoloashade, Abosede, actress, 27
Agbaje, Bola, playwright, 204–5, 207
Alsop, Will, architect, 113, 179
Amoo, Shola, director, 208, 216
Apraku, Andrew, actor, 198
Artur, Liz Johnson, photographer, 197
Asante, Gyearbour, actor, 63
Atkinson, Rick, memoirist, 104
Attoh, Rienkje, producer, 208
Atuona, Nneka Diana, playwright, 208
Auerbach, Frank, artist, 74, 76–7, 86
Ayres, Gillian, artist, 72, 74, Figure 4.2
Ayrton, Michael, artist, 72

Bamtefi, Moji, actress, 198
Barber, James, writer, 208
Barclay, Humphrey, producer, vii, 61, 62, 63
Barrett, Syd, musician, 75
Barry, Hannah, gallerist, 163–4, 182–5, 186, 188
Baxter, Glenn, artist, 87
Beasley, John, historian, 107
Beaton, Norman, actor, 63–4, Figure 3.5
Beattie, Basil, artist, 82
Berger, John, artist and writer, 84, 142
Bell-Jones, Gareth, curator, vii, 160
Bhimji, Zarina, artist, 92
Blake, William, artist and poet, 16–17, 26, 33, 144–5

Bloch, Martin, artist, 73
Bohay-Nowell, Vernon Dudley, teacher and musician, 80
Bokinni, Yinka, broadcaster, 99
Booth, Charles, sociologist, 18, 25–7, 28, 31, 166, Figure 2.8
Boughton, John, urban historian, vii, 48
Bourne, Stephen, cultural historian, 52, 60, 61
Boyega, John, actor, 205–7
Boxer, Frank, restaurateur, 182, 185
Brar, Dhanveer Singh, musicologist, 201–2
Brighton, Andrew, artist-philosopher, 83
Broadbent, Jim, actor, 43
Brown, Charmaine, sociologist, vii, 217
Brown, Glenn, artist, 84, 86, 87
Buckstone, John Baldwin, actor-manager, 227
Bulloch, Angela, artist, Figure 4.5
Burne-Jones, Edward, artist, 69
Burne-Jones, Georgiana, philanthropist, 69–70
Burney, Elizabeth, housing expert, 52
Burrell, Heather, sculptor, 131
Burton, Clive, artist, 132, 215
Bussey, George, manufacturer, 22
Butt, Lorraine, designer, 135

Cage, John, composer, 84, 148
Camp, Sokari Douglas, sculptor, 131
Capper, James, sculptor, 164
Cardew, Cornelius, composer, 79
Carter, Tony, artist, 87
Chadwick, Helen, artist, 82
Charles II, King, 26, 231

Chesshyre, Robert, writer and journalist, 49, 59, 117
Chesterman, Ross, warden of Goldsmiths College, 80, 82
Choumert, George, landowner, 18, 19
Clark, Kenneth, art historian, 71
Clark, T.J., art historian, 76
Codjoe, Eugene, photographer, 197
Coldstream, William, artist and teacher, 72–3, 74
    reforms, 75–6, 78
Collings, Matthew, artist and critic, 87
Collishaw, Matt, artist, 84, 92, Figure 4.5
Compston, Joshua, curator, 124
Conn, Eileen, campaigner, vii, 103, 107, 118, 128, 130, 171, 172, 175, 176, 178, 181, 182, 223
    "The field of possibilities", 222, Figure 8.12
Corbett, Ronnie, comedian, 41
Cornell, George, 41
Cornish, Joe, comedian and filmmaker, 205
Craig-Martin, Michael, artist and teacher, 84, 93
Crane, Walter, designer, 70
Craxton, John, artist, 78
Cresswell, Peter, artist, 81
Critical Décor (David Pugh and Toby Morgan), artists, 92
Cunningham, Merce, choreographer, 84

Daniels, Leonard, artist and teacher, 73, 74
Dannatt, Trevor, R.A., architect, vii, 28
Davenport, Iain, artist, 88, 125
Davis, Alan, council leader, 109
De Crespigny family, landowners, 19
De Francia, Peter, artist and art historian, 80, 82
De-lahay, Rachael, playwright, 207
De Monchaux, Cathey, artist, 87
D'Offay, Anthony, gallerist, 89, 92
Debra, Kate, director, 208
Deller, Jeremy, artist, 137
Denis, Dominic, artist, Figure 4.5
Dennis, Jo, artist, 185
Dickens, Charles, novelist, 18
Dhondy, Farrukh, writer and editor, 61
Dorriman, Rev. Graham, 49, 59
Dowler, Bobby, artist, 163, 164
Drake, Lettice, architect, 187
Driver, Charles Henry, architect, 172
Duffy, Niall, council leader, 111
Duncan, Shane, director, 208

Eales, Oliver, artist, 164
Eckersley, Toby, councillor, 104
Edwards, Passmore, philanthropist, 70
Eggerue, Chidera ("Slumflower"), blogger and writer, 197
Einstein, Albert, physicist, 148
Ekaragha, Destiny, director, 204
Elliot, John, scriptwriter, 60
Emin, Tracey, artist, 92, 137
Eno, Brian, musician, 182
Errol, John, actor and writer, 60

Fantoni, Barry, cartoonist, 75
Faramawy, Adham, artist, 163
Farkhas, Rósza, gallerist, 214
Fawkes, Wally, cartoonist and musician, 74
Fear, Tanya, actress, 208
Feaver, William, critic and biographer, vii, 78
Femi, Caleb, poet and filmmaker, ix, 48, 54, 63, 193, 203–4, 207, 217
Fisher, Andrea, artist, 82, 91
Flanagan, Barry, sculptor, 145, 146
Forde, Brinsley, musician and actor, 56
Foreman, Freddie, 40–2
Foreman, George, 40–2, 53
Forge, Andrew, artist, 81
Francis, Geff, actor, 63
Fraser, Jeremy, council leader, 90, 110
Fraser, Neil ("the Mad Professor"), music producer, 53
Freedman, Carl, gallerist, 89, 91

Freud, Lucian, artist, 78
Frost, Terry, artist, 74
Frye, Maxwell, architect, 28
Fuller, Peter, critic, 84

Gallacio, Anne, artist, 91
Gandolphi, Louis, camera-maker, 22
Gardiner, Clive, designer, 78
Gavron, Sarah, director, 198
Giggs, musician, 202
Gilbert and George, artists, 92
Gilroy, Paul, historian, 64
Glaswegians, 54
Glücksberg, Luna, sociologist, 117–18, 218
Goddard, Camilla, art consultant, viii, 128, 132, 137, 151
Golub, Leon, artist, 92
Gormley, Antony, sculptor, 87, 123, 124, 130–1
    Bollards, Figure 6.5, Figure 6.10
Gormley, Paloma, architect, 182
Goss, Sue, councillor, 107
Gowing, Laurence, artist, 72
Grace, W.G., sportsman, 22
Green, Christopher, artist, 164
Gregory, Clive, astronomer, 142
Griffin, Oliver, artist, 164
Gwyn, Nell, actress, 26

Hallett, Dido, artist, 185
Halliwell, Albert, artist and teacher, 71
Hambling, Maggi, 137
Hancock, Matt, politician, 213
Hancock, Tony, comedian, 37
Harman, Harriet, politician, 104
Harrison, Helen, sculptor, 133
Haselden, Ron, sculptor, 91, 112
Hatherley, Owen, architectural critic, 5, 8, 214
Hatoum, Mona, artist, 91
Hebdige, Dick, cultural critic, 41, 56, 58
Heller, Margot, curator, viii, 92
Henriques, Julian, professor and filmmaker viii, 58, 216

Hennessy, Peter, historian, 213
Hero, Dilip, writer, 55
Heseltine, Michael, politician, 108
Hill family, landowners, 21
Hill, Octavia, philanthropist, 27
Hirst, Damien, artist, 88–9, 91, 92, 95, 125, 137, Figure 4.5
Hodgkin, Howard, artist, 74
Holder, Ram Jam ("Porkpie"), actor, 63, 108
Howard, Charles, artist, 74, 76
Hume, Gary, artist, 88, 92, Figure 4.5

Imafidon, Kenny, social researcher, 197, 208
Innes, Neil, musician, 80, Figure 4.3
Irvine, Michael, council officer, 127
Irwin, Bert, artist, 82
Isham, Chris, physicist, 155, 156

Jack the Hat, 42
Jacobs, Jane, urbanist, 6
Jacobs, Nicola, gallerist, 87
James, Fraser, actor, 205–6
Jarvis, Will, gallerist, 215
Jason, David ("Del-Boy"), actor, 37–8, 227
Jeffrey, Ian, art historian, 89
John, Peter, council leader, 119
Johnson, Linton Kwesi, poet, 58–9
Johnstone, William, artist and teacher, 71–3
Jones, David, artist and writer, 71
Jopling, Jay, gallerist, 89, 92, 124, 229

Kaufman, Pat, artist, 91
Kay, Elisa, curator, 159
Keating, Tom, forger, 78
Keeble, Sally, council leader, 111
Kelly, Mary, artist, 82
Kemp, Lindsay, mime, 84
Khan, Akbar, merchant, 194, Figure 9.3
Kieffer, Anselm, artist, 92
Kieffer, John, arts consultant, viii, 89
King, Sam, mayor, 50
Kirby, Neil, council officer, 187, Figure 8.12

Klein, Randy, sculptor, 16
Kohsen, Anita, psychologist, 143
Kossoski, Adam, muralist, 114
Kray twins, Ronnie and Reggie, 40–2
Kruger, Barbara, artist, 92

Lamming, George, writer, 54
Landy, Michael, artist, 88, Figure 4.5
Latham, Harriet, choreographer, viii, 150
Latham, John, artist, 2, 125, 135, 141–60, 230, Figure 7.5
   Report of a Surveyor, 143–4
   One-Second Drawing, Figure 7.2
   Time-Base Roller, Figure 7.3
   Face or *How the Univoice is Still Unheard*
      sketch for, Figure 7.4
      maquette for, Figure 7.5, Figure 7.6
      detail, Figure 7.7
      as installed, Figure 7.8
Latham, John-Paul, geologist, viii, 150
Latham, Noa, philosopher, viii, 160
Ley, David, geographer, 219
Linke, Simon, artist, 87
Livesey, George, philanthropist, 21
Logan, Peter, filmmaker, 82
Logsdail, Nicholas, gallerist, 145
Long, Richard, sculptor, 13
Lord Beginner, musician, 54
Lord Kitchener (Aldwyn Roberts), musician, 54
Lord Woodbine, musician, 54
Lowe, Adam, sculptor, 133
Lucas, Sarah, artist, 92, Figure 4.5
Lyndhurst, Nicholas, actor, 37
Lyttleton, Humphrey, musician, 75

McDowell, Sean, artist, 163, 164
MacInnes, Colin, writer, 73
McLaren, Malcolm, artist-manager, 80, 81, 82
McNab, Andy, writer, 38
McQueen, Steve, artist and filmmaker, 82, 207
McTernan, John, councillor, viii, 99, 150–1

Male, Marcia Bennett, sculptor, 134
   Path Marker, Figure 6.9
Manheim, Julia, sculptor, 126
Mann, Sargy, artist, 76
Manson, Fred, architect and council officer, viii, 90, 100, 111, 112, 117, 127, 160, 182
Marley, Bob, musician, 55, 56
Marshall, William, historian, 26
Matthews, Anne, council leader, 110, 111
Medley, Robert, artist and teacher, 74, 77
Mellish, Bob, politician, 109
Merryfield, Buster, actor, 38
Michael, Adeyemi, filmmaker, 207
Milner, Simon, artist, 164
Milroy, Lisa, artist, 87
Minton, John, artist, 72
Monroe, Carmen, actress, 63–4
Moody, Dr Harold, campaigner, 137
Moral, Heather, sculptor, 131
Morris, Bill, architect, 179
Moses, Robert, town planner, 6, 7
Mould, Oli, cultural critic, 216
Muir, Gregor, curator, 48–9, 76–7, 117
Muir, Jane, ceramicist, 126, 176–7, 215
Münder, Sven, gallerist, 182
Mundy, Henry, artist, 74, Figure 4.2

Nairn, Ian, urban historian, 31, 45
Newell, Russell, photographer, vii, 48, 56–8, 100, 104, 193, Figure 3.3, Figure 5.1
Newman, Beatrice, knitwear designer, 196

O'Brien, John, council officer, 103
O'Grady, John, council leader, 102, 109
O'Looney, Benedict, architect, vii, 179, 194
O'Neil, Paddy, council officer, 128
Odewale, Yetunde, actress, 198
Odutuyo, Debrah, writer and director, 198, 199
Ogbonnaya, Clement, pub landlord, 197, 208, 217
Ofili, Chris, artist, 137

Oguns, Femi, agent, 204
Ojo, Wale, actor, 198
Okafur, Kelecha, trainer, 197
Okwula, Nicholas, social entrepreneur, 197
Ono, Yoko, artist, 156, 157
Onwubulo, Andrew ("Rapman"), writer and
    director, 200
Opie, Julian, artist, 87
Osayami, Andrew, producer, 198
Ové, Horace, director, 60, 63

Paley, Maureen, gallerist, 84
Pardoe, Enrique, artist-philosopher, 82
Parker, Cornelia, artist, 91
Parry, Eric, architect, 125
Parsons, Vicken, artist, 87
Passmore, Victor, artist, 72
Pateman, Trevor, artist-philosopher, 83
Peake-Jones, Tessa, actress, 38
Pearce, Leonard, actor, 37, 38
Pearse, Innes, M.D., 27–9
Philips, Carrol, writer, 60, 63
Phillips, Tom, artist, writer, composer, vii,
    11–13, 76, 77, 79, 87, 124, 132–3, 159,
    182, 231
  garden arch, Figure 6.6
  lamp-post, Figure 6.10
  South London Dreaming, Figure 2.1 (detail),
    Figure 2.2
  We Love Peckham, Figure 6.1
Pippen, Stephen, artist, 92
Plackman, Carl, artist-philosopher, 82
Plunkett-Greene, Alexander, restaurateur, 76
Podro, Michael, art historian, 76
Poitier, Sydney, actor, 62
Poncelet, Jacqueline, ceramicist, 125
Porter, Roy, historian, 39, 43
Porter, Russell, pub landlord, 215
Powell, Enoch, politician, 50
Power, Anne, urbanist, 45, 48
prisoners of war, 31
Profitt, Russell, council officer, 118–19, 167,
    168, 173, 182

Pugh, Gareth, designer, 163

Quant, Mary, designer, 76
Quinn, Mark, artist, 92

Ranks, Buckey, musician, 58
Reckford, Lloyd, actor and director, 60
Reid, Ebony, sociologist, 200–1
Rhodes, Zandra, designer, 134
  bollard, Figure 6.8
  lamp-post, Figure 6.7
Richardson, Charlie, 40–3, 131
Richardson, Eddie, 40, 85
Richards-Turner, Cecilia, director, 208
Riley, Bridget, artist, 79, 90, 124
Rio, Ferdinand, sportsman, 201
Ritchie, Tony, council leader, 109, 110
Robb, Steven, architectural historian, 179
Roberts, Perry, artist, 87
Rodgers, Franklyn, photographer, 205–6
Rodney, Donald, artist, 92
Rogers, Claude, artist, 72, 73
Rossitor, William, philanthropist, 23, 69–70
Rosso, Franco, filmmaker, 56, 61
Rowlett, George, artist, viii
Ruskin, John, art critic, 17, 70
  Ruskin Gallery, 70

Saatchi, Charles and Doris, art collectors,
    86, 89, 93
Saffran, Yehuda, artist-philosopher, 83
Sassoon, Ben, architect, gallerist and bar
    owner, viii, 163
Sayle, Alexei, comedian, 11
Schnabel, Julian, artist, 92
Schubert, Karsten, gallerist, 88
Scott, George Gilbert, architect, 17
Sellmann, Billee, fundraiser, 88–9
Sennett, Richard, sociologist, vii, 5
Shakespeare, William, playwright, 40
Shaw, Raqib, artist, viii, 93, 228–9
Shone, Richard, art historian, 86
Shonibare, Yinka, artist, 87
Sinclair, Iain, writer, 126

Slolely, Glenn, musician, 55
Smith, Malcolm, council officer, 116
Smith, Mickey, arts entrepreneur and DJ, viii, 171–2, 173, 216, 217, 226
Smith, Neil, geographer, 218–20
Smith, Paul, designer, 137
Smyth, Bob, journalist and councillor, 103, 109
Spark, Muriel, novelist, 7, 32
Stellman, Martin, writer, viii, 61
Snow, Nick, councillor, 109
Spencer, Gilbert, artist and teacher, 70, 74
Spragge, Helen Foster, artist, 150
Staunton, Claire Louise, curator, 159–60
Stevini, Barbara, arts activist, viii, 142, 146, 154
Stone, James Matthew, artist, 163
Strevens, David, council officer, 182
Strong, Gwyneth, actress, 38
Sullivan, John, scriptwriter, 37–9
Summerson, Sir John, architectural historian, 32, 117
Sunshine, Monty, musician, 74
Sutherland, Graham, artist, 78
Swan, Lucy, landscape artist, 131

Tagg, John, artist-philosopher, 83
Talfourd, Thomas, lawyer and playwright, 18
Tatchell, Peter, campaigner, 109
Taylor, Damilola, 99–100, 114, 117
Taylor, Ken, architect and gallerist, 126
Teddy Boys, 38, 40, 85
Ternan, Nelly, 18
Thatcher, Margaret, politician, 39, 47, 63, 85, 86, 110
Thompson, Jon, artist and teacher, 69, 71, 81–9, 93–5, Figure 4.4
Thorn, Rev. Ernest, 55
Thornton, Pat, artist, 91
Thorp, David, curator, viii, 90–3
Tilling, Thomas, transport entrepreneur, 21
Toscano-Heighton, Emily, artist, 131
Travellers, 54
Turner, Corinne, photographer, viii
Tunstall, Rebecca, urbanist, 45, 48

Turk, Gavin, artist, 92
Turner, Edward, inventor, 27
Tyabji, Joy, director, 166

Uglow, Euan, artist, 74, 76

Vaughan, Keith, artist, 72
Vietnamese boat people, 54
Vogel, Karl, sculptor, 73

Walker, Audrey, textile designer and teacher, 85
Wallinger, Mark, artist, 87, 137
Walters, Ashley, actor, 205, Figure 9.5
Washington, Denzil, actor, 62
Watts, Mary, artist and ceramicist, 23
Watts, G.F., artist, 23, 69
Wearing, Gillian, artist, 93, 137
Wentworth, Richard, sculptor and teacher, viii, 84, 87, 93, 184
   Agora, Figure 8.1
Whybray, Simon, artist, 184
Williams, Cephas, entrepreneur, 196
Williams, E. Owen, architect, 28
Williams, Raymond, cultural critic, 2, 3
Williamson, George, M.D., 27–9
Willis, Clair, historian, 54
Willis, Ted, writer, 60
Wilson, Jane and Louise, artists, 93
Wilson, Jonathan, owner of Bussey Building and Copeland Park, vii, 163, 169, 171, 172, 183, 185–6, 188, 190, 225, Figure 8.12
Wollacott, Bob, artist, 107
Wongs (also Wo), Natalie, fashion facilitator, viii, 197–8, 203, 208, 217
Wood, Sam Taylor, artist, 97
Worrell, Trix, writer, viii, 61, 64–5

Yates, Edward, developer, 18
Young, Roger, council officer, viii, 128, 137, 151, 156, 157, Figure 7.5

Zukin, Sharon, sociologist, 6

Places

221 Balham High Street, nightclub, 42

Addington Square, 40
Albany Road, 29
All Saints Church, 131
Anstey Road, 44, 142
Area 10, 186
Asylum Road, 25, 183
Avondale Rise, 217
Aylesbury Estate, 45, 119
Aylesham Shopping Centre, 93, 167, 177, 188

Baldwin Crescent, 32
Balham, 37, 38
Bar Story, 163, 176, 215
Bellenden Road 18, 44, 141, 215, Figure 6.3, Figure 6.4, Figure 6.10, Figure 7.1. *See also* Bellenden Area Renewal
"Bellenden Village", 216, 219
Bellenden Ward, 127, 136
Bermondsey, 23, 38, 42, 44, 134
Best Western Hotel, 38, 227
Bim's African Food Store, 195
Blackpool Road, 194
Blenheim Court, 163, 176, 215
Blenheim Grove, 107, 163, 176
Bouncing Ball (aka "Mr Bees", "Chicago", "Kisses"), nightclub, 55, 56
Brick Brewery, 176
Bristol, 38
  riots, 59
Brixton, 39, 50, 202, 208–9. *See also* riots
Brockley, 53
Building One, 89
Burgess Park, 2, 45
Bussey factory, later Bussey Building, 23, 126, 169–73, 175, 177, 185
  as CIP House, 126
  as Museum of Fire Arms, 22
  as Notevision Building, 169, Figure 2.7, Figure 8.4, Figure 8.5
  as Sports Manufactory, 22

Calmington Road, 29
Camberwell, 17, 23, 32
Camberwell Green, 32
Camberwell Grove, 17, 25
Camberwell New Road, 18
Camden Chapel, 53
Camden Estate, 45, 47, 115, 116
Central Hall ("The Church of Strangers"), 55
Chadwick Road, 188
Chanell Tunnel, 107
Choumert Road, 18
Choumert Square, 18
Clayton Arms, pub, 164, 166, 197
Clifton Crescent, 104
Clifton Rise, 78
"The Coal Line", 42
Collyer Place, 163
Commercial Road, 26
Copeland Road Industrial Park, 126, 169–73, 176, 177, 185–6, 193, 194
Costa Street, 44
Crystal Palace, 16, 21

De Crespingy Estate, 19
Danby Street, 141, 152
The Denes, 45, 137
Denman Road, 18
Denmark Hill, 16
Dovedale Court, 163, 176
Dulwich Village, 16
Dundas Road, 44

Edison Bell factory, 27
East Dulwich Road, 134
Elephant and Castle, 38, 45, 50, 119
Elm Grove, 18, 26

Fenwick Road, 53
"The Five Estates", 43, 115, 167, 219, Figure 5.6
Flaxyards development, 106, 111, 173
Frank's Café, 182, 216, Figure 8.9
Freeman, Hardy and Willis, department store, 18

Friary Estate, 201
Friary Road, 163

Ganapati, restaurant, 133
Gantry Road, 58
Glengall Road, 27
Gowlett Arms, pub, 164
Gloucester Grove Estate, 45, 110, 115, 116
Goldsmiths Road, 27
Goose Green, 2, 134
Gordon Road, 50, 53
Grove Park, 11, 13
Grummant Road, 227

Hartley's Jam Factory, 31
Herne Hill, 16, 17
Heygate Estate, 45, 119
Highshore Road, 18
Holdron's, department store, 18, 22, 106, 169, 171, Figure 8.3, Figure 9.3
Holly Grove, 18, 187
  conservation area, 107
Howden Street, 127

Ivanhoe Road, 188
The Ivy, pub, 189

Jones and Higgins, department store, 18, 29, 106, 166, 179, 209, Figure 2.4

Kennedy's Sausages, factory, 226–7, 228, 229, Figure 10.1, Figure 10.2
Kennington Park Road, 50
Kentish Drovers, pub, 19
Khan's Bargains, store, 194, Figure 8.3, Figure 9.3
King's Arms, pub, 29
King's College Hospital, 16, 49

Lane ward, 14
Lewisham, 2, 39
Library Square, 226

Linden Grove, 18
Livesey ward, 14, 166

McDermott Grove Wildlife Garden, 133, Figure 6.6
Maudsley Hospital, 16, 49
Meeting House Lane, 32, 137
Millard Building (Goldsmiths), 85–7, 97, Figure 4.7
Mr Smith's, nightclub, 41
Moncrieff Street, 19, 104
The Montpelier, pub, 215
Myatts Fields, park, 85

New Church Road, 41
New Cross, 2, 17, 224
Newington ward, 50
Nigel Road, 127
North Dulwich Station, 16
North Peckham, 38, 43, 200, 225, Figure 3.2, Figure 5.6, Figure 5.7
North Peckham Civic Centre, 114
North Peckham Estate, 45, 47, 48, 49, 59, 100, 107, 110, 115, 116, 217, Figure 3.3
Notting Hill Gate, 2, 50
Nunhead All Saints Cemetery, 16, 19, 107
Nunhead Lane, 18, 41
Nunhead ward, Nunhead and Queens Lane ward, 14, 26, 166, 220
Nutbrook Street, 104

Old Kent Road, 17, 21, 25, 40
Old Kent Road ward, 14
One Tree Hill, 16
Overground rail network ("The Ginger Line"), 151, 173

Peckford Place, 40
Pecheham Manor, 14, 17
Peckham *passim*, maps
  A–Z map, Figure 1.1

Index | 241

bomb damage map, Figure 2.9
Booth poverty map, Figure 2.8
Greenwood map 1830, Figure 2.3
map 1897, Figure 2.5
Peckham Arch, 112, 115, 186, Figure 5.4
Peckham High Street, 2, 17, 25, 26, 27, 40, 44, 226, Figure 2.4
Peckham Hill Street, 21
Peckham Liberal Club, 26, 189
Peckham Library, 99, 113, 114, 115, 177, 179, 187, Figure 5.4, Figure 5.5
Peckham Lido, 17
Peckham Mosque, 194, Figure 9.2
Peckham New Town, 21, 25
Peckham Palms, 19
Peckham Peace Wall, 167
Peckham Police Station, 137
Peckham Pulse, 112
Peckham Road, 21, 25, 38, 227–8
Peckham Road Fire Station
 new, 227
 old, 92, 226, 228, 230
Peckham Rye Common, 2, 16, 22
Peckham Rye Conservation Area, 173–5
Peckham Rye (street), 25, 26
Peckham Rye Park, 17, 22
Peckham Rye Station, 16, 18, 21, 22, 42, 58, 151, 163, 173, 178, Figure 2.6, Figure 2.7, Figure 8.6
Peckham Rye ward, 166, 220
Peckham Springs, bar, 176
Peckham ward, 14, 166, 220
Peck River, 16
Pelican Estate, 207, 227
Pelican House (aka Winnie Mandela House), 227–8
Pentecostal Faith Chapel, 141, 152
Petitou Café, 135
Prince of Peckham, pub, 197, 208
Print Village, Chadwick Road, 188

Queen's Road, 25, 26, 27, 137
Queen's Road Station, 16, 21, 137

Raul Road, 44, 104
Red Cross Cottages, 27
Ronan Point, 47
Rotherhithe, 21, 53, 86
Ruskin Park, 70
Rye Lane 2, 17, 18, 19, 21, 22, 25, 26, 31, 102, 168, 215, 226
Rye Lane ward, 14, 220
Rye Wax, store and club, 172

St Giles Church, 14, 17
St Luke's Primary School, 53
St Mary's Road, 28
Sainsbury's store, 105–6
 multi-storey car park, 177, 181, Figure 5.3, Figure 8.8
Sassoon House, 28
Savage's corset factory, 31
Sceaux Gardens, 45
Shakespeare Road, 89
Sheepcote Lane, 46
Sheney Road, 12
South Metropolitan Gas Works, 21, 25
South Street, 17
Staffordshire Street, 27
Sumner Estate, 44, 45, 115, 116
Surrey Canal, 2, 21, 25, 44, 45, 54, 102, 106
Sydenham Hill, 16

Talfourd House, 227
Talfourd Road, 12, 28, 230
Telegraph Hill, 16
Tower Hamlets, 45

Victoria Inn (formerly the Wishing Well), pub, 131

Waghorn Street, 127
The Walmer Castle, (later Pharoah's), pub, 42, 53, 72, 75, 77, 227, Figure 4.2
Walworth Road, 25, 50
Warwick Gardens, 107, 108
The White Horse, pub, 75

242 | Index

Willowbrook Estate, 45, 107, 115, 116
Wilson's Cycles, shop, 59
Wingfield Street, 127
Woolworth's, store, 18
Wyndham Road, 40

Culture and Creativity

African hairdressers, 196
Albany Theatre, 61
Arcadia Missa Gallery, 214
A Moving Image, film, 208
Ariwa Music Studios, 58
Artists Placement Group (APG), later O+I, 146–7, 154, 157, 159
Assembly Point, studios, 27
Attack The Block, film, 205

Babylon, film, 56
The Ballad of Peckham Rye, novel, 7, 32
Bellenden Arches Open Day, 126, Figure 6.2
Black Music, magazine, 55
Black Theatre of Brixton, 63
Bonzo Dog Doo-Dah Band, 79, Figure 4.3
Blue Story, film, 200, 205
Bold Tendencies, exhibition, 164, 182, Figure 8.2
 organisation, 182–5, 188
Bullet Boy, film, 205

calypso, musical genre, 54–5
Camberwell Beauty, butterfly, 26, 231
Chisenhale Gallery, 90
Chronic Love Foundation, 171–2, 204, 207
 Art Lounge, 173
 CLF Café, 172
Citizen Smith, sitcom, 38
Cooke Fawcett, architects, 184
Copeland Gallery, 185
Crisis, punk group, 104
Crossing The Line, documentary, 207
Crown Theatre, 26

Desmond's, sitcom, 61–4, 108, 141, 198, Figure 3.5
Dino and Ernesta Santarelli Foundation, 160
Dolehouse Crew, squatters, 163–4
drill, musical genre, 56, 202–3, Figure 9.4

ECAD Gallery, 197, Figure 6.4
Electric Theatre, 22
Entitled, film, 207

Flat Time House (210 Bellenden Road), living sculpture, 157–60, 223, Figure 7.1, Figure 7.8
For Queen and Country, film, 61
The Fosters, sitcom, 61
"Freeze" exhibitions, 87, 95, Figure 8.8

Gaumont Palace Cinema, 26
gIRLS aBOUT pECKHAM, fashion group, 198
Gone Too Far!, play and film, 204–5
grime, musical genre, 56, 201–3

Hannah Barry Gallery, 182, 184
Health and Efficiency, magazine, 29

jazz, musical genre, 74–5, 79, Figure 4.3

Liberian Girl, play, 206
Lisson Gallery, 87, 89, 145, 154, 159
Livesey Museum, 21
Love Thy Neighbour, sitcom, 61
Lyndhurst Way artists' group, 164, 186, Figure 8.2

The M^2 Gallery, 126
Meet The Abesanjos, sitcom, 198–9
Mental Furniture Institute, 159
"The Minky Manky Show", exhibition, 91, Figure 4.6
Moscow 17, drill group, 202
Multi-Story Orchestra, 182–3, Figure 8.10
Museum of Contemporary Art (Bellenden Road), Figure 6.4

Index | 243

"Nelson Mandela House, Nyrere Estate", 37, 39, 49
No Problem!, sitcom, 61

Off The Endz, play, 205
Only Fools and Horses, sitcom, 37–9, 42, 43, 60, 64, 227–8, Figure 3.1

Passport to Pimlico, film, 1, 3, 43
Peckham Heroes, video series, 208
Peckham Levels, creative industries centre, 188, 215, 220, Figure 8.13
Peckham Observatory, architectural feature, 184
Peckham Palazzo (Venice), 184
Peckham Pavilion (Venice), 184
Peckham Peculiar, magazine, 191
Peckham Platform, arts centre, 187
Peckhamplex, cinema, 177–8, 188, 206
Peckham Portraits, photography exhibition, 206, Figure 9.5
Peckham Shed Youth Theatre, 166
Peckham the Soap Opera, play, 207
Peckham Theatre (old), 26, 227
pirate radio, 201–2
Practice Architecture, 182

Rastafarianism, 55–6
reggae, musical genre, 55–9, 201
Rocks, film, 198
Roof Top Film Club, 185, 216, Figure 8.11
Royal Court Theatre, 60, 61, 172, 204, 205, 207, 208
Ruff Ruff & Ready, post-punk band, 164
R. White's lemonade, 22

Safehouse 1 and 2, exhibition space, 185
Sassoon Gallery, 163
Scratch Orchestra, 79
Sensation, Royal Academy exhibition, 93, 96
Serenade in Sepia, radio and television music programme, 55

Situationists, 13
Small Axe, drama series, 207
Sodiq, documentary, 207
Spike Surplus Scheme, squatters, 164
Sunday Painter, studio space, 214
Sun Gallery, 214

The TBoy Show, sitcom, 199
Theatre Peckham, performing arts academy, 205
This is Brixton, This is Peckham, This is Croydon, documentary series, 208
Till Death Us Do Part, sitcom, 61
Top Boy, drama series, 205
Tower Cinema, 26

Underexposed Arts, arts organisation, 206

Victoria Miro Gallery, 228

We The Ragamuffin, film, 56–8, 216, Figure 3.4
West Indian World, newspaper, 58
Whitechapel Art Gallery, 90
!WOWWOW!, artists' collective, 163

Zone 2, drill group, 202, Figure 9.4

Organisations and Institutions

Aladura Spiritualist African Church, Figure 9.1
Amalgamated Union of Engineering Workers (AEUW), 39, 227
The Arch Company, 176
Arts & Business (formerly Association for Business Sponsorship of the Arts), 131, 217–18
Arts Council, 61, 89, 145, 146, 150, 153, 159, 172, 224

BBC, 38, 39, 53
Bellenden Advisory Board, 136
Bellenden Area Renewal Scheme, 127–36, 160, 217–18, 224–5

Index

Bellenden Residents Group, 119, 136, 181
Bellenden Residents Renewal Committee, 128
Bermondsey Labour Party, 109
Bermondsey Mafia, 103, 104, 22
Black Majority Churches, 193–4
Bloomberg Philathropies, 224
Blue Beat, record label, 54
British Land Company, 18, 141
Bussey Cricket Club, 23

Camberwell Art School, 2, 12, 42, 61, 70–7, 95, 106, 187, 226, 227, Figure 4.1
Camberwell Fair, 19
Camberwell Metropolitan Borough, 19, 29, 45
Channel Four, 56, 58, 60, 61, 207
Charity Organisation Society, 27
Charter 88, 61
Chatham and Dover Railway Company, 21
Cheap Trains Act, 21
Civic Trust, 103
Clear View Research, 197
Community Outreach Ministries, 194
Creative Land Trust, 224
Cross River Tramway project, 169, 171, 173, 194

D&R Scaffolding, 42
Dub Vendor Records, shop, 58

English Heritage, 167, 173, 174, 179
Everlasting Open Arms Ministries, 114

Goldsmiths College, art school, 77–89, 93–5, 113
Goldsmiths College, 2, 43, 59, 72, 77–8
 as Goldsmiths Technical and Recreative College, 69
Goldsmiths Electronic Music Studio, 80
Goldsmiths' Livery Company, 69, 77
Greater London Authority (GLA), 167, 176, 189

Greater London Council (GLC), 19, 44, 167
Greater Peckham Alliance, 118, 119

Harris Academy, 26
Henry Moore Foundation, 92, 152, 159
Heritage Lottery Fund, 174
Historic England, 221
Hornsey College of Art, 80

Institute for the Study of Mental Images, 143, 148, 157
Institute of Race Relations, 51
Imperial War Museum, 44
Inner London Education Authority, 77, 78
Isaac Newton Institute, 156
Island Records, 55, 56

Kiss FM, 55, 201
Kyrle Society, 27

League of Coloured Peoples, 50, 137
Licensed Victuallers Institution, 17, 185
London, Brighton and South Coast Railway Company, 21
London County Council (LCC), 14, 16, 19, 44
London Docklands Development Corporation, 85, 88, 108
London Institute, 77, 91
London Wildlife Trust, 131

Make Shift Limited, 188
Mayor of London Office artist studio study, 219
Melodisc, record label, 54
Mountview Academy of Theatre Arts, 187, 206, Figure 5.5

National Film School, 61, 207
National Front, 61
National Institute of Economic Research, 213
Neighbourhood Renewal Fund, 126
Network Rail, 175, 176, 178

Newington Community Development Project, 103, 109
North Peckham Project, 106–7, Figure 3.2

Outset Contemporary Art Fund, 224

Peckham Action Group, 104, 105, 109, 163
Peckham Experiment, 27–9, 31, 112
Peckham Fair, 19
Peckham Heritage Regeneration Partnership, 175
Peckham Partnership, 114–18
Peckham Planning Network, 181
Peckham Programme, 118, 167, 168, 175, 182
Peckham Settlement, 27
Peckham Society, 103–4, 107, 171, 173, 178, 179, 225
Peckham Vision, 171, 172, 174, 176, 178, 181, 184, 187, 188, 189
Pempeople (People Empowering People), 197
Pioneer Health Centre, 27, 112
police, 114
    censorship, 202
    corruption, 43
    Operation Swamp, 59
    racism, 53
    Special Patrol Group, 197
Port of London Authority, 88

Railway Heritage Trust, 180
Rowntree Foundation, 45
Royal Academy Schools, 87
Royal College of Art, 77, 87, 197
Rye Lane and Peckham Station Action Group, 119, 173, 178

St Martin's art school, later Central St Martins, 81, 82, 125, 142, 145, 229
Scarman Report, 48
Slade School of Art, 74, 87, 93
Sojourner Youth Truth Association, 53, 58, 197

Southern Rail, 175
South London Gallery (SLG), 2, 11, 23, 69–71, 90–3, 95, 154, 197, 226, 230, Figure 4.3, Figure 4.6
Southwark Arts Forum, 124
Southwark Borough Council, 4, 8–9, 21, 29, 44, 45, 99–103, 111, 115, 118, 159, 171, 173, 178, 186, 214, 220–1, 225, Figure 5.2
    housing policy, 52
Southwark Community Development Project, 50
Southwark Educational Research Project, 151
Southwark Planning Network, 181
Survey of Race Relations in Britain, 52

Tara Fabrications, 176
Tate Gallery, Tate Modern, 12, 111, 123, 159
Transport for London, 167, 169

United Girls' Schools Mission, 27
University of the Arts, 77, 95

Concepts and Themes

agency, 46, 224, 226

Black Lives Matter, 207
bomb damage, 1, 29–31, 44, 107, Figure 2.9

civil society, 222–3
community assets, 189, 221
commuting, 225
Covid, 4, 8, 14, 188, 213–14, 226
Creative Enterprise Zones, 189, 224
creative industries, 3, 216, 220
"Creative Southwark", 220
creativity, working definition, 2
culture, working definition, 2
    cultural economy, 213

decanting, 114, 117–18

gentrification, 5–8, 43, 62, 101–2, 123–6, 160, 166, 173, 176, 207–9, 214–22, 224, 230

home-working, 214
housing, 44–50
   Conservative policy on, 46, 114
   Holland Report on, 51
   Labour policy on, 46
Housing Action Trusts, 110
Housing Associations, 47, 114, 116, 119
housing legislation
   House and Town Planning Act (1919), 44
   Housing Act (1891, 1900), 44
   Housing and Planning Act (1988), 110
   Housing (Homeless Persons) Act (1977), 100, 110
   Labouring Classes Dwellings Act (1866), 44
   Land Compensation Act (1973), 100
   Local Government and Housing Act (1989), 126
Housing on Trial, report, 52
housing: "Right to Buy", 47, 48, 117

inter-community rivalry, 63
inter-community separation, 216–17, 226
   vertical apartheid, 216

New Southwark Plan, 178, 181, 188, 189–90, 194

"on road" culture, 199–201

Peckham and Nunhead Action Plan, 167, 177, 178, 179, 181, 186

"Peckham Paradigm", 6–9, 214, 228
planning, 5, 7, 8, 31, 167–9, 221
   listing, 221
   zoning, 220
planning legislation
   Localism Act (2011), 189
   "Section 106", 221–2
   Town and Country Planning Act (1990), 221
Planning for the Future, White Paper, 220

race legislation
   Commonwealth Immigrants Act (1962), 51
   Race Relations Act (1965, 1968), 51
racism, 3, 5, 8, 53, 60, 61
   New Cross fire, 59
regeneration, 7
   Single Regeneration Budget, 107, 114, 115
   theory of, 101–2, 217–18
rent gap theory, 218–19
resistance, 3, 40, 43, 60, 222
riots
   1958, 50, 51
   1981, 8, 48, 56, 58, 59, 107
   1985, 8
   2011, 8, 118, 166, 175, 204

squatting, 48, 163–4, 186

Urban Housing Unit, 106
Urban Programme, 50

Windrush generation, 50, 53, 54, 194, 20